Simply put, it's just a joy to read. Emi[...] complex journey of motherhood. Even [...] be the same, Emily makes us mothers fe[...] all [...] understood and seen. So many smart and intelligent concepts unpacked in a witty, uplifting, light-hearted, and easy-to-read way.

— JANE ROSS, MOTHER OF THREE

In today's world of mass information, we don't need more "knowledge"; what we need is wisdom. Emily is a carrier of that wisdom. Self-initiated through her journey as a teacher, coach, and student of the healing arts, Emily has combined all of her experience into one easy-to-follow step-by-step book. Like a Mother will be my #1 recommendation to all my clients who are embarking on the journey of motherhood. Emily, you are a gift to this world.

— RICK WILLIAM, COACH, SOMATIC THERAPIST, AND FOUNDER OF THE FREEDOM ROADMAP

There is no parenting without guilt. Like a Mother shares the real truth of motherhood in a deeply honest and validating way, creating a profound awareness of much of the self-blame and self-shame that is an inherent part of being a parent.

— DR RUSSELL KENNEDY, BEST SELLING AUTHOR OF *ANXIETY RX*

Jumping into bed and reading a chapter after a busy day felt like a meaningful debrief with a friend. It was so refreshing to hear someone else articulate how I felt and put relevant science behind why I felt that way. I found it lighthearted and playful but also meaningful, raw, and relatable. It's heartwarming to realise I wasn't alone in the big feelings and identity shifts that come with motherhood.

— RAYCH FINDLAY, MUM OF TWO

Like a Mother *had me giggling, tears rolling, all the feels. It felt like a big warm hug of support written into 200 pages. Finishing the book felt like I could take a huge sigh of relief because it leaves you feeling heard. The journey of motherhood is no easy feat, but Emily's words are so relatable and comforting that it makes you feel as though you can breathe easy knowing you're not alone.*

— MELANIE BRENNAN, MOTHER OF THREE

It's as if Emily has taken a peek inside my soul, gently observing every insecurity and worry, and then taking my hand and walking through the mess beside me. She holds space for every vulnerability you have as a new mum, providing comfort, solace, and a new vision. This is the book I will be sharing with all the new mums in my life.

— LILLIAN DALEY, MUM OF ONE, @THE.TEACHER.COLLECTION

Like a Mother

Like a Mother

Emily East

HOW MOTHERHOOD IS THE KEY TO
UNLOCKING YOUR GREATNESS

AWAKEN ✿ VILLAGE

——— PRESS ———

This is a work of non-fiction. Any resemblance to persons living or dead should be plainly apparent to them and those who know them, especially if the author has been kind enough to have provided their real names. All events described herein are true from the author's perspective.

The content of this book is for general instruction only. Each person's physical, emotional, and spiritual condition is unique. The instruction in this book is not intended to replace or interrupt the reader's relationship with a counsellor, physician, or other mental health professional.

Printed in the United States of America.

Editing by Awaken Village Press
Cover and interior design by Andrea Gibb
Author photo by Charlotte Rogers

ISBN 978-1-957408-04-0 (paperback)
ISBN 978-1-957408-05-7 (ebook)

Library of Congress Control Number: 2022914618
Category & Genre: Non-Fiction, Parenting, Self-Help, Spirituality

Published by Awaken Village Press,
Sioux Falls, South Dakota, U.S.A.
www.awakenvillagepress.com

Emily East acknowledges the Traditional Owners of the country on which she works, the Dja Dja Warrung people, and recognises their continuing connection to the land, waters, and culture. She pays her respects to the Elders past, present, and emerging.

Emily East
10 Dunvegan Terrace
Strathfieldsaye VIC, 3551
emilyeast.cfs@gmail.com
@emily_east
+61 429 604 866

TAG! YOU'RE IT!

To _____

I'm gifting you this book because when it comes to being a badass mum, you came to my heart. You are incredible.

Thank you for everything you do and offer the world. All the love that you give and have created.

Thank you for your hard work. Thank you for your lessons. Thank you for your patience. Thank you for transforming and blossoming into this beautiful creature that is you. I see you, I hear you, I love you. Welcome to the sisterhood.

I'm so grateful we are on this beautiful Earth at the same time.

Let's do this – together!

All my love,

From _____

DEDICATION

To all the women before me and all the women who will come after. The reason we are all here is because of our ancestors. Like them, we are the creators. We are the pure essence of divine feminine energy, put on this planet to create and birth new love and new life. We have birthed every single human life on this planet and are incredibly strong. We are also soft and gentle and loving and caring. We are everything. We embody everything. We are not only in this universe; the universe is *within us*. Let's remember and spend time reminding ourselves of this sacred role we share together. We are a part of the most beautiful and sacred sisterhood there is. We are mothers.

And to my two boys, who chose me. Thank you for being here. Thank you for being my light and showing me the way home to myself. You help me remember who I truly am. Love, Mum. And to Zac – for everything.

CONTENTS

PREFACE

When my first son, Zephyr, was born, I played the waiting game. I wasn't working, I wasn't practising yoga, I wasn't playing my competitive team sports that I loved, I wasn't going out with my friends anymore, and my sex life? Non-existent. All aspects of my life had changed, all the way down to my thick fingernails, dry skin, and balding head, and the only solution I could come up with was that once my baby wasn't so dependent on me, I could just pick up where I left off and start doing all the things I'd done before as if nothing had changed. I saw this as just a phase I was going through. *I'll be able to live my own life soon enough*, I told myself. *I'll be me again.*

This way of viewing the situation led me to try to start running again just three weeks after giving birth – and as we know, birth is no easy feat on the ol' pelvic floor – just so I could try to get back onto my beloved netball side. I thought that to feel like myself again, I just had to reassemble the pieces that started to come apart when I started this motherhood journey.

The problem was that I didn't yet understand that what looked like my previous life falling apart was actually my new life coming together. Mind you, it took me a good long time to even be open to this idea, let alone embrace it. If you'd suggested it when Zephyr was a newborn? Well, let's just say you'd better be able to run faster than a lady who's thirty kilos overweight (that's how much I put on with my first pregnancy) with abdominal separation and incontinence issues – so, in other words, not very fast at all.

Back then, I would spend my days waiting until naptime to do something for me or something that gave me glimpses of my past life. *Waiting* for my husband to get home. *Waiting* for the weekend. I wish I could say that I had an epiphany that woke me up one day like a slap in the face, but instead, it dawned on me slowly that I needed to stop waiting. I came to understand that my life would always be different from now on, and it was time to mourn the death of the old me so the new me could be born.

I realised with some dismay that I'd been spending my days just waiting for the time to pass – which really meant I was waiting to die. *Oh my god.* Hanging on too tightly to my old life and who I used to be was causing me to waste the life I had in front of me.

Not only did this realisation cause me to change how I was doing things, it made me feel I wanted to share it, had to share it. When, as new mums, we chase after our old lives or spend our time waiting and wishing for them to come back, it keeps us from fully appreciating what's in front of us. It is my hope that this book can help someone to see that, without taking as long as it took me or even to see it at all since there are certainly mums who keep on fighting the losing battle of trying to fit into their old lives and feeling like they're failing. I can't blame them since that seems to be what our culture encourages with a million magazine articles about how to 'Get Back to You after Baby'.

If I'd been able to let it go with grace, maybe even have a little funeral for that part of me, grieve it, say some nice things about it, read a moving poem, then I could have been more open to receiving something just as wonderful (or even more so). Think about it as if you're arriving at a party, stepping into a room full of people, and noticing that the dress code appears to be 'neat casual' – but you're wearing a sparkly bikini and angel wings. You have a choice in how you can approach this situation. You can leave the party, or you can stay and feel self-conscious – or you can choose to strut into that party with confidence and own this new and fabulous you, as different and out of place as you might feel at first. Because in time, I bet, you'll be the life of the party and everyone will want to be near you.

Some women take to the destruction of their old selves and the birth of their new selves (aka motherhood) like fish to water. Others, like me, take some time to find our feet and stumble often. In writing this book and sharing my experience, I want to assure you that if you're in that second group, you're not alone. But I also hope that mums in the first group might find something in this book as well. You'll learn as you keep reading that I'm proposing (or maybe more so describing) a new paradigm of motherhood. People used to believe you had to choose between having kids and having a life. It's true that you can't have *the same* life as before you became a mum (and, as I've laid out in this preface, trying to force that is a frustrating and disappointing endeavour). But I don't believe that our only other choice is to dissolve our identity and place all our hopes for satisfaction and fulfilment on our kids. In fact, this is a dangerous path as well, for reasons I'll explain in this book. In motherhood, we don't lose our identity; we develop a *new* identity. By having kids, we haven't ceased to exist; we still have an identity, and motherhood is a core part of it. We haven't lost ourselves; we are still ourselves *within the context of motherhood*. It can take some time for a new mum to figure out what that means, but I hope this book will be a useful guide on the path.

Trust me when I say that finding your new normal is a good thing. Actually, it's an even better thing than you can imagine. Becoming a mum gave me strength I never knew I had, and I found a sisterhood I never believed possible. The concepts in this book have led me on an adventure that has changed my life and the way I experience mother-hood. It's okay if you're not convinced yet. Just keep reading – come on this journey with me, and I'll show you.

When we have children, words and phrases like *lost* and *finding ourselves* are thrown around a lot to describe the space between the rhythm of life we felt before we were mums and the way we feel once we've settled into our new and a different rhythm. It can certainly feel like we are a bit lost in this space between; we don't know who we are anymore, our bodies feel different, we relate to our loved ones differently, and our daily life of going to work or socialising just doesn't happen the way that it used to. I think the words *disconnected* and *distracted* describe this transition better than *lost*. Let me explain to you why.

As women, we go through this incredible rite of passage that is *supposed* to change us. Becoming a mother requires us to go deep within ourselves and do things we never thought we could. We menstruate every month, which in itself is a rite of passage from girl to woman. Those who live in a male body don't get that chance. Still, if we look back at history and various cultures around the world, there are so many rites of passage created for boys because they don't get the natural rite of passage we are gifted at birth just by virtue of being women. The first Australians took young boys on 'walkabout', where they spent up to six months in the wilderness to make the spiritual and traditional transition to manhood. In other cultures, adolescent boys are required to spend days on the water fishing by themselves for survival or have hooks put into their mouths, get tattooed or even put their hands into a hole filled with fire ants (as if puberty wasn't hard enough). In some cultures, the young boys were given new names upon their return because they were no longer returning as the boys who left but as men. Rites of passage were designed to push young boys to their limits so they could discover what they were capable of and achieve things they never thought they could. Rites of passage were meant to mark a transition. A time of change. A time of awakening. A time when they could achieve the next level spiritually, physically, and emotionally. Nowadays, a rite of passage here in Australia might be a fishing trip with your dad or a trip to watch the football or maybe even having your first beer.

As I pondered the rites of passage in other cultures in preparation to write this book, I felt right away that, 'They have to go to those extremes to push and challenge males as far as we are pushed as women'. It's a pretty special and sacred thing when you think about it that we are given at birth an inbuilt rite of passage and an open invitation to spiritual awakening and reaching consciousness. I mean, really, I think it's magical! And we shouldn't lose sight of how special and sacred these rituals are. We mustn't take them for granted just because they are naturally part of our lives and not explicitly created by human beings for the sake of marking a transition. They are meant to push us and change us, to get us to achieve things we never thought we could. Once we create life, it's a given that we'll be different – more aligned, more spiritual, more conscious. It comes with the territory.

The thing is, we may not be aware of these newfound superpowers. That's why I say new mums are disconnected or distracted, not lost. We've always had the codes to be who we are; we just forgot them. The world helps us forget because we are programmed and encouraged to fit inside boxes society shows us that we should. But you're here because you're ready to lean away from the path that was paved for us, and you're ready to start dancing to the beat of your own drum. You're ready to sing the song that only you can hear inside of you. You're ready to use your motherhood experience to awaken the parts within you that have been hiding in the shadows. You're ready to become whole. You're ready to reclaim your inner wisdom and personal authority. You're ready to use the demands of motherhood to wake you up to who you really are, to who you've always been but just forgotten. This is the unveiling of you.

We have everything within us that we need already; motherhood just brings it all out of us. When a flower doesn't bloom, we don't fix or change the flower; we change the environment. We are in need of nothing, and if we couldn't handle it, then it wouldn't be assigned to us. The life you dream of living is yours to have; otherwise, you wouldn't be capable of even seeing it. If you're currently feeling a bit lost inside of motherhood or looking ahead to motherhood and feeling fear about losing yourself, know that you are not 'becoming' mum – you *are* mum.

We are born with this innate wisdom and intelligence within us to express our true selves. We just need the right nurturing and the right fuel for the fire. When we aren't stepping into our power, it's not because we can't or we don't have what it takes, but it's just that we haven't learned how to yet. We're still in that transition phase or the space between. We're still down the metaphorical well. (Don't worry, that will make sense in a little while.) Life is full of transitions, and we're always learning and evolving, but the transition to motherhood is by far the most profound and life-changing.

Some people can learn to ride a bike in a day; others need more time and maybe some training wheels until they find their balance. Perhaps they need a mentor or a personal trainer, maybe even a bike mechanic to help them along the way, or maybe what's needed is a lycra specialist, an energy bar sponsorship, or a physiotherapist. We all need different nurturing to get us to where we want to go. But know this: You have what you need already. It's woven into your inner fabric, sister. You have legs and arms and a cardiovascular system and a central nervous system that will help you coordinate your limbs and keep your balance. You have everything you need to ride a bike. You've always *been* able to ride a bike.

In the same way, you've always had the knowledge and capabilities to be a mum. That doesn't mean you won't have to pull the old training wheels out from storage and use them from time to time because shattering our old worn-out belief that we're incapable takes time. We can go back and forth, we make mistakes, and sometimes we nail it. It's about bringing awareness to our superpowers – to the fact that we're capable of living the life we desire and experiencing motherhood as we desire. It's all within us; it's just about getting the right support to help with the unveiling. That includes the support system around you and the resources within you.

I'd encourage you to move away from terms like *lost* and *finding* because they imply you are looking for something you don't have. You have it, sister. Just like our rites of passage are inherently built into our lives, you've got everything you need within you. Within you lie the wisdom of the ancients, the power of the Earth, and the primal power of the feminine. You are a descendant of the women of the ancient past who knew beyond a doubt that they belonged and that they were capable. It's just a matter of becoming less disconnected and distracted from that truth.

When I look back on my life before kids, it feels like motherhood has made my life twice as good *and* twice as bad. I had no idea what I was in for until I lived it. It's truly profound how our children can take us to hell and back, but there is nothing they could possibly ever do that would make us stop loving them. The love a mother has for her child is the truest and deepest love around – selfless and forgiving, unconditional and non-judgemental, expecting very little or nothing in return. And for all the time we spend engulfed in feelings of love and light, our children also put us in touch with the darker sides of ourselves and our nature. It's a lot.

As mothers, we discover that life is no light experience. We have responsibilities, pitiable amounts of time to ourselves, and desperate worries about whether our children are healthy or 'normal'. We suffer from guilt that we're not doing enough, being enough, or attending to the things we feel we 'should' be or provide. We agonise over our careers and, in many cases, lack of. In our darker moments, we might doubt ourselves and whether we're doing anything right, or struggle for self-esteem while we watch the worry lines set in, our faces age, and our body parts begin to point down.

Mothers of very young children, in particular, can feel like they are on their own. If we are lucky enough to have paid maternity leave or a partner whose salary can provide us with the luxury not to work, the result is that we're physically isolated from other adults as we spend most of our time in the familiarity and comfort that our home offers. This can make us feel like we have no one we can turn to, even though it's connection and support that we crave. In our 'old' lives before we became mothers, we were most likely surrounded by people: work friends or school friends. We were involved in a community where we felt we could joke and vent about whatever was annoying or bothering us. We go from laughing at our office or lunchtime desks with friends about our troubles to spending most of our time home alone with our babies. For new mums who work outside the home, the challenges are different, but it can feel similarly isolating – with an extra helping of mum-guilt, thanks to people who cast judgement for not being with our kids full-time.

Our old friends might not understand us, and our partners can feel like they sure don't. And it always seems to be the case that mothers who struggle with sleepless nights are surrounded by mothers who have babies who sleep through the night. Or maybe the mother who can't get her children to look in the direction of a vegetable is surrounded by mothers who have little gems that sit up at the table and eat what they're given. Or, in my case, I have two wild boys who take up a lot of my energy navigating and managing their big emotions, and I spend most of my time with my sister's kids, who are freakishly placid and gentle. Even if we do find we can surround ourselves with others, often they have different struggles than we do. Or maybe we do discuss our problems and don't get the support we're after; they don't understand or give us the response we need. Particularly our opposite-sex husbands or partners. In all fairness, how could they possibly understand the physical and psychological challenges we confront as mothers? Besides, even if they did, they're most likely at work all the time. Even if we get through all that, we then struggle to unload because we feel like we're 'too much' or being a burden by venting. Or worse, we feel like we're being ungrateful for what we do have and, of course, our children. Cue the guilt loop again. (Are you sensing a theme here?)

Motherhood is a rite of passage, a feminine initiation, if you will. It gobbles us up, sends us down the rabbit hole of darkness where we're confronted with the deepest and darkest parts of our souls. But if we meet this journey with curiosity, humility, and an open heart, we will return to the light with gifts to share. We can bring to light the parts of ourselves that have been kept in the dark. The parts we don't like about ourselves can offer golden nuggets of wisdom that allow for more compassion and kindness towards ourselves and our children. Motherhood opens up a portal that enables us to return to ourselves and our mysterious purpose inherent at birth. Like any initiatory experience, it cracks us open, reveals resources we never even knew we had, and ignites new strength and resilience. It's transformative. And with transformation comes pain as we grow into the person we are meant to be.

This is what I've learned on the path of motherhood. And though this path forces each of us into a new kind of self-sufficiency, it's also nice when we don't have to go it alone. That's why I'm inviting you to join me in revisiting some milestones from my path as you walk your own (or prepare to). Shall we?

INTRODUCTION

I had some pretty funny ideas about parenting before I became a parent. I would think more about what I would do for and with my children, and not much thought went into who I would be or become. I also didn't understand who the hell I actually was and how much motherhood would change me. I mean, I thought I had a pretty strong sense of self before having children, thank you very much. I felt stable. I was friendly, nice, and confident. I would have claimed to know *exactly* who I was, but what I knew about myself turned out to be very little.

Once I actually had children, it triggered an identity crisis that, as it turned out, became a spiritual awakening of sorts. Prior to this experience, I had desperately wanted to believe in spiritual awakenings. I'd read countless books about people having them but didn't think I'd ever experience one for myself. They all seemed to follow miraculous (and unlikely) circumstances, like being stuck in a caved-in mine for three weeks or dying in an ambulance after a car crash, only to be brought back to life with a new appreciation and perspective. My own awakening would come in a messier, stickier version, covered in Spider-Man stickers and biscuit crumbs.

When I became a mum, there was all this stuff about my mothering journey I so wanted to change – this led to some pretty extreme guilt as I tried to deny the feelings I was having. I mean, I was doing pretty well – I had two healthy babies and a husband who loved me. My family was supportive, and I even liked my in-laws. I had a house, a car, running water, hot showers, and money to buy daily coffee and a weekend cocktail. Compared with the majority of the world, my life was as easy as watching an episode of *Friends*.

Meanwhile, the dissatisfied thoughts were non-stop, like some sort of depraved laugh track designed to torture me. *Is this really all there is? Will I be forever waiting for my baby's nap time until I can have any peace? Do I really have to burn myself out and peel myself off the floor with a spatula at the end of every day? Am I really going to be in a sexless marriage forever? Will my libido continue to be as sparse as my hair with post-breastfeeding baldness? Do I have to return to work and pretend I'm the same person sitting at the same office desk like nothing has changed when I feel like everything about me has? Do I need to sit around yet another mother's group circle and talk about how our babies sleep and what they're wearing instead of the things I long to talk about, like: Is anyone else losing their marbles and finding new ways every day to dislike their partner? Is anyone else feeling like they are desperately trying to fit back into their old life but failing? Am I the only one questioning the very purpose of my existence?*

It was all too much.

I felt like I was going through the motions of what every other mother was doing. *Pregnancy. Birth. Newborn. Toddler. Go back to work. Add being a mum to the to-do list. Don't let anyone see you burn out. Don't yell. Don't scream. Don't cry. You're meant to love it. Don't be ungrateful. Don't give your kids sugar. Don't let them have more than twenty minutes a day of screen time. Put your kids first. Get on with it.*

I knew there was more joy to be found in motherhood, and I knew I could find a way to hope it would last longer instead of wishing it were bedtime already. If you're reading this, I'm assuming you also long for another way.

Maybe you feel like you could do better. Maybe you're living with your dream husband and a baby who sleeps through the night, but you're yelling more than you'd like to. Maybe you feed your children organic homemade treats while you mist lavender oil through the air vents, but your sex drive has gone AWOL. Maybe you're proud of yourself for finally getting the paint out of the cupboard for your toddler and braving the mess so they can have a good time, but you cry yourself to sleep because you're consumed with loneliness and resentment. Or maybe you feel like you suck at everything and spend your time drinking or binge eating or scrolling social media. Or maybe you have everything you ever wanted, but it still feels like something is missing.

If you saw yourself in any of those statements, this book is for you – but note that this book isn't about being the 'perfect' mum. It's not about how to get your grocery shopping done without giving your kid an iPad or how to get your kids to eat broccoli. What this book *is* about is claiming your authenticity, standing in your knowing even amidst criticism, building rock-solid trust in yourself and your instincts, feeling more connected to yourself and your loved ones, and allowing your self-realisation story to unfold as your divine gifts inherent at birth make the world better.

A *new* paradigm of mothering, if you will.

The old way is just that – old and tired and saggy. We get to be the generation that changes the rules. **We have the power to turn doing into being, control into surrender, judgement into acceptance, and separation into connection.** You'll probably have to do things you've never done before. And you're definitely going to have to let go of some limiting beliefs like your children's lives depend on it. Because, guess what? They do.

This new paradigm makes you feel energised, worthy, self-compassionate, and connected to the infinite. And it's not about being *more* or doing *more*. In fact, this belief that we need to be more or do more can keep us stuck feeling 'less than'. Comparing ourselves to others or an unrealistic ideal is very much the old paradigm. The new paradigm allows us to see that we *can have what we want – it's accessible to us right here, right now, when we open ourselves to receive it.*

The paths of parenting and the spiritual are, more often than not, one and the same. The two paths can start around the same time. Mothering teaches us all those spiritual truths that we resist and hide in the shadows but finally can no longer avoid – that life can never be perfect, we can't control everything, nothing lasts, and we are not who we think we are. With practice, we can live in a state of receptivity. What are my experiences teaching me about myself? Can I see that my children, in so many ways, are raising me?

If you're thinking, 'Great. As if being a mum wasn't hard enough, now I have to add enlightenment to my to-do list as well?' trust me, that's not what this book is. I'll take you on the journey of how I surrendered control and embraced my shadows, but this isn't as brutal as it might sound. You don't need to hit rock bottom or have a near-death experience to make this shift. The transition to motherhood is made up of tiny a-ha moments that compound and magnify one another rather than one discrete, life-altering incident. That's the gift of expanding your awareness while mothering: it includes all the love and chaos and grit and imperfection. It's not based on control or keeping things tidy. There's room for old pieces of toast hidden under the couch, the train set in the middle of the lounge room floor, last week's dishes in the sink, and teenagers sneaking home after curfew. We don't have to slip away during nap time or when the kids are in bed to 'find' ourselves. We discover that at home.

And instead of thinking you don't deserve it or your needs aren't important because you have mouths to feed and bums to change and you're too busy giving everyone else what they need and what they don't even know they need and staying consumed with things that you 'should' be doing – it's time to create the life you desire and be open enough to receive it instead of not knowing how to take steps to get it.

Up until becoming a mum, I'd made a professional career supporting other people's mental and emotional wellness – teaching stress-coping strategies, personal resilience, meditation, mindfulness, positive psychology tools, you name it. And I thought, to climb out of the black hole I felt trapped in, I would have to keep pushing through and doing what I thought I knew. Brain, intellect, and rationality over soul and intuition. I felt like I had an intellect that was quite sufficient, thank you very much. But add that to my list of limiting beliefs and programming, and it's a wonder I didn't have a breakdown sooner.

I was stuck in the old paradigm, meaning I didn't trust my instincts and inner wisdom when I started parenting; I was more focused on research and information out there from the 'experts'. I was consumed with outside noise, and my inner wisdom was dulled to a whisper. I remember listening to a podcast about managing your child's emotions, and it hit me like a wooden toy block to the face. I was learning about how to master my child's emotional fitness, but most of the tips I was learning, *I needed myself. How was I going to hold space for my children's emotions if I couldn't do that myself? How was I going to support my children through emotional turbulence if I was drowning in my own? How was I to live a life of integrity and fulfilment if I was faking my way through parenthood?* In that moment, it all made sense. To be what I needed to be for my children, I would have to be that for myself. I didn't just need to mother my children; I needed to mother myself with the same compassion and understanding. I knew this on an intellectual level, but how was I going to put this into practice? Because that was the gap for me. I knew things; I was smart; I was intelligent. I knew the power of positive thinking and how the mind works. So why was I still feeling stuck? Self-help books already filled my house. What else could I do?

Eventually, I realised that I couldn't do it myself anymore, and my emotional, mental, and spiritual health wasn't going to take care of itself, so ... with the support of my working husband, we reworked our budget and forked over the money to hire my first coach. Within the next six months, I finished my manuscript (the one you're reading right now), found my dream publisher, began my own coaching business, landed my first big clients, bridged the gap between my heart and my brain, kicked prolonged loneliness and resentment to the curb, and grew into a place of emotional mastery. And all this has allowed me to mother with such integrity and fulfilment that I count my lucky stars that I get to be me each morning.

This book contains the lessons I learned during that transition as I came to see motherhood and myself in a whole new way. Motherhood isn't about 'having it all' in the sense of simply doing more – that's the old paradigm. It is also not about losing yourself completely in motherhood. It is about *being* yourself and claiming your unique gifts *within* motherhood and, at the same time, forgiving yourself for not being perfect. Motherhood isn't about trying to control every little detail and feeling like you have to do everything yourself. In the new paradigm, we accept ourselves as we are and don't expect perfection, either – because we treat ourselves with the same acceptance and forgiveness we desire to offer our children.

No matter how much of a mess you might feel at this moment, remember that (as a mother or someone who wants to become a mother) you are part of a grand collective of strong, gentle, capable mothers. We have birthed every single human on this planet. And that is no small thing.

At this point in the book, you may still be deciding if this is a journey you'll take with me. It can be tempting to stay in the old paradigm, the way we are used to doing things. So let me tell you why your decision to step into the new paradigm matters.

We *need* smart mums with big hearts and creative minds to make a difference in this world.

We *need* mums to feel happy and fulfilled so the legacy that is their children lives on, paving a way for conscious, loving beings well after they're gone.

We *need* mums to be surrounded by other mums who radiate self-love and abundance so we don't program our future generations with untrue beliefs about how showing vulnerability is weakness.

We *need* mums to raise conscious leaders who take charge of our planet and care for it in the same way they were mothered, with love and acceptance and unity, making heart-led decisions.

We *need* mums like you to start living large and on purpose so they can inspire others who want to rise up, too.

A mother can be – no, a mother *is* – the most influential person in someone's life. Let that land. With that comes great responsibility. Let's use this mothering experience to change the world.

SURVIVING IS THRIVING

We've all had those days when the sleep deprivation, the constant smell of baby vom on your shirt, and the dishes piled in the sink leave you counting down the hours (actually minutes, let's be honest) until bedtime – not to mention the constant search for a clean pair of underwear because you have yet to tackle Mount Washmore. Yes, you enjoy smashed avo as a snack, but not smashed into your carpet. Or perhaps it's the tantrum that ensued after you dared suggest your child have a banana for a snack – 'Oh, I'm sorry, you don't like bananas today? I must have mistaken you for the toddler who ate three yesterday'. And that's just the physical load. What about the mental load of worrying about your career, or lack thereof? The resentment you feel towards your partner for having useless nipples and a penis that is somehow a ticket for him to continue his life seemingly unchanged while you're left feeling misunderstood and confused?

And on those days, it seems like the best you can do is just *survive*.

This observation can feel quite defeating. After all, when it comes to our children, we aim a lot higher than survival. Of course, we want them to get through tough times, but the ultimate goal is for them to *thrive*. But when you get into the headspace of comparing your own 'barely surviving' moments with the thriving you'd wish for your children, I want you to keep two things in mind.

First, the hard moments are the ones that feed our feeling of living a purposeful and meaningful life. Just for a moment, think about the proudest moment of your life (without saying your kids, but it could be childbirth, etc.). Hold that vision for a moment and let me ask you, was that moment easy? Most likely not. Challenges give us opportunities to step up and show ourselves what we are made of.

Second, sometimes merely surviving is, in fact, a laudable accomplishment! When the sleep deprivation kicks in and your toddler has pushed your friend's daughter over for the sixth time, or your toddler is crying for you to pick them up and has pulled your pants down around your ankles while you're settling your newborn, these are survival moments, no question. Or maybe you've turned your back on your one-year-old for literally five ten-thousandths of a second, and they've managed to not only find a dog poop but also made the decision to take a nibble. But, I look back at these moments and think, *Wow. I'm pretty amazing. I managed to get through that*.

Those *surviving* moments are actually *thriving* moments. If we can just stop judging ourselves, getting through these moments is what makes us proud of ourselves and gives us a strong sense of well-being. Smooth seas never made a skilled sailor.

We don't need extra things on our to-do lists. We don't have to carve out time to be the best parents ever. We're already doing it. We're already amazing. We don't have to do anything else but be ourselves. We can use all of the interactions we share – the angry, stressful, overwhelmed, resentful, adorable, and miraculous – as opportunities to nurture caring and capable children. But that's not even the best part. Better than caring and capable children? Really? Yes, sister! This isn't a parenting book. Even though we will discuss how approaches covered in this book relate to our children, this is a book for you. The nurturer. The authentic, rollin'-up-your-sleeves-and-gettin'-it-done, doing-the-best-you-can mum. You.

The following pages describe my struggles as a new mum and how I'm using them to be a better person and a better parent. I explain the ways I am practising resilience, discovering who I really am postpartum, keeping my husband as my lover rather than feeling like we're just really good roommates that run a small daycare centre, and how I'm working on myself and caring for myself in the chaos of being a mum.

So, how do we do it? How do we turn our struggles into triumphs? The first step is to know we are already triumphant. Then, we have to start with ourselves. We have to lead the way. We have to show our children and be the role models they need, not the picture-perfect, unrealistic, have-it-all-together side of us. Showing them all sides of us and modelling evolution, learning, and growth is what it's about. That's what this book is about: using everyday moments to build strong, connected relationships with yourself, your partner, and your children. To thrive and to blossom. To survive *and* thrive all at once.

REWILDING OURSELVES

Lately, I've been thinking about the way our parents were raised and how their parents, or our grandparents, were raised. It wasn't that long ago that children were punished in school for stepping a toe outside the very small box within whose confines they were expected to stay. Children were to behave in a very particular, well-mannered way – to be seen and not heard. I have memories of my dear grandmother correcting my posture. She would tell me she would be punished if she slouched and always had to stand and sit up straight.

The way we were parented can become the default when we ourselves become parents. Have you ever said something to your own kids and then stopped in shock to realise, 'Oh my goodness, that's what my dad says!'? This is natural – and yet, we are living in a completely different world now.

When children grow up being punished for not conforming, they learn to suppress anger, frustration, and guilt – any emotions that may have been inconvenient for the adults around them. This is why so many of us, as adults, need to relearn how to be okay with these emotions. We are relearning to be okay with who we are, to accept and acknowledge the inner voice that we (and our parents before us) have been taught to ignore. We need to unlearn the lesson that listening to adults and people with authority is more important than trusting our gut and intuition. I was in a coaching session with a group of over sixty women learning how to set boundaries and say no when this hit home for me. We were investigating how saying no felt in our bodies because, for most of us, potentially displeasing or putting someone out is deeply uncomfortable. I was thinking of my children during the practice. They have no issues whatsoever in saying no with total conviction. They say it with their whole bodies, not worrying about looking silly or upsetting anyone. I was unlearning the conditioning that I had to please everyone. Learning that it's okay to say no when I need to in order to honour myself and my intuition.

This is a new paradigm of parenting, and it's also a new paradigm of relating to ourselves. It's not so much about learning something new as it is about exercising skills we haven't used in a while (like honouring our embodied wisdom when it's telling us to say no) and learning to listen to voices we've become used to tuning out. One of the most beautiful parts of rewilding ourselves this way is that our kids can be our guides in the process because they haven't yet learned to ignore what their bodies and inner wisdom are telling them. They trust themselves innately as we once did.

This isn't a book about how to parent. It's a book about a mother (or mother-to-be) learning her own unique birthright, personal authority, and inner wisdom — learning to trust her instincts and intuition. In learning to find the gifts in even the most challenging moments — and letting those moments teach us instead of feeling that we have to control them — we are saying yes to motherhood as a spiritual awakening. And the best part is, it's waiting for us at home.

At times, it may feel like we are swimming upstream. We live in a world where logic, intelligence, and rationality are idolised and an intuitive approach is sometimes discounted or met with a disapproving raised eyebrow. But this is preferable to feeling like we are spending our lives waiting and wishing away the time – and it's also the most important work we can do.

I used to feel sadness for the world my children were being born into until I realised that this is exactly *why* my children are being brought into the world at this exact time. *They are the generation that's going to change things. And we are the ones who will raise them to do it.*

Imagine a present, serene mother who accepts whatever life brings. Unexpected or unwanted events don't break her. She never overreacts. She's aware of the times when she lacks wisdom or compassion both for herself or her children, but she doesn't waste time feeling guilty – she might do better next time. She's self-aware, but because she's fostered a deep, loving connection with herself, she is not self-conscious or self-absorbed when she talks to others. Her friends say she is gentle and kind in a genuine way. Her brothers and sisters add that she is clear in her thinking and makes good, heart-led decisions. She makes others feel comfortable, even special, and there's no shortage of people who love her. Her children light up in her company because she makes them feel seen and heard. She's creative, spontaneous, magnetic, sexy, and quick to laugh and smile no matter what she's doing – because she feels that life with children is play, not work.

If this all sounds a little too Stepford Wife-esque, know that my intention with this book is not to create a mass of clone-like perfect mothers that all progress at the same time in the same step-by-step ways – there are millions of ways to be like this mother and still fulfil your own unique purpose and let your own story unfold. This book has come after years of mere wishing, then some commitment and discipline. Then after a few more years, it came from gradually learning that progress comes not from yearning to change yourself or your experience but from a measure of self-acceptance and compassion for yourself.

Lisa Marchiano uses the analogy of a well in her book, *Motherhood: Facing and Finding Yourself.* Becoming a mother is like finding yourself at the bottom of a dark well. It's dark, it's frightening, it's lonely. We're forced to surrender control and are confronted with the very depth of our being. But if we meet such an experience with humility, curiosity, and an open heart, the experience can be transformative.

I wrote this book from the thick of my early child-rearing years to help with my own practice as much as the readers'. I mapped what I was experiencing alongside universal cycles of feminine initiation as a coping strategy to claw myself out of the hole I felt I was stuck in. I was interested in using my relationship with my children and my identity shift as an opportunity to study my mindstream and cultivate self-awareness.

Becoming a mother shook every cell of my being, and the way I saw it, I had two options: I could try to rebuild and piece back together the life I'd had, or I could build a better one from the ground up. And as you know by now, I realised it was time to shatter the old paradigm and create a whole new one. Motherhood has been my spiritual awakening. The potential to learn from loving our children and apply that knowledge to other aspects of our life is limitless.

What I wanted for myself was to stop missing the point – to stop waiting around until my children didn't need me so much so that I could either return to my old life or start a new one. I wanted fewer moments of 'this is so overwhelmingly hard' and more of 'oh my god, I love my life and my children and my family. Every cell in my body is radiating with gratitude right now'. It's inevitable there will be both, but I wanted to savour the good more and be kinder to myself during the hard times. I wanted to learn how to enjoy all the stages of life, accepting that I will rise and fall and knowing that this is how we live life to the fullest. I wanted to be the present and serene mum, radiant and magnetic.

Now, don't get me wrong. Feeling present and serene, radiant and magnetic doesn't mean you'll never have moments or hours or days that are chaotic. Just the other day, I found myself desperately waiting for my husband to get home because I'd been pushed to my limits with the kids. I'd lost my cool and yelled at them. And as soon as Zac walked in the door, I excused myself to have a good cry in the bathroom as I reflected on the highlights of the day, which included my second son spreading poo all through the house after his nappy was so full it fell down past his knees and – yes, on the same day – copping an elbow to the head (which may even have been deliberately intended for me) while trying to pull my sons off each other when a play fight turned serious. The new paradigm does not mean everything goes smoothly according to plan. It means we are able to stay present, refrain from judging ourselves, and find the hidden gifts, even on days that end in tears. (And by the way, it also means not making ourselves wrong for those tears, but accepting our feelings instead of fighting them.) This is the path I've been learning to walk as a mother, and in this book, I'll share tools and lessons I've picked up along the way.

We can return from the well, back to our families, back to our children, back to ourselves with our expansive gifts. So, this book aims to be your guide – your light at the bottom of the dark well, to remind you that good times are coming. Your gifts are emerging. You have something within you that you never thought was possible. And you've got this. Even when you don't think you do.

PART ONE
Doing vs Being

The need of feeling responsible all the livelong day has been preached long enough.

William James, *The Gospel of Relaxation*

CHAPTER ONE

Surrender Is the New Hustle

Surrender – what an amazingly powerful word. It often engenders the thought of weakness and cowardice. In my case, it required all the strength I had to be brave enough to follow the invisible into the unknown.

Michael A. Singer, *The Surrender Experiment*

When my first son was born, a dual birth unfolded. My son was born, and with that, so was I. Sharing my body with another was a radical transformation on so many levels. I feel like I've journeyed through every emotion on the spectrum, at times swimming in the low vibrational pools of loneliness, depression, and confusion and then scaling the highest frequencies of love and joy and empowerment I'd ever experienced. Moments of 'I can't do this anymore' to 'How the hell did I do that!' entangled together. This transformation has been a potent catalyst for change for me. I've been forging my own unique, unconventional path, falling into deep union with my intuition, and slowly but surely rewilding myself. In this moment now, I feel both vulnerable and confident with who I am. I'm proud of who I was, where I've been, and what I'm becoming. I still travel through the full emotional scale on the daily raising children. I still have healing to do, sleep to catch up on, and patience to discover. Learning to live life to the fullest doesn't mean I don't experience the absence of satisfaction from time to time. I'm learning to love all the stages and accepting that I will rise and fall with cycling energies. Parenting wild children, keeping them wild, has been my biggest homecoming. My boys have shown me the purest, most nourishing ways to heal and be my own medicine. They've entirely shifted the lens through which I observe the world. Today and every day, I'm humbled and in absolute awe.

My reflections, May 2022

Ironically, but not so surprisingly, just as I sat down to write this, my eighteen-month-old came over and tried to push my laptop buttons. I felt the urge to distract him with a toy, put the TV on, or send him to his father just so I could get some space to work. I witnessed my urge and decided to do something different because I knew how the story would go if I didn't. He would get upset, he would fight harder for my attention, I would get frustrated, and we'd all end up in tears. Instead, I closed my laptop, and I held him. I stroked his baby-soft skin, noticed the curl of his eyelashes, and smelt his sweet head. I kissed him, held him, and was simply in the moment with him, just being together.

Then, before you know it, his little attention span was up, and he'd run off to play with his trains – and I was free to dive into writing. If I'd insisted on pressing forward with my writing, not only would it probably have caused a tantrum, but I would have missed out on this sweet moment of connection.

When we can go with the flow – that is, surrender to the flow of life – it can help those moments of conflict feel lighter and open up new possibilities. Unfortunately, this doesn't come naturally because so many of us are stuck in 'doing' mode instead of 'being' mode, feeling like we always need to win, to come out on top, to be productive and efficient, to fix everything.

(Now before I go any further, I just want to make sure you've read the Preface and Introduction. I say this as someone who's often tempted to skip the front matter and turn straight to Chapter One. You're short on time, I totally get it – but if you're like me and you tend to skip ahead, I'm urging you to go read those introductory portions right now before you go any further. They contain some really juicy material as well as key concepts you won't want to miss.)

This 'doing' way of seeing the world makes sense. After all, we're surrounded by the idea that in life, there are winners and there are losers. Apple claims to provide the *best* user experience, there is a *number one* song in Australia, and L'Oréal is the world's *best-loved* beauty brand.

When we become mothers, this idea follows us into a new arena. When your baby sleeps through the night, you're winning. If your child doesn't throw a tantrum at the supermarket, you're winning. If your pram is top of the range and has more features than most other prams, you're winning.

Competition is all around us, and we've been sold the idea that there are winners and losers. But bringing this attitude into motherhood is a losing proposition. This competitive instinct guides us to focus on things that don't bring us fulfilment (Nancy is a way better mum than me), and it envisions motherhood as a zero-sum game, where if you can't be the best, you're doing it wrong. Not only that, but it activates the inner perfectionist that so many of us have brought with us from our earlier lives into motherhood. If we're fixated on feeling bad because our child had a meltdown or didn't follow the nap schedule we so carefully plotted out for the day, then we miss out on being in the moment and appreciating all the small, beautiful moments that did happen – even on a day with a meltdown and no nap.

That competitive instinct exists in all of us, and most of the time we're unaware of it. It's one of the reasons saying 'sorry' can be so hard. We don't want to admit when we're wrong because it can be tough for our ego – but we can't win all of the time, so what happens when we lose?

Consider this: If I asked you why your friends or your partner or your children love you, they wouldn't say it's because you have the dopest pram at the mothers' group. It's because of who you are – shared history, experiences you enjoy together, the unique perspective you bring. But it's not because of any particular goal you accomplish, and it's definitely not because you're determined to win and always come in first. I don't think there's ever been a partner whose response to that question was 'Because she wins at all costs. Even when she knows she's wrong, she'll go down swinging. I just love that I can never reason with her, and we can't play a friendly board game because it always ends in tears'. (#worriedsmileyface)

If we can see ourselves as we're seen by the people who love us –
and if we can learn to value the qualities in ourselves that they value in
us – then we can escape from this 'comparisonitis'. We can stop being
so goal-oriented and learn to enjoy the process, enjoy the journey.

One particularly ugly way this comparisonitis comes up is when we
measure ourselves against other mothers. Personally, I feel my days are
full to the brim, just keeping my kids alive. It can be hard not to compare
myself with my sister or the Instagram influencers who feed their kids
organic, homemade snacks while reading to them in French and listen
to classical music in the car with lavender oil misting out of the air vents.

The thing is, this comparisonitis can cut in all directions until it has
us completely paralysed. I sometimes feel guilty for sharing that I've
had a hard day because I have so much to be grateful for. I am a white
female with an amazing support system. I grew up in a loving family,
had choices about further education, then married my husband and
moved into his house. I got pregnant fairly easily and had uncomplicated
births. I haven't faced the discrimination or oppression that I know a lot
of mothers have. It's important to be aware of our privileges, but this
can all too easily become a breeding ground for shame and guilt, to the
point where we feel we can't share if we've had a tough day. And in the
process, we invalidate our own feelings and cut ourselves off from our
own instincts and inner wisdom.

The bottom line is that we are allowed to feel whatever we're feeling,
we can be both grateful *and* have a bad day, whether those feelings might
seem rational to others or not. The truth is that reality is subjective. How
we react to a given set of circumstances varies from person to person
and might even be different for the same person on a different day. For
example, two commuters on their way to the same job are stuck in traffic.
One sees it as an opportunity to enjoy their coffee and feels optimistic
about their day. The other feels anxious about being late and whether
or not they will get done what they need to get done. Giving birth could
be a comparable physical event, without any medical complications, for
two new mothers, but one might suffer from postpartum depression
while the other is filled with maternal joy.

When we finally come to experience motherhood, the fact that we desired it for so long can make us feel that any emotion other than sheer delight is a sign of a lack of gratitude – but that isn't it at all. Motherhood can be joyful *and* hard at the same time. It's important to let ourselves experience every emotion we feel – the good, the bad, and the crazy. It's part of enjoying the journey – accepting when we're *not* enjoying the journey – instead of forcing it to be a certain way.

By the way, this small (but not simple) shift in focus is one of the things that helps the most with lifestyle change and forming new habits. Think about the person who embarks on a new fitness routine with a weight loss goal. If hitting that number on the scale is their main focus, it might seem like 'more is better'. It might be tempting to overdo it and go to the gym for six hours a day to hit their goal faster. But that's not how it works. Focusing on finding a form of movement you enjoy – and that you can keep doing *for life* – makes the process enjoyable. That means you'll keep at it even if it takes a little longer to reach your weight loss goal. It also means you won't stop and return to a sedentary lifestyle once you reach your weight loss goal. The goal-oriented competitive mindset causes us to lose sight of the reason we set the goal in the first place: to lead a healthier life. If you discard the win/lose mentality and focus on enjoying the journey instead – if you become 'someone who exercises' instead of seeing it as a temporary means to an end – reaching the goal comes with the territory. Still, it doesn't define your worth as a person.

Simon Sinek, author of such books as *Start with Why*, calls this an *infinite mindset,* where there is no end in mind when striving for the success you're after. You add value for the sake of adding value, not because it makes you a winner. The value that we add to the world is more than the win. It can drive us even when we're not winning and keeps us inspired regardless of the outcome. That's why our children love us, our clients love us, our family loves us. Not because we win. You're loved because of who you are, period. When we have this infinite mindset, we're less distracted by outside noise. We're so focused on adding value by being ourselves that we don't care what anybody else is doing or thinking. It doesn't matter how many Instagram followers you have; if you're making a difference, then you're making a difference. If your mission is to act with love and inspire others to do the same, you can do that whether you get that promotion or not. You can inspire children whether you're the janitor or the principal. It doesn't matter who is 'winning' or has a higher ranking. The infinite mindset helps us focus less on the outcome and more on the infinite ways to be better and do better.

In that moment with my son that I shared at the beginning of this chapter, I could have stayed focused on the goal of starting to write *not one minute later* than I had planned for the day. Instead, I was able to go with the flow and stay in 'being' mode rather than 'doing' mode – and because of that, when I finally did begin to write, I felt I was sitting on a cloud, buzzing with love from the moment I had just shared with my son. And what a special feeling I was able to give to him, too. Simply being doesn't cost me any time at all; if anything, it makes time slow down a little, so it feels like I'm getting time back. When I go about my day in this space, I'm actually much more productive in the ways that matter. Simply being with our children and how this makes them feel is more important than what we do for them. When we move from doing to being, we embody our most radiant selves and manifest joy, lightheartedness, and pleasure.

This doesn't mean we don't default back into doing mode from time to time. I, for one, love a good course or training that requires me to shift into student mode for a bit. I've spent truckloads on coaching programs and e-courses over the years, and I've noticed that it feels really good to learn and check all the video modules and worksheets off the list. But unless you put what you're learning into practice, it's just busy work. All the videos and worksheets in the world won't make a difference if you're just doing without being. It might sound counter-productive, but I've learned that slowing down, giving myself time to connect and open, digest, and integrate – time to soften and let what I'm learning land – can be much more effective and transformative than just ploughing ahead through more video modules.

The same thing applies to being in full 'mum mode'. When it can be tempting to rush around and get things done simply to check more items off the list, I've learned to ask myself, 'What's the rush? What's the race?' I let myself slow down. Embrace my pace. I know that I spend most of my time with my children, so I'm going to do things a little slower. Some days I'll be too tired or lack the motivation to do any work. A lot of wisdom comes with the time and space it takes to integrate what you learn into your life. You cannot be embodied in anything if you are bingeing on your personal development. Let it digest properly instead. Marinate on one question for a whole week. Chew on it slowly. At the end of the day, the woman we are becoming in this thing we call motherhood is more important than what we *do*.

That's the new paradigm right there. The old way of mothering was focused on what we did, what we provided. But we're evolving past that. The energy we transmit, the way we feel about ourselves and our lives, will impact our children just as much as – or, I would argue, *more than* – what we do for them. What you do for your children doesn't replace how you make them feel. If you're providing for them and it's burning you out, then they feel your fatigue more than they appreciate the snack you've just put in front of them or the clean shirt they are (or were) wearing.

You might be thinking, 'If I'm not doing anything, how does anything get done around here?' We can still do the same things and get things done with a different energy and a different focus point. The dinner and bathtime ritual for me at the end of the day used to be something that I dreaded. I was usually at the end of my tether. Most often, what food I was going to cook was an afterthought, so it was always stressful finding something last minute to rustle up to feed the animals (by animals, I mean children). I'm exhausted. I'm scanning the pantry for something to feed them and decide to whizz up a quick pasta because I can't be bothered to fight the 'you need to eat *something*' battle. I'm stressed and burnt out, the kids are feeding off my energy, and they become stressed too. Food is thrown, and it's a big mess (physically and emotionally), and I'm checking the time every excruciating two minutes, hoping my husband will be home soon and I can go to bed myself. Who am I in this moment? I'm stressed, I'm burnt out, my focus is more on feeding them and getting them bathed than it is on my own emotional state and presence, and I'm wishing the time away.

Now imagine this. Let's, for a moment, flip the paradigm and relive the same scenario. It's dinnertime again. I'm in the kitchen, staring at the empty shelves because I didn't conjure up the energy to go to the supermarket *again,* and I start to feel a little stressed. So I pour myself a soda water and get a slice of lime, a fancy straw, and some ice. I put some sexy music on, and I start to dance. I shift my focus from what I was doing and, instead, bring my attention inward and change my energy. My kids come and join me, and we dance together and share some sips of my special drink. I don't even mind the backwash because I'm immersed in the moment and feel energised by how I'm feeling. Food is still thrown when we make it to the table, but I'm less reactive and less bothered by it. I feel the irritation within me, but it's much easier to let it go because the joy I feel while dancing and sharing this moment with my children trumps it. And, when they're fed and bathed and in front of the TV, I think, *Wow, that was a doozy.* But not the type of doozy where I'm wishing it to be over; more like, 'Damn girl, where did I get the energy for that?'

That's who I want to be. Imagine the implicit lessons you're teaching your children in this new paradigm. Imagine your children witnessing and feeling that energy. Imagine someone walking into your home at that moment or your husband walks through the door. Imagine how they feel walking into that space compared to the old paradigm, the air so thick with stress and anger and impatience. When we flip the paradigm, everybody wins. When you shine, so does everybody else. When we focus on who we are in each moment and the person we are becoming, it's less about what we do and what we provide. Yes, those things are important, but just imagine providing and doing things for your children from a place of presence, confidence in yourself, feeling connected fully to your purpose and inherent gifts and pure love and trust you have in your life. Imagine your child witnessing that and absorbing that energy. Now *that's* something worth working on.

Now and then, I do still find myself in overdrive 'doing' mode – caught up in the endless washing, cooking, and cleaning, more concerned with getting everything done by the end of the day than with enjoying the small moments along the way. But I'd say that these days, the ratio is more 70/30 than 99.8/0.2 like it used to be. With practice, I've gotten pretty skilled at catching myself when I feel pushing and compromising who I want to be just to get things done. In those moments, I choose to soften into myself and do the same things with different energy. I cut myself some slack and focus on who I am, not what I can do.

If this feels very far off from where you are right now, know that all you need to do is catch yourself in doing mode and soften into being mode one moment more each day. Nothing transforms without loving awareness. And it's easier than you think.

This first section of the book is about facing the challenges that come with a changing identity and how we see ourselves. Motherhood is a challenge on a whole new level. Even if we're familiar with the idea of being instead of doing, the level of surrender and loss of control inherent in motherhood changes the game entirely in ways that can make us feel we've lost sight of who we are. We'll unpack how to be the mother and person we desire to be and how to use this identity shift to our advantage. The question is, who do you *want* to be? You get to choose. And when we do, we get to live a fulfilled life of meaning, purpose, and alignment with the cosmos (too much?).

Just do it

Jerry Uelsmann, a professor at the University of Florida, divided his film photography students into two groups on their first day of class. He explained that everyone on the left side of the classroom would be in the 'quantity' group. They would be graded only on the amount of work that they created. When it came time to grade them, he would tally the number of photos each student took, and the more there was, the higher the grade.

The other side of the classroom was the 'quality' group. They would be marked on how good their work was and only had to submit one photo during the semester – but it had to be nearly a perfect image to get an A. At the end of the semester, can you guess who produced the better photos? It might or might not surprise you, but the *quantity* group produced the best photos. During the semester, these students took many photos, experimented with lighting, tested different methods in the darkroom, honed their skills, and learned from their mistakes. God knows they had the opportunity with the amount of work they produced because that was their focus. Meanwhile, the *quality* group spent most of their time speculating about perfection. In the end, they didn't have much to show for their efforts except for one photo that was just okay (this story was told in the book *Atomic Habits* by James Clear).

CHAPTER TWO

Flexible Identity, Defined Purpose

Everyone has a purpose in life ... a unique gift or special talent to give to others. And when we blend this unique talent with service to others, we experience the ecstasy and exaltation of our own spirit, which is the ultimate goal.

Deepak Chopra, *The Seven Spiritual Laws of Success*

I don't know about you, but I never really gave much thought to my purpose or the meaning of life until I became a mum. Not until my identity completely shifted and I felt like I didn't have it anymore did I realise something was missing.

Purpose gives us something to live for, a reason to get out of bed in the morning. This purpose helps us feel connected to something greater than ourselves. It connects us with our creativity and passion and can help propel us forward when things get hard. Without it, life can feel like, 'What am I here for? What's my contribution to the world? Would anyone notice if I wasn't here?' At the core of this purpose is identity; when that identity shifts, our purpose can also start to feel shaky and uncertain.

Of course, motherhood provides entirely new answers to the questions of 'What am I here for?' and 'What's my contribution to the world?' Yes, your baby would notice if you weren't here. But remember that it's not just any person who is this baby's mother. It's you, with your unique and special qualities and attributes. *This* is a mother's contribution to the world. It's not just about meeting your baby's needs. We must hold on to our individuality to be the best mothers we can be.

When we get lost in comparisonitis or disconnected from our inner wisdom or intuition, we start to feel that our children might be better off with a different mother. And when we allow ourselves to become so wrapped up in our children's needs that we forget our own, we lose sight of this powerful new purpose that is birthed alongside our children when we become mothers.

This purpose is what gets us picking vegetables off the floor a billion times but continuing to serve them. It's what gets us out of our warm bed to lie on the floor next to our baby's cot to keep them settled. It's what gets us cleaning the highchair for the seventy-two billionth time. It gets us doing the hard things because we see the bigger picture. This is both a virtue and a downfall. Because motherhood connects us so deeply with our role of caring for and nurturing another, we forget that we are important too. We forget that being connected to the bigger picture without being connected to ourselves leaves us depleted and lacking the energy to serve. We almost lose ourselves in the idea that motherhood is our only purpose because it's so consuming.

But I've found the truth of our purpose is not found in our role – whether that be motherhood or in our careers. It's not found in what we accomplish. It's found in who we are. This lesson is one we all need to learn at one time or another; it's just that motherhood puts us on the express train to confronting it.

I was on a coaching call with a client who had hurt her back and had stopped practising yoga. She was feeling all out of sorts within herself and was struggling to find what brought her joy and who she really was. When we unpacked it further, she shared with me how much she loved yoga and all the wonderful things she experienced from it. She obviously enjoyed the movement and mindfulness, but yoga to her was more than just exercise. It was her way of connecting to herself and feeling a sense of purpose and belonging. So when she stopped practising yoga, she felt disconnected from all those things and herself. She had placed so much weight on her yoga practice because it was so sacred and deeply tied to her identity and how she saw herself. When we place so much importance on one thing, like yoga or competitive sports, we don't have as much flexibility to ebb and flow along with the ebbs and flows of life. When just one thing (yoga) was taken from my client's life (just like netball was taken from mine), it felt like everything changed for her, and she was left floundering. It felt like she was missing out on so much. In a way, she made it hard for herself to adapt and evolve as life unfolded. For this client and me, moving forward was reliant on discovering other ways to meet the needs that yoga and netball used to meet and detaching our sense of identity from that one activity.

The more we feel that certain activities define who we are, the more we defend them and cling to them, no matter the circumstances. If we believe 'I am a fit and capable person who is good at sports', an injury can really strike a blow to this identity – or can drive us to keep training even when our bodies need to rest and recover. If we can look deeper into the essential qualities of the activity and the underlying needs it fulfils for us, we can find new and different ways to connect with those qualities and meet those needs. When our identities are not sufficiently flexible, they work against us, letting a sense of pride get in the way of growth. Our egos do their best to make sure we don't change our identity – but the good news is that we can.

As new mums, we cling to what was normal before we created life. We cling tightly because it's familiar and what we know, but this pride can get in the way because we think, to find ourselves again, we have to pick up the old threads and carry on with our previous life. It's hard to make room for new beginnings this way. For me, my sport stopped, my house was no longer clean (ever), and I wasn't working. And all these things were tied closely to who I felt I was. So when all this changed, I was left asking myself, *Who even am I?*'

The average age of becoming a mother in Australia is around thirty-one. So you can see how long we spend defining ourselves in a certain way, and then when that disappears, we can be left asking, *who are we now?*

Schoolteacher, yoga instructor, netball player, mother. These are things that I *do,* not who I *am.* Strip all these things back, and what are you left with? It's you. Are you bubbly? Reserved? Friendly? Loyal? A dog lover? Lovable? (Of course, you are.) As life ebbs and flows, the constant is always you. You are more than your occupation, parental status, passions, and personality type, so detach from the labels you've clung to in the past. You exist here, in the present, and you matter. And there's not a label in the whole world that can articulate or encompass your captivating intricacies.

Other examples of making your identity flexible might look like:

'I'm a schoolteacher' becomes 'I'm the type of person who is organised and patient and cares for children.'

'I'm a netballer' becomes 'I'm the type of person who likes being a part of a team and likes a physical challenge.'

'I'm a clean freak' becomes 'I'm the type of person who likes to be organised and know where things are.'

When we have an identity that is flexible rather than brittle, we can go with the flow instead of swimming upstream. Avoid making any single aspect of your identity an overwhelming portion of who you are. The more we let a single belief or story define us, the harder it is to adapt when life changes. When the world is shifting around us, flexible thinking can keep us sane. Broadening our identity and loosening the grip on it a little will ensure we aren't held back in our previous patterns of thinking and acting. Because post-babies, nothing is the same. We can go back to doing the things we were pre-babies if that's what we are called to do, but if we can't for some reason, that's okay, too. A lack of self-awareness is poison. Checking in periodically to see if our new and old habits are still serving us is the answer.

You can live a meaningful and purposeful life by just being you. It's about knowing who you are, what you enjoy, what you don't, what needs you have, how to get them met, what parts of you need healing. We love being mums, and we also love having hot coffee. And getting acrylic nails put on despite knowing we'll get poo under them the next time we change a nappy. Knowing yourself, understanding yourself in all contexts (not just motherhood), is your purpose. Living as your most natural and authentic expression is your purpose. When we have this understanding of ourselves at our core, we quickly see the ripple effect this has on our children, our loved ones, our community, and our planet.

Just in case you were thinking you're behind the curve, I *did not* learn this lesson with my first baby. After Zephyr was born, I still fully expected to return to the life I'd had before. I only learned to surrender and go with the flow after life slapped me forcefully in the face with that lesson in a way I couldn't ignore.

The story starts at the engagement party for my twin sister, Jane, about a year before Zephyr was conceived, when I overheard one of our mutual friends talking about a yoga teacher training course starting the following week. I shimmied into the convo and learned that this intensive two-week training just happened to line up perfectly with school holidays, so I'd have those two weeks off from my teaching job. *Excellent.* Life had presented me with an opportunity, and I took it.

The training was taking place in Noosa, a popular vacation spot where finding somewhere to stay during school holidays proved difficult. The only place I could find, with the help of a friend, was an Airbnb that would be shared with two men – not ideal. I almost called to withdraw from the course, but because I went, I met Dave (not his real name) – one of my flatmates at the Airbnb. Dave was the owner of a successful, nearly forty-year-old company that worked with large corporations facilitating well-being interventions. This chance meeting kicked off a sequence of events that unfolded over the next three years. Dave invited me to work with him and eventually offered me the opportunity to take over the company.

I took it and signed all the papers when Zephyr was just a couple of months old. I'd started this venture before getting pregnant and felt determined to see it through and make it work. I wanted to prove to myself that I could have a successful career *and* be a mum. I so badly wanted the shoe to fit that I ignored my inner guidance telling me it wasn't right.

We'd negotiated a five-year handover, and I was committed to learning from Dave during this time to prepare to take full ownership. As Zephyr got older, he'd be easier to leave in someone else's care for blocks of time, and our plan was to have another baby after the five-year transition was complete. I was determined to give this business my everything and make the most of these five years to establish myself as a successful business owner. I had this idea before becoming a mum, and I was determined that becoming a mum wasn't going to change my vision.

Little did I know that life had bigger plans for me. The first sign was when my health seemed to take a turn. Zephyr started refusing my milk, I was next-level lethargic, and my period had stopped. My doctor thought my iron levels might be low or my thyroid might be off. Talking to my mum and sisters about my symptoms, they asked if I was pregnant, but being only five months postpartum, I thought – *surely not.* Still, while visiting my older sister, I took a pregnancy test and found myself sitting on the toilet looking at a stick that read 'pregnant'. Holy. Shit. Like, what?

It was an excruciating two-and-a-half-hour drive home to see Zac and share the news. When I showed him the pregnancy test, he just sat on the end of the bed in silence. His first response was, 'How did that happen?'

We're not as stupid as we might seem. We weren't having a lot of sex, and when we did, it wasn't in my ovulation window (or so we thought) – but all it takes is one slippery fellow to sneak through. And I've come to believe that if a little starseed wants to come through, and is capable, it will.

I spent the next week wandering around the house like a zombie, trying to process what was happening. I was at a loss for what to do about work, feeling sad about not being able to have a cocktail with my friend at her hens party on the weekend, feeling like I wasn't ready to divide the attention I was giving Zephyr. I'd just started to feel like *me* again, and now I had another one on the way. Then I'd find myself in the fetal position, crying because my first reaction had been shock rather than gratitude.

But as they say, life is what happens while you're busy making other plans. I rang Dave and opened the difficult conversation of withdrawing from the business. I was surprised to feel an inner knowing that it wasn't right for me; this was one of my earliest and most powerful signs of how I'd been stuck in the old paradigm of motherhood, trying to fit my new self into my old life.

My second baby set me free. I knew I couldn't commit to working the hours needed for this business with two babies under two.

At my first ultrasound with Knox, the technician was shocked to hear that number two was coming so quickly after number one. 'Are you disappointed?' she asked me. Her question hit me like a punch to the stomach. Perhaps I *was* feeling that way, and that's why it struck me the way it did. 'No,' I answered, 'not at all. Just a wonderful surprise'. And for the first time, I really meant it.

From then on, I fully committed to being a mum – and to being a mum in the new paradigm by surrendering and letting go of who I thought I was and what I thought I was meant to be doing. Knox completely changed the direction of my life, and I found myself whispering to him every day, 'Thank you for being here'.

There is a deep peace that can come from surrendering to life's perfection that is far beyond our comprehension. But only direct experience can help you see and feel that for yourself.

There is a difference between diving completely into what life offers you and chasing something that isn't for you. Because I believed meeting Dave had been no coincidence, I felt I needed to see it through. At one time, I'd been open to what life had been presenting me, but now I was trying to force it and ignoring all the signs to surrender.

Yoga, Dave, Knox – all led me to the work I'm doing now through 'coincidences' – otherwise known as life's opportunities that I took. Meeting Zac was the same way. We first met in a nightclub in Melbourne with hundreds of other people (what are the chances?) at a time when I'd just gotten out of another relationship that I'd known deep down wasn't right for me but had spent so much time and effort trying hard to make it work. It wasn't my decision to end that relationship, but even when it had just freshly ended, I never doubted or questioned it. It was that deep feeling, that deep knowing inside where it felt right, even though my mind was scrambling to make sense of it. By not getting what I thought I wanted, something better came along for me.

When I think about my friends, too, I see how each of them came into my life magically just when I needed them. I didn't go looking for them or chase them down. And it was the same with the publisher of this book, by the way. I was invited by a friend of a friend to do an interview, and while researching this new connection, I noticed he'd written a book. I checked out who his publisher had been – Awaken Village Press. *Interesting.* By that time, I'd been looking for months for the right publisher and had gotten a couple of offers, but nothing felt right. The process of writing book proposals made me feel like I was moulding myself into what each publisher was looking for. It didn't feel good, and it didn't feel true to me. Through this 'coincidental' connection, I found the publisher that would support my story and my manuscript and how they were meant to unfold.

Life rarely unfolds the way we want it to – and thank goodness, really. When I look back on my life, the biggest and best things that have happened to me haven't happened *to me* but, rather, have happened *for me*. Can I take a moment to ask you to think back on your life and pinpoint the best things that have happened in it – were they something you forced or chased? Or where are they 'coincidences'? When I first asked myself this, it literally made me laugh seeing that all the best things were because life guided me. When we let go of forcing ourselves into what we think we need to do or be, we can see how life is our biggest teacher, friend, and ally.

When we think about the word *surrender*, it can call a sense of weakness or giving up. But in reality, surrender is anything but that. It requires all the strength we little ol' mums have. We must surrender who we think we are to allow a greater version of ourselves to be reborn – which is seriously a deeply courageous act.

We surrender control of our sleep patterns, our routines, our ability to leave the house whenever we want (without packing the kitchen sink), or we don't even know if we'll ever be able to pee in privacy or wipe our flaps in peace ever again. That's pretty courageous if you ask me. And quite possibly scariest of all, we learn that we can't control everything in our children's lives – and if we don't learn to surrender that, too, we will either damage our children by trying to control everything or drive ourselves crazy with worry, or both.

When we become mums, the enormity of the unknown is terrifying. Will my baby choke if I give them solids? Will my baby like their new babysitter? If I let my baby climb the stairs at the park, what if they fall? It's relentless. The thing is, control is only an illusion anyway. No matter how tightly we try to cling to control, we can never eliminate uncertainty or make life predictable.

When you look back on your life, can you identify times when life has shown up for you in ways you couldn't have planned or predicted? I know we all have them, and being aware of them can help us let go of control in the moment. Knowing that life is happening *for* us can help us trust that it will all work out in the end. It can help us not sweat the things outside of our control – like how much dinner our fussy toddler will eat tonight or whether or not they'll nap today.

There's a sense of peace and comfort in knowing there are forces at play much bigger than my little agenda. When I notice what's stirred up in me and consciously choose to let go, I feel taken care of. I feel a sense of trust in life – and I want that for you, too.

So, we've established that your identity has to shift upon becoming a mother (der) and that keeping your identity flexible is one of the ways to do this without feeling like you've completely lost the plot. And we've established that surrendering to the flow of life can bring unexpected gifts – but at the same time, can fiercely challenge the identity that contributes so much to our sense of purpose. But what does the research show about what brings a sense of purpose to life?

Studies commonly find four types of experiences that promote meaning and purpose:

Physical and mental well-being (taking care of your body and your mind – e.g., meditation, eating well, moving our bodies);

Belonging and recognition; being a part of something larger than yourself (finding a community to be active in, whether it be a netball team, your family, group coaching containers, an online book club, or the mafia);

Personally treasured activities (sports, hobbies, being a parent, being a dope aunty, completing the Sunday sudoku); and

Spiritual connectedness (whether you find that in going to church, trusting in the universe, prayer, setting intentions, or connecting to nature).

Having a sense of purpose comes not just from a connection to something bigger than yourself but from a deep sense of connection *within* yourself – and this sense of purpose, in turn, leads to better physical health and increases your life expectancy. There are places in the world known as 'Blue Zones', which statistically have the longest-living people. What they have in common tells us a lot about how to live a long and healthy life (because it's not just about living a long life, it's about living an active and able one). Alongside moving their bodies, eating a certain way, and living a life of minimal stress, the people in Blue Zones also report feeling connected to their meaning and purpose. It makes sense that you'd live longer when you feel like you have something to live for. When we see how we fit into the bigger picture, then we're more motivated to care for ourselves because it's not just about us anymore – it's about everyone.

MEET YOUR EGO

Sigmund Freud gave us the term *ego* when he created a model to explain the human psyche. Many theorists, including Carl

Jung, have developed their versions and conceptualisations of the ego. Here's my understanding of it.

The ego is not our true **self**. It's a wounded, past version of ourselves that wants to protect us at all costs – and it's part of the reason we might have overly identified with the activities we enjoyed doing before becoming mums rather than letting our identity be more flexible.

Protection in the eyes of the ego means we must stay where we are, make no changes, and certainly don't question anything. It's the voice that says we can't do something. It's the voice that worries about what people will think of us. Don't show anyone the 'real' you, just the facade you think people want to see and how you want people to perceive you. The ego never admits when it's wrong, never genuinely apologises (only when it makes it look better), and absolutely knows everything.

There's nothing wrong with the **ego**. We are all born with one. You probably have noticed young children are very egocentric and consumed by how they fit into the world themselves until they grow and learn that there are other people in this world. It's an essential part of development to be egocentric, but there comes a point when it's time to grow out of it and expose the real you and become aware of when the ego is running the show. When it comes to our identity, the ego resists this change and is super resistant to letting go and transforming. It's too scary. It's too vulnerable. I mean, what will other people think if you don't fit the norm? What if you struggle and don't love every experience of motherhood? If you admit that you're not perfect and you're not always right? People might think you're a bad mum. No. I'm staying put. I'm digging in my heels because it's all too hard.

When we recognise our ego **and** understand that it's just an inner part of our psyche trying to protect us, we can say thanks, but no thanks. I'm choosing growth and vulnerability and courage instead. You understand that it's not the real you.

It's the voice that speaks both internally and out loud, always analysing how you will sound, look, and be perceived. But when we start to peel back the layers of our true selves, the ego starts to loosen its grip on us, and we are free to be one hundred percent authentic and true to ourselves. We also start to observe it in others more easily. Nowadays, when I notice it in Zac, instead of being the ego police and shining a light on it in a judgy way, I can just take a deep breath, know that that isn't the real him, and see beyond it to who he is deep down. It's like being an empathetic and spiritual ninja.

Our sense of purpose is influenced by the culture and surroundings we grew up in – a concept we'll explore more in the next chapter. But at some point in our lives, we can step back and take a look at the purpose we absorbed from our upbringing – like the desire to be rich, famous, and successful – and ask whether it's really what we want for ourselves. When we let the direction of our lives be determined by external influences, we give away our power. We can surrender to the flow of life but, at the same time, be crystal clear about our own unique values and how those may be different from the culture around us – and *this* is the legacy we give to our children.

Because, remember, motherhood in itself is a deeply meaningful, even magical, purpose that connects you to something much bigger than yourself. You and I are part of the most ancient and sacred life force. We have birthed every baby on this planet. We have created every living human life. And we are incredibly strong. Creating environments for our children to thrive in and supporting our children to be in alignment with their hearts, minds, and souls and contribute and make a positive difference in this lifetime is our shared purpose, but it's also an individual one. You are contributing to your community by 'just' being a mum, and you are a part of this amazing sisterhood that is way bigger than just you and me.

You instinctively do hard things for the sake of your children without even thinking about it because you have this innate and built-in understanding of this purpose. This subconscious understanding propels us forward in challenging times of motherhood. Motherhood gives us an opportunity to make the subconscious conscious. We might think we lack purpose simply because it's not what we thought it was before having children. We used to think our mission statement was found in our careers, in what we accomplish. Motherhood is a mission statement – but within that, our purpose, our mission statement, is us.

My purpose is me and my unique way of being. And when I'm aligned with that, being connected to myself isn't about me at all. It's about all of us. It's about the unity of the planet. It's about the prosperity and abundance life offers so that we live in integrity, alignment, and free-flowing synergy.

Now that we've arrived at what identity looks like and why it's important, the next two chapters will delve into *how* to find ... no, create ... no, *choose* the identity that gives life to your purpose. Because it absolutely is a choice that belongs to each of us. Know that it's there bubbling with magic just beneath the surface, ready to be claimed.

CHAPTER THREE

We Create Our Realty. Who Do You Want to Be?

This is my wish for you and for all of humanity, for people to find their true calling. A call for deeper integrity, to listening to the inner knowing. A call for deeper listening to the note of our instrument. A call to feel our sacred obligation to do great work for humanity and the Earth, recognizing that we all have our individual truths and strengths. To be clear, grounded, and giving yourself fully in humble service, without coming from a place of fear. Fear will still come up from time to time, but you no longer have to live there.

Jacqstar Davies, *Source Unkown*

Every newborn baby enters the world and is bombarded with so much new information that it can be overwhelming. Their higher brain is flooded, and it's impossible to absorb and process all of this raw data and hubbub in its totality. Think of trying to find your car in the parking lot of Chadstone (a massive shopping complex in Melbourne) or IKEA. It's crowded, the parking lot is full, and people are everywhere. To find your car, you don't visually take in the pavement or the colour of the sky or every single car or person you see. Instead, with a focused mental image of *your* car, you edit out the information that is irrelevant at the moment to find it (some of us find this easier than others, which we will explore further in Chapter Thirteen in a discussion of the differences between the male and female brain).

Over time, as our brains develop, human beings gain the ability to focus on what's most important and tune out everything else – and we're not the only animals that have this ability. Deepak Chopra writes in *Metahuman*: 'When penguins and other seabirds that nest in huge colonies come back to the shore with their crops full of food, they somehow find the one specific fledgling that belongs to them in the overwhelming din of noise created by thousands of chicks. The arctic fox can detect the movement of mice underneath several feet of snow in the winter and pounce precisely on its prey. Monarch butterflies can follow an exact migration pattern to and from one locale in Mexico where they breed'.

It's amazing how we are hard-wired to take the information that contributes to the survival of our species and prioritise it amid the flow of all the other stimuli our senses process every hour of every day. Over time, this becomes habitual and subconscious – and this has both pluses and minuses. Of course, we don't want the monarch butterfly to decide not to fly to Mexico for the winter, and we don't want to lose our car in the parking lot because we're so busy admiring all the other cars. But we can bring loving awareness to these habitual patterns, too. In cases where it makes sense, we can make a different choice – but first, we need to see that we *have* a choice.

The details we notice are deeply tied to our identity. What we notice makes up who we are. It's the most basic editing tool our minds possess: 'me' or 'not me'. And it sometimes leads us to exclude possibilities that can enrich our lives. Take the example of my dad's love for his flip phone. (Remember those?) My dad thought of himself as 'someone who doesn't need a smartphone', so he resisted it for the longest time. We insisted on buying him a new iPhone because we knew he would love it. He's not 'someone who loves smartphones', but he *is* 'someone who loves keeping in touch with his family and seeing pictures of his grandchildren'. This is a simple example, but do you see how a flexible identity could have allowed him to enjoy the benefits of group chats with all the family and Snapchat sooner?

Now consider a mum who thinks of herself as 'someone who doesn't think kids should have screen time, ever'. Experiences like being out in a restaurant and seeing another family with a child glued to an iPad reinforce this 'not me' feeling, as the mum who holds that opinion judges the other mums harshly for allowing her child that zoned-out, glassy-eyed time in the restaurant. So then what happens when the mum who doesn't believe in screen time finds herself at home with a needy child, and she's not feeling well and her husband won't be home for another three hours? She hands her child the iPad so she can lie down – but she's unable to rest because her mind is so noisy, turning all her judgements back on herself, insisting that parents who give their kids screen time are bad parents. That moment is an opportunity not only to forgive herself but to let her identity be flexible and, instead of defining any parent who lets a child use an iPad as a bad parent, perhaps consider the deeper values at play. This mum views a parent who is connected and engaged with their child most of the time as a good parent, and by noticing that 'not me' and holding it more loosely, she can come to see that even great mums sometimes set their kids up with the iPad for a while.

Also, in *Metahuman*, Chopra writes that in the human mind, reality is constructed so that:

- The available information isn't overwhelming and chaotic;
- We feel free to accept or reject any aspect of reality we choose;
- We seek to repeat the most familiar, safe, and agreeable experiences;
- We avoid the most threatening, strange, and disagreeable experiences; and
- The ultimate judge of what's real is the ego, which is highly personal and selective about how we interpret the world.

As you can see, the human mind and body are so clever at keeping us safe and engaging in activities that keep us alive and evolving. But from a neutral standpoint, it can be limiting. Without conscious awareness, our minds silently filter, censor, and judge every experience we have. And if we edit out too much reality, we can miss the important things that could expand love, kindness, creativity, compassion, growth, and evolution. Just like Dad was missing out on me sending a video of Knox's first steps.

When you ask the average person what their life's purpose is, you'll most often get a response like 'Ah, I dunno'. But if I asked you, girlfriend, you probably have something in there about raising happy and healthy kids. Good for you. The average person can't articulate what gets them out of bed in the morning, what drives them or motivates them. More often than not, little people get us out of bed quite literally, and they're a big part of our 'why' to do whatever it takes to fulfil our mission in life. But what scares the bejesus out of me is the thought of getting to the end of my life and feeling like I didn't reach my full potential. It's terrifying.

This isn't to say we should measure ourselves against some impossible standard. What I mean is that when we go through life on autopilot, living according to the choices our parents made for us or the decisions we made several decades ago, we are missing an opportunity to consciously choose the identity and purpose that will bring us the greatest fulfilment. I refuse to get to the end of my life and think, *Feck, that went quick*. Or worse, I look into my children's eyes and feel that they were only little just yesterday, and I missed it. I don't want just to get by and through day to day. I want to live purposefully, right now. And I want to create and live the life that I know I can.

So, who do you want to be? What do you actually want, not just what you don't want? What gives your life purpose, and what is your why? You get to choose. It can be anything that you want. Anything that resonates or inspires you to wake up and live in alignment with your purpose.

With so much expansion and choice, it can be a little overwhelming. You don't have to know right now. But the brilliant thing is you can make it up. You can create it and change it. And you can keep it small and simple. In fact, I encourage you to keep it small and flexible, just like we talked about earlier. As we grow and evolve, so do our purpose and identity. You don't have to have it all figured out. Your purpose doesn't have to be a thing; it can be a way, like how you dress, what you post, all the things you create, what you attend, and how you eat.

When I started doing this work on purpose, I pinched mine from my sister, Jane. Hers is to *add value to other people's lives.* I like it. You can borrow it, too, if you like. I love it because it means I can add value in any way that I'm capable of that particular day or moment. On some days, I have lots of value to add; on other days, I just have a little, like a smile or a hug. And I can add value to my own life, too. I have a post-it note with my purpose written on it up in my bedroom as a reminder to connect with it every day. It drives me and motivates me and reminds me of why I'm here. I'm here to add value. The best way for me to add value is to be my true self. And when I feel valued and seen and heard, this takes me places. I'm living my potential.

Here are a few more ideas you might like to pinch:

- To raise conscious and radiant children who will change the world;

- To express your true, authentic self;

- To create around what drives and excites you;

- To inspire your children to live a full life;

- To leave endless ego chatter of the mind and live free;

- To love everybody, always, even the people who are hard to love;

- To be love and spread love;

- To own your energy and raise your vibration (and those around you);

- To leave everyone you see and meet a little happier; and

- To have your inner child's back, even when they get it wrong.

Our identity and what we decide is 'me' or 'not me' shapes our reality, how we experience the world, and how we connect with others and contribute to society. There is no greater force on Earth than our identity. Our identity is how we see ourselves, but it also holds so much more power than what we are consciously aware of. It's our subconscious energetic instruction to the world. It's the stories that we tell ourselves and how we see ourselves that shapes our reality. And this gets a massive hit when we are mums. I don't think you will get a mother out there who says her identity doesn't change in some way when she has children. And there is no better place to start with our purpose than understanding what encompasses it. Our identity comes in the rubric of our highest selves and living a life of meaning.

We are constantly filtering and judging all incoming information based on how we see ourselves and what we identify with. So breaking down this 'me' or 'not me' way of thinking can open us up to new possibilities and make us more resilient and adaptable when faced with transitions. And I don't know about you, but becoming a mother has got to be one of the biggest transitions there is. Not to mention all the transitions our babies make when they grow. Sleep suit to no sleep suit. Cot to bed. Daycare to preschool. Car seat to bolster seat. Purees to solid foods. Baby bath to big bath. To counteract this 'me' or 'not me' pattern of thinking and identifying, we can keep our identity flexible and bring loving awareness to the judgements we make every moment.

As we start to evolve and cocoon into this different motherhood identity, clinging to old beliefs can hold us back from the next level of growth. This can happen consciously or subconsciously – as in, we can be aware of these limiting beliefs, but more often than not, they are so sneaky and ingrained that it's hard to pull ourselves up on them.

This interpretation of our reality is run through a filter of the belief system we've established via all the information we've picked up over the course of our lives. Our beliefs have also been passed down to us from generation to generation, and when we don't investigate what is really going on, we risk stumbling through life on autopilot, living and breathing a product of our environment and societal conditioning. The way we parent is a massive example we've spoken about before. The way we were raised is ingrained in us, and with or without conscious awareness, we can automatically pick up these habits and paradigms. We mindlessly regurgitate stuff we have seen or heard before unless we tune in and start to pay attention to what we tell ourselves, the words that we use, and the thoughts that we have because these things essentially form our beliefs and, in turn, our actions, our behaviour, and our life.

This mental programming and conditioning have almost exclusive control over our habitual behaviour – and almost all of our behaviour is habitual. This serves us because it means we don't use a lot of brainpower on the simple things and have more space for creativity and freedom of thought. However, on the flip side, we can get stuck on autopilot, cruising through life and allowing this subconscious paradigm to control our behaviour and reality. And our subconscious mind is where our habits come from because they don't require much awareness or conscious thought. The next chapter is all about habit change and consciously choosing our behaviour. But before you go down that path, you first have to know *who* you want to be and how you want to show up in life – and that requires conscious awareness.

This doesn't mean questioning all of our instincts. (Remember, we don't want the monarch butterfly to ignore their flight patterns. Some of these ingrained habits are pretty beneficial!) If anything, conscious awareness allows us to choose when to surrender to our instincts and to *stop* second-guessing ourselves during those times. Childbirth is a great example. It's the highest level of surrendering to the body's innate capabilities. You simply let your body do its thing. Of course, there are times for intervention, but often we go straight to intervention, forgetting what the female body can do. When we trust our inner knowing and instincts, this frees up our brainpower for focusing our conscious mind on other things. When we mother using our deep knowing, it's habitual. When we don't trust our instincts, motherhood can be hard because our brains are full of making decisions, then changing our minds, then calling a billion friends for advice, then scrolling social media for 'expert' opinions, then buying forty books and downloading thirty-eight podcasts about how to parent. We have the answers within us; we just have to quiet the noise sometimes so we can hear it. Then we have more time for other things like creativity and freedom of thought.

With our subconscious mind, rather than the conscious mind, driving behaviour, we act on emotion, not logic. The subconscious mind is where feelings reside. This is why repeating positive affirmations doesn't work if we are just saying the words and not *feeling* them within ourselves. We need to let them land in our nervous system. (*Much* more on that coming up in the next section of the book.) We need to reach the subconscious to make a change. The surface level won't cut it when it comes to changing habits; it's got to go deeper. The mind might be a 'yes', but if the body is a 'no', it's a no.

Scientists say we have about 60,000–80,000 thoughts a day. (So if you're a mum, we probably have double that.) We aren't aware of most of those thoughts; they're just repetitions of the thoughts we had the day before. *Yawn.* But when we bring conscious awareness to our thoughts, we have the ability to choose which ones we pay attention to – the good, the bad, and the freaky. Without judgement, just start to pay attention to the good ones and the helpful ones. Our conscious mind is where we have choice. We can create thought, choose thought, accept or reject it.

The subconscious mind is hard at work without us knowing about it. It can't accept or reject thoughts. It takes everything literally. It's why visualisation is so powerful – because our subconscious mind and nervous system don't know the difference between what is imagined and what is reality. You can run a race in your head all in your imagination, and the same parts of your brain will light up exactly the same way as if you were actually running the race in real life. We can even start to take short, shallow breaths that simulate running a race, and our physiology will change. So use your conscious mind to see what you want to see and be who you want to be. Feel it and embrace it. Focus on the feelings and sensations within your body, not the thoughts, and you will begin to shift your subconscious paradigm.

Don't rebuild, transform.

Habits are more than just nasty things we want to get rid of, like smoking or eating junk food. Habits are practices we have done so often that they've become automatic responses we do without thinking. We save a lot of brainpower that way. Think about how easy it is to brush your teeth. You don't need much conscious effort to do that. In fact, you can clean your teeth, feed a toddler, and pop a load of washing on all at once. Why? Because cleaning our teeth is a habit ingrained in us and our behaviour and doesn't require much conscious effort.

This is a good thing when it comes to cleaning your teeth – but for other habits, not so much. For example, just think how often we pick up our phones, how often we fill small pockets of time scrolling social media, how often we make breakfast for our children before our own, how we check our emails or see if there's a load of washing to be done before we sit and read our book or do something we enjoy. Or how we feel like the only way we can relax or switch off is to make sure everyone has what they need and everything in the house is done before we give ourselves permission.

Creating a new healthy habit can feel impossible. Even with bursts of motivation and good intentions, things like exercise, doing the dishes before bed, or replacing choccy time with herbal tea when all kids are in bed can be put into the 'too hard' basket after a little while. But when you change your identity – when you shift what you consider 'me' and 'not me' – the habits that align with your new identity have an easier time taking root.

When you change how you see yourself within your subconscious, you're going deep instead of just focusing on the outcome and surface thoughts. We need to go deeper, and this is your personal invitation. Let's open our conscious mind and use it to shape the way we see ourselves and mix up our subconscious beliefs and the stories we tell ourselves. Let's change the system at its roots. Because if we're comfortable, we are living in habits. And comfortable is not where your idea of success lives.

It's not just new mothers who experience a shift in identity. Think of those who have lost or changed careers, moved towns, or started a new job or relationship. When these shifts happen, people tend to focus more on what they want the outcome to be, what they want to have, what they want to achieve. We go out and set goals and make plans to achieve them without considering the subconscious beliefs or how our nervous systems are functioning that drive the actions in the first place. But the identity shift as new mums is so extreme that, in a sense, it forces us to take a different approach. We can use the loss of our old identity to step into the new paradigm.

With all this talk of habit change and identity change, you might think I'm trying to fix you. That's not the point. You are not broken. You are perfect just the way you are. Becoming aware of our patterns and consciously shifting them allows us to bring the life we have more in alignment with the life we want. If we're trying to force ourselves to be a certain way, becoming aware of that self-judgement can actually help us let go of it and move into self-acceptance. If we're applying other people's values to our own lives, we can't reject that paradigm as 'not me' until we first become aware of it.

Becoming a mother is, in a sense, like wiping your slate clean. Our identity is shaken right down to the foundation, and instead of just rebuilding, we can transform. Just like Puerto Rico after Hurricane Irma and Hurricane Maria, if they rebuild their township exactly the way it was before being destroyed, it would simply be destroyed again when the next hurricane hits. Instead, they are building new, improved, sustainable, ecological, and stronger houses that will withstand any hurricane. Just like Puerto Rico, we have an opportunity not just to rebuild our identity and reality but to *transform*.

CHAPTER FOUR

The 'Being' Approach to Habit Change

Most of our difficulties come from losing contact with our instinct, with the age-old forgotten wisdom stored up in us.

Carl Jung, *The Earth Has a Soul*

Doing one thing differently is often the same as doing everything differently.

Matt Haig, *The Midnight Library*

In today's instant-gratification world, we've been conditioned to see and want things instantly with a single click, the push of a button, the promise that we can buy now and pay later. Patience is in short supply; we want big results, and we want them quickly. But for true, lasting habit change, we can learn from the 'one percenters'. In his book *The Slight Edge*, Jeff Olson advises us to focus on taking baby steps toward making change – actions so small that we underestimate the difference they can make.

Done consistently over time, these actions add up to the very biggest accomplishments. Not only is this approach the most effective, but it's perfect for busy mamas who sometimes (okay, most of the time) only have the energy to do the small things. There is magic in the mundane that motherhood can offer us. The fact that we can't always see the difference it's making doesn't mean it's not there. Just as we know the small ways we show up for our children on a daily basis add up to create something as grand as the canyon, showing up for ourselves in small ways adds up to big change over time. Rome wasn't built in a day, hey, hey, hey.

Doing the little things consistently over time adds up to big change – and this is true in both directions (behaviours that benefit us and those that don't). If you eat a cheeseburger every day, eventually, it will have a detrimental effect on your health. The problem is that those results don't happen instantly. A single burger seems so insignificant that it's tempting to do it 'just this once' – but each time we repeat the behaviour, we contribute to it becoming a habit. A simple error in judgement, compounded in time, *will* ruin your health. Not immediately, but eventually.

If you read ten pages of *The Whole Brain Child* today, would that change your life or your parenting? Probably not. But if you read ten pages every day, in one year, you've read ten books and have been inside the minds of the world's most influential people. Would your life change then? I'm going to say yes.

When you make a conscious decision to act the way that aligns with your highest self, or towards the direction you know you want to move in, you don't see the results, at least not today. That's why it's so easy to say 'just one more piece of chocolate' or to pass by our yoga mat even though we've laid it out on the floor in a convenient location. But we have to realise that these decisions *do* make a difference. So why don't we do them?

Jeff writes in *The Slight Edge* that it's because:

1. They're super easy to do and frighteningly easier not to do;
2. Results are invisible at first; and
3. These small acts seem invisible.

The things that create success, in the long run, don't look like they're having any impact in the short run. For example, I love butter. I have offensively embarrassing amounts of it on my toast and crumpets and a fresh scone out of the oven. Forget about it. I want to make a change in this. I want to make better decisions about my health and unattractive obsession with butter. But it's just too easy to say, 'one more chunk won't hurt'. Go cold turkey, you say? Now you're just asking for trouble. But putting just one percent back into the butter dish? I can do that. If I put just one percent back each time, in just one year, that's 365 percent better. In other words, *three-and-a-half times* better. One percent is so 'slight edge' we don't even know that we're doing it. The same goes for anything and everything. The way we love ourselves, connect with those around us, our health, our exercise. Everything.

Let's look at it through the lens of our parenting. I don't have to be the best mum every day. I don't have to make big gestures, play the best games, or serve the best meals. I just have to get one percent of all that right a day. I can do that. We can all do that. Forget about working on getting my fussy toddler to eat *all* his veggies; a one percent win is just having him not throw them on the floor! Eventually, he'll taste some more. It doesn't feel like much of a win, but I'll stick with it day in and day out, knowing that we're getting better each day.

Because these changes are so miniscule in the short term, it's easy to get down on myself like I'm not doing enough. But knowing what I know about the power of one percenters, if I stay patient, I know that in the long run, Zephyr will be able to go out on dates and confidently try and taste everything and anything on the menu and enjoy experiences food can offer. My mum said that my dad didn't eat broccoli when she first met him. He was your typical meat-and-three-veg farmer who didn't stray too far from familiarity. Now he eats Japanese seaweed. His favourite thing to order from Niko's is tofu soup, and he's cooking vegetarian lasagnes. Who would have thought? It's not something that happens overnight, but as the saying goes – 'A year from now, you'll wish you started today'. This goes for everything – your relationships, your spiritual journey, your health, your marriage, your financial habits, your diet, your knowledge – anything and everything. So keep going;

you've got this, even when it doesn't feel like it. Being a good mum isn't dramatic or about the big things. It's so easy to overlook the simple and small actions we do every day and realise how much of an impact they are having. They're things that we do every day, and we don't even notice. Little virtues or success habits done over time yield big results.

If your little actions – saying 'I love you', adding broccoli to a plate, ten minutes less of mindless scrolling, sitting down on the floor with your kids for two minutes longer than usual, putting music on to dance to for just one song, walking for just fifteen minutes, swapping ten minutes of TV to listen to a podcast or read a book – each represented a one percent improvement towards who you want to be, your level of achievement in a year's time *would not be doubled but more than tripled*. And that's just pure addition. What about compound interest? Because the better we get, the better the better gets!

Those little things that will make you successful in life – that will secure your health, your happiness, your fulfilment, your dreams – are subtle, simple, and so mundane that nobody will see, nobody will notice or applaud. They are those things that, at the time you do them, often feel like they make absolutely no difference – things that are so easy to do but just as easy not to do. These things don't bring any visible results, at least not straight away. Things that seem so insignificant they couldn't possibly matter. But they do. Things that, when you look at them in isolation or as single occurrences, don't seem to have any influence or impact at all – yet when compounded over time, they add up to outrageous success. The Grand Canyon can be seen from space, and it started with a teensy amount of running water. My dad eats seaweed. Google says it took over two thousand years to build the Great Wall of China. You get my point?

Now, we don't want to have to wait *that* long to see results; we just have this lifetime. But it's an amazing and precious life, aren't you just a little bit curious about what you can create? Any aspirations that you have can start with just one percent. You don't have to try twice as hard or even three times as hard to improve yourself, your relationships, your happiness, your self-worth, your household. Besides, you're already trying. We all are. It's not a matter of trying harder. Well, maybe a little harder – but just by one percent.

Another reference from Jeff Olson's *The Slight Edge* is his example of the Apollo rocket's journey to landing on the moon. He states that on the way to the moon, the rocket was actually on course only two to three percent of the time. From the time it took to get from Earth to the moon, it was off course *ninety-seven percent* of the time. On a journey that's nearly 500,000 kilometres, it was only on the right track for 12,000 of them. In other words, for every half hour the rocket was in flight, it was going in the right direction for less than one minute. And it safely made it to the moon. Think about this next time you think of your own goals. If something like the Apollo rocket, with millions of billions of dollars of engineering and technology a lot fancier than Google Maps, *still* got it wrong most of the time, you can do it, too. Give yourself a break. If you think this sounds like a lot of wasted time – being so off track – perhaps it is. But what if being off track *is* the process? What if correcting yourself every so often and flexing your self-awareness muscles is how you get to where you want to go? Those miniscule adjustments in our behaviour in pursuit of our goals can make all the difference. Focus on those one percenters. Remember, Armstrong and Aldrin did (unless you're into conspiracy theories) walk on the moon. The reason being is that the rocket got there eventually. And so can you.

Decide who you want to be and prove it to yourself with little wins.

The ways we behave are reflections of our identity. Now is the fun part of deciding what is important to us, and what we want to be a part of our identity. For example, being environmentally conscious is important to me, being healthy is important to me, and being a good mother. Wbu?

Let's take being healthy as an example and see how we can use this to shape our identity and reality. Yes, I can get myself all pumped up and motivated to start eating healthier and going for more walks with the boys or stop eating so much ice-cream. But these are all outcome-focused and just scraping the surface with my conscious mind. But if

I start to tell myself a different story, like 'I *am* a healthy person' rather than 'I'm *trying* to be healthy', it dives a lot deeper and lands differently within the body. I can start to identify myself as a healthy person and ask myself, what would a healthy person do? And make those choices regularly until I *become* that person. Each time I'm faced with an opportunity to be what I call 'healthy', I can ask myself what a healthy person would do until that healthy person becomes me. Then it becomes, what would *I* do?

Another example is if you are determined to quit drinking. When someone offers you a drink, you might say, 'No thank you, I'm trying to quit' – but to change this story and inspire real change, you can respond, 'No thanks, I'm not drinking tonight'. Notice the difference? That's the difference between using our conscious mind and reprogramming our subconscious. I'm not a drinker *trying* to quit; I'm actually not a drinker. We can start to shape our realities any way we like and create our desired identity. When we tell ourselves stories and have the same thoughts for long enough, they seep into our subconscious and form our habits and reality – and then they don't leave much wiggle room when we want to behave a different way or when our old identity no longer fits us.

Consider, for example, these statements.

I'm terrible with names.

I'm bad at directions.

I'm not a good sleeper.

I was never a good speller.

These are all stories we tell ourselves that we have to start pulling ourselves up on because they form our identity. They create limiting belief systems that trip us up whenever we want to level up and increase our vibration. What if you told yourself a different story?

I'm working on getting better at remembering names.

I give myself tools to help find my way around.

I'm becoming a great sleeper.

I can learn to be a strong speller.

The language we use is so important. Take the word 'can't', for example. It implies that we don't have a choice when, in fact, we always do. Even words with less pull, like 'need' and 'want', have the same effect. 'I *need* to go to the gym'. Says who, the gym police? Even that has such a pull and is so loaded. It can make you feel like you have to, or you 'should,' go. But a simple change like 'I'd *like* to go' or 'I'd *enjoy* going to the gym right now' is much more freeing. When it comes to our children, our voice becomes their inner voice. Have you ever heard your child say something that makes you stop in your tracks and think, 'Where did you hear that?' and then realise it came from you? My son said to me the other day when he wanted to go to the park without pants on, 'I'm going to get a bit cross' when he was feeling frustrated (gulp). He also said to my husband with a stern and serious voice, 'Listen, Dad. I'm talking'. As funny as it is, it can also be such a wake-up call to hear your voice in their little mouths. Not to mention, you say a billion words a day, and the one time you let the f-bomb fly, it's the only word they pick up on and start repeating. *You don't hear me when I'm right in front of your face asking you to put your pants on, but when I mutter 'fuck' under my breath while vacuuming and the TV is so loud the neighbours can hear it, you magically hear me then.*

It goes to show how attentive and absorbent our children are when it comes to our language. English is one of the hardest languages to speak, and they learn it by listening, copying, and absorbing what we say. If that's not a big enough reason to be more mindful of your language, I'm not sure what is. But it's more than the language. Language is much more than the words we speak; it's our tone of voice, it's our body language, it's our energy. I've done sessions with Zac about how to relate to each other authentically, and one of the facilitators said this, which has been burned into my memory: 'I think couples would get along way better if they didn't speak words'. *Ouf.* Think about that for just a minute. Even when our children are still learning to speak, they make it clear to us whether they're happy or not just by screaming and using their little bodies to communicate with us. So, for example, if you feel bad about yourself, you feel a low sense of self-worth, or you feel ugly, flabby, and unworthy, even without speaking a word of this, the people around you will feel it (more about this when we dive into energy later in the book).

When you catch yourself or someone else using these words, it can be helpful to ask some questions. One of my students once came up to me and said, 'I can't go on the school excursion because I'll miss football training'. 'What will happen if you miss training?' I asked. 'Well, I'll have to start the game on the weekend on the bench. So I can't miss training. I have to go', he told me. My response: 'So, what you're saying is, if you choose to go on a school excursion, you will be benched come game day. But if you choose to miss the excursion, you will be in the starting team'. 'Yeah', he admitted.

'It might not seem like you have a choice, but you always do. What you're saying here is that you would rather miss the excursion and go to training because you don't want the repercussions of missing training. That's a choice! And it's always up to you.'

It's like when Zac says he can't turn his phone off to stop clients ringing on the weekends. He absolutely can; his arms aren't broken. But he chooses not to because he wants to do what he sees is right for his business and his clients. The point here is that he *has* a choice. We always do, and words like 'can't' have us thinking that we don't – and after a while, we start to believe it.

Zac even corrects me now when I say things like 'I have to meditate' to 'you'd *like* to meditate'. Bless his cotton socks. This type of talk seeps into our subconscious, drops into our bodies, and surfaces in our actions and behaviour. The words we use turn into our thoughts, those thoughts become feelings, and our feelings become our actions. Take a peep at these goodies:

I want (= lack)
I need (= lack)
I wish/I hope (but I'm not in control = disempowering)
I'm trying (you're either doing it or not doing it; there's no in-between)
I hope (might happen/might not = lacks faith)
I should (I don't really want to, but the expectations I have on myself are pressuring me into it)

I don't know (spoken as truth, slams the door shut on finding out)

I can't (obvs – You always have a choice).

Replacements:

I have

I create

I trust

I'm grateful for

I enjoy

I can

I choose

I love

Studies have shown time and time again that the language we either use ourselves or are exposed to influences our behaviour. One of my favourite examples of this is an experiment that tested how fast participants walked down a hallway when called in to partake in an experiment. Participants were told they were involved in a language acquisition experiment and blinded to the fact that the researchers were actually testing the speed at which they walked into the building *before* they participated compared to the speed at which they *left* the building. The participants were split up into two groups. Both groups were asked to participate in a number of linguistic tasks, including sorting words printed on cue cards. The only difference between the two groups was the types of words they were working with. Group one was only exposed to words associated with the word 'young', like fast, bouncy, flexible, nimble. Group two, on the other hand, was only exposed to words associated with the word 'old', like frail, slow, tired. The participants in group one left the building and walked down the hallway *quicker* than when they entered after participating in the language tasks. The researchers even recalled participants in group one 'skipping' up the stairs to leave. However, the speed at which group two left the building decreased compared to when they first arrived.

The words we choose, the movies we watch, the books we read, the paintings in our houses – all impact our thought processes and how we behave. How do you want to feel? Plaster those words around your house and start eliminating the words that are seeping into your subconscious and driving your behaviour. Always saying that you're tired? You probably are. But hearing the word 'tired' over and over again will amplify the tiredness and make it bigger than it needs to be. The moral of the story is, choose your words carefully, girlfriend, because they turn into profound influences on how we live our lives and how our children live theirs. It might not seem like that big of a deal, but remember the power in one percenters. Call yourself out the next time you use a limiting word or phrase – replace it with what you *do* want. One of my favs is replacing the word 'busy' with 'full'. Call out your own BS; just give it a whirl for a week and see how you go, girl.

You'll then come to feel and realise that your mission statement isn't just a statement. It's a way of being. Your legacy and your mission are just a way of being yourself. They're not something that you have to push or prove. Being your unique and special self *is* your purpose. Language is a tool to help us feel into the person we want to be, so the process of habit change becomes one of coming into ever greater alignment rather than swimming against the current.

Practise loving discipline

Due to having Zephyr and Knox so close together, there was a period of almost three years where I didn't work. I started back for a short time, teaching two days a week in a secondary school. It made for big, messy, flat-out days, but I was enjoying it – at first. About five weeks in, I hit a wall. I was totally run-down and exhausted. My mouth was filled with ulcers. I was physically drained, and my spirit was running on empty.

In an attempt to be kind to myself, I'd accepted the fact that I wasn't journalling or reading or writing or any of the usual things I would do for self-care, creative expression, and nourishing my spirit. Instead of doing a short meditation or breathwork, I'd crash into bed exhausted and fall asleep the instant my head hit the pillow. My intentions were good, but they led me to a very dark place. Negative thoughts consumed me, and I found myself in a big dark hole. My habits weren't serving the person I wanted to be, but by the time I realised it, I was too sapped of energy to do very much about it.

Thankfully, I already knew about the one percenters. I decided to make one tiny change – so small it might even seem insignificant. I decided to fill up a glass of water each night before bed and place it on my bedside table. That way, it's the first thing I see when I wake up, and the first thing I do in the morning is drink that glass of water – before touching my phone, before doing anything else. (Credit to Dr Nicole LePera's book *How to Do the Work* for this idea.)

What does drinking a glass of water have to do with meditating or breathwork or nutritious meals or journalling? It might seem uncon-nected – but this one small thing, this new habit, has had a ripple effect. It's my daily reminder that I am worth taking care of, even if drinking this glass of water is the only act of self-care I get in that day – but many days I do more, and seeing this glass of water first thing in the morning sets the tone for that. It's a subtle reminder that I'm building self-trust and that I've got my own back. For me, it's helped me turn 'I'm such a failure, I'm not doing enough' into 'I can keep promises to myself, and I won't let myself down'.

What will be your act of loving discipline? It doesn't have to be a glass of water. It might be flossing your teeth or washing your face. The key is to make it simple and easy and do it daily. No one will applaud you; nobody else might even notice. But you will know.

This act of loving discipline differs from the other 'one percenter' habits and small wins. This is a promise you make to yourself to prove that you're worth showing up for. It's the catalyst to help you bring loving awareness throughout your day and embrace the new identity you're choosing for yourself. Doing it first thing in the morning is key. Shift your attention to yourself before you turn it on to everyone else.

Once you choose your habit, you can watch it grow. It may be the start of a morning routine where you cook yourself breakfast and then read ten pages of an inspiring book while drinking a cup of hot tea. But there will still be days when that original miniscule act of loving discipline is all you get to – and that's still enough. More than enough, in fact. And when you build that deep self-trust, there will be days when you don't keep your promise, but your trust is so unwavering that everything doesn't fall apart because of it.

HOW YOU CAN BE WITH THESE CONCEPTS

For each section of the book, I've pulled together my favourite tools and practices to help you implement the concepts covered in that section. I'd initially given these 'toolkit' sections the title *What You Can Do,* but it didn't sit right with me given the New Paradigm of motherhood is less about the *do* and more about the *be.* So, with help from my editors, we've renamed these sections 'How to be with these concepts'.

Can you feel how a small shift in language changes our perception? The exercises below are not something to put on your to-do list and work through mechanically, checking each one off. Take it slow and really feel into each one. Take the time to be with it. And if today is one of those days when drinking a glass of water is as much self-care as you're going to get in – well, there's nothing to feel bad about. No one living life and loving it to the fullest doesn't experience a lack of love and satisfaction from time to time. We're learning how to enjoy and honour all our stages, accepting that we will rise and fall and be all of the things. This is about following the breadcrumbs of love and laughter in your life, knowing they are within your reach.

In this section of the book, you've learned that reality is personal and is shaped by what we choose to pay attention to and what we tune out. By becoming aware of the filters and judgements we make, we can choose who we want to be and prove it to ourselves with little wins. We can use the transformative process of becoming mothers not just to *rebuild* our lives again but to *transform* for the better. But we must bring our body and intelligence to the party – as well as a healthy dose of self-acceptance. Your purpose is your driving force, your fire. And as mothers, we have a unique opportunity to create our reality and new identity from the ground up, knowing that we are a part of something so sacred and significant on the largest scale there is. We share a purpose, you and I. Taking some time to connect with that purpose every day is what makes a fulfilling life. Look into your baby's eyes and remember that they chose you. They knew you and how you would parent them before you even did. They trust you, and the universe has also entrusted you with this assignment. Because it is your calling. Relax and enjoy the ride – even when it's at its roughest.

Visit my website *emilyeast.com.au* and follow the prompts to download my meditation 'Activating Your Best Self' – in this activating meditation, I take you on a journey where you embody memories from when you felt gratitude, pride, purpose and meaning, love and connection, and powerful and courageous. We bring them forward to strengthen these parts of you, honouring that they are not something outside of you that you have to 'find' or develop but are already within you and arm's reach.

Visit my website *emilyeast.com.au* and do the free feminine archetype quiz. Learn more about yourself and the feminine collective in the process. I'm super proud of this one!

What does a day in your perfect life look like? What are you doing? Where are you? Who are you with? Journal on this for a minimum of thirty minutes, and just when you think you've finished, keep writing. If you can envision it, you can create it.

Call yourself out on your own BS – the limiting dialogue you express either internally or out loud. Write it down in your journal and then, right along next to it, replace it with something helpful. Use the examples from this chapter if you need a little help.

Brainstorm some ideas of what your act of loving discipline will be. Is it drinking a glass of water? Looking in the mirror and saying 'I love you'? Setting your alarm tone on your phone to music or words you want to hear first thing in the morning? (Just kidding, mums don't have alarm clocks, we have children for that – so choose an inspiring ringtone instead). Write out some ideas and then try them out this week to see which one works best.

A FEW WORDS ABOUT PLAY

How many of us ignore or suppress our creative sides in favour of more practical pursuits? How many of us give up on activities we do just for fun because we're supposed to be 'working' or we don't have time for them? How many of us opt to empty the dishwasher or fold one last load of washing before we lie on the floor and play with our children? (Me!) The reality for most of us is that we feel like we need to be productive over being 'creative' or having fun. We feel the pull to do practical things that will produce a certain outcome before we engage in the things that seem to lead nowhere. *If I fold this washing, I'll be up to date. If I empty the dishwasher, I'll feel productive for the day. If I have dinner ready before my husband gets home, I will have done a good job.* These things can certainly be fun, but the question is, do they leave us feeling empty when we're done, or do we feel nourished and refreshed?

In *Play: How It Shapes the Brain*, psychologist Stuart Brown describes how play opens the imagination and invigorates the soul. He calls play a 'public necessity' after studying the lack of play in the childhoods of young men who went on to commit homicidal acts. *Scary.* He has since studied the role of play in the lives of thousands of people. He found that a life lived without play contributes to the development of depression, chronic stress-related illnesses, and even criminal behaviour. He explains that a lack of play should be treated like malnutrition; it's a health risk to your body and your mind. I think this speaks so loudly, not just for the importance of fostering play in our children but of allowing and giving ourselves permission to play as well. As adults, it's crucial for us to prioritise the things in our lives that bring us joy in themselves, not because of any secondary gains. We can re-engage our sense of childlike wonder. Just watch your children play; that's a good place to start! What I've been doing to engage in this is playing music. Playing music, singing, and dancing! When I'm bathing the kids, when I'm folding washing, when I'm just being with my children. We can do something off the cuff, be impulsive, follow our passions. We can try something new that we've always wanted to do without needing to perfect it or be good at it. Learn how to cook, study a new language. Get your hands dirty in the garden. Buy a sewing machine. Compliment a stranger on her outfit. These examples share one component: doing something for enjoyment, not for any external reward. Let's stop punishing ourselves if we take a moment to rest and play and not do those things we see as 'productive'. The question is, what do you do just for the mere joy of it? What do you do not because of any secondary gains (like money, success, adoration, or to keep others alive and well) but just for the pure enjoyment it brings?

If you're not sure, here are some questions you can journal on to discover more about what brings you joy and how you can bring more play into your life. Catherine Price has a brilliant book called *The Power of Fun* that helps you unpack what truly lights you up and how you can get more of it. I highly recommend it! (Since reading her book, I took up guitar lessons and do Shirley Barber fairy puzzles that I loved when I was a little girl, which has been *so* fun. I've found that by bringing more fun into my life, I'm less stressed, less tired, more motivated, more creative, and more engaged in my life).

- When in your life have you laughed the hardest? What were you doing? Who were you with?

- What is a time or a memory when you felt playfully rebellious or harmlessly deviant?

- What are some moments from your life where you felt most alive? What were you doing? Who were you with?

- Which people are often present in the moments when you have the most fun?

LESSONS FROM THE MOON

☾ WHY THE MOON?

The moon is the divine mother herself. She represents life's seasons and teaches us that whether we are full, half full, or just a sliver of our potential, we're still shiny and magical. Connecting with her is powerful because her natural rhythms can show us how to connect to our inherent wisdom and truth within ourselves. You can google the full and new moon dates (there's one of each in every month) where you are living and pop them in your calendar. Whether you believe the moon holds powerful energy or not, the routine of having two dates per month in your diary to check in with yourself will be powerful in itself. I can't stress enough how these rituals have changed my life. I have a close group of girlfriends, and we used to meet on the new moon and do the ritual together. There's nothing like a group of women getting together for the sole purpose of lifting each other up. Women coming together to give energy and support is in our bones and DNA. The full moon, to me, seems a lot more sacred. Give the ritual a whirl and reclaim your feminine ancient wisdom by practising on your own or in a group. Here are some rituals I like to get you started; feel free to use them or make your own. Get creative, sister. And enjoy. I run workshops and rituals like this monthly inside our Soul Nation online community – pop over to *emilyeast.com.au* to join us, and I'll guide you through one!

☽ FULL MOON

On a full moon, the Earth, moon, and sun are in approximate alignment, with the Earth in the middle, so that the entire sunlit part of the moon is facing us and the shadowed portion is entirely hidden from view. To harness the power of the full moon, we can embody her energy by practising the elements of her phases ourselves. The full moon is about cleansing. It's the perfect time to trust, surrender, and let go. We can take this time to release the things that are no longer serving us and to forgive the people and experiences that have hurt us (including ourselves).

You will need:

- Loose/scrap paper (something you can burn);
- Lighter or matches;
- Pen;
- Palo santo (the wood, resin, or oil of *Bursera graveolens*, used to clear negative energy) or sage or selenite rod to cleanse; and
- Favourite crystal (optional).

What to do:

1. Cleanse your space and your aura using either your sage or palo santo;

2. On the paper, use the journal prompts to write down the things you desire to let go of. Feel into them completely when you write them; you can use music to help you get into the zone. Ask yourself, What do you want to let go of? What is no longer serving you? Which thoughts, feelings, or actions would you like to relinquish before the next moon cycle? Which beliefs are you aware of that are holding you back? It's important to let them go with love, not out of hate or out of thinking these emotions or actions are wrong. They are all part of your experience. They have come to you to draw your attention to something, and now it's time to give them a big hug, say thank you for the lessons, and send them on their way;

3. Burn the paper to ashes, either in a sink or outside (with the motto of safety first, of course), to symbolise the cleansing and releasing. As you watch the paper burn to ashes, whisper to yourself 'let' on the in-breath and 'go' on the out-breath;

4. Pop your favourite crystals outside on the Earth under the full moon; this will charge up and enhance the energy in the crystal.

Mantra / Mirror Work for the Full Moon

| I trust | I surrender |
| I let go | I am safe |

☾ NEW MOON

A new moon occurs when the Earth, moon, and sun are in approximate alignment, but, unlike on a full moon, the moon is in the middle. In this alignment, the entire illuminated portion of the moon is the half that we cannot see.

The new moon is like an empty vessel. It symbolises new beginnings and new opportunities. It's the perfect time to reflect on your goals and ways of living, spend time manifesting and visualising whatever it is you desire, and feel into the emotion of already having these things. I like to think of the full moon as making room for new things, like cleaning out old clothes to make room for new ones. The new moon is about bringing *into* your life to fill the space you have cleared. You wouldn't buy a new couch without anywhere to put it, right? It's like saying to the universe, *'Hey, girl – I've made some energetic space, and I trust you'll fill it with something awesome and meant just for me, even if I don't know what this is yet.'* The full moon and new moon rituals go hand in hand. They work together.

You will need:

- Your journal and pen;
- Oracle or tarot cards (optional);
- Palo santo or sage or selenite rod;
- Lighter or matches; and
- Favourite crystal (optional).

What to do:

1. Cleanse your space and your aura with your chosen cleaning tool;

2. In your journal, write about who you'd like to be and what energy you'd like to encompass coming into the new moon cycle. You could ask yourself, What do I want to feel during this cycle? Are there some things I can put in place to help me

soften into this desired energy? What emotions do I feel in the perfect day for me?

3. Place your favourite crystal (perhaps the one you charged up under the last full moon) on top of your journal to use the crystal's energy to bring your words to life;

4. Draw yourself some tarot cards for an extra juicy dose of inspiration and guidance.

Mantra / Mirror Work for the New Moon

I am capable   I am creative
I am worthy and deserving   I am safe

HOW TO USE TAROT CARDS

You can usually buy tarot cards in those tiny shops with so many crystals and lamps and things hanging from the roof that you can't move around in there without making something chime. Usually, it is a place that smells of incense and sells those hippie pants and salt lamps. That's a good place to look. Look at all the card deck options, and listen to your intuition. See if a deck stands out to you. Don't overthink it, just touch the cards, feel them, and see which ones ask you to take them home. Those are the ones for you. But, if online is more your game, I'll give you full permission to judge a book by its cover and decide that way. If that still freaks you out a little, my favourite decks are by Chris-Anne, and you can find them online.

You will need:

- Deck of cards;
- Journal and pen; and
- Cleansing tool of choice.

What to do:

1. Before you draw your cards, cleanse the deck with your palo santo or sage. You can additionally (or alternatively) cleanse them by touching each individual card to inject your energy into them;

2. Shuffle the cards until you intuitively feel they're ready, then place the deck face down;

3. Using your dominant hand, split the deck three times;

4. Still using your dominant hand, split the deck in half, and place the bottom half on top of the other pile. Then draw three cards from the top of the pack and lay them face up so you can read them.

Let the cards tickle your senses. Play with them. Use them to springboard your curiosity and stir up inspiration and mind's-eye imagery. Let the cards stimulate your subconscious mind, and let the beauty of the cards speak to your soul.

The card decks will include a booklet on how to use them – but I also found that the book *Make It Happen* by Jordanna Levin was pivotal for me in my spiritual journey; I highly recommend it. She will also give you powerful tips for reading your cards.

THE SIGNIFICANCE OF FIRE AND HOW TO CLEANSE

Fire is a powerful force of destruction, creation, transformation, and purification. It has been used across various cultures for centuries as part of core spiritual and ritual practices. In some Native American traditions, a shamanic fire ceremony is performed to clear negative energies and any unnecessary attachments to make way for the new energy and intentions.

In the Hindu Vedic ritual 'Havan', offerings are made to the sacred fire for worship energy and protection. Some Indigenous Australians perform traditional smoking ceremonies to ward off bad spirits, pay respect to the departed, celebrate, and to clear and heal. Esoteric Buddhists hold a Goma fire ceremony to burn away the roots of suffering and to pray for their intentions to manifest. In Paganism, the celebration of Litha, or Summer Solstice, is often accompanied by a fire ceremony as a form of worshipping the sun.

Incorporating fire into a full or new moon ritual mirrors all of the above traditions. Fire can be a powerful tool for releasing things that no longer serve us.

The art of cleansing or 'smudging' is an ancient spiritual ritual for purification, dispelling negative energy, and improving mood and can easily be incorporated into your weekly routine or meditative practice. Smudging is the ritual of cleaning the energy of a physical space, object, or person. If you have a meditation ritual, you can burn Sage or Palo Santo before your practice. This will help prepare your energy and mind for meditation and allow you to more easily connect.

1. First you start with a simple intention of focusing on clearing the negative energy out of your space and mind.

2. Once you have your intention in mind, light the Sage or Palo Santo and hold at a 45-degree angle pointing the tip down towards the flame. Allow it to burn for 30 seconds and then blow it out.

3. If left to rest on a heat proof surface, the stick will smoulder and release smoke for about 5 minutes. If used for smudging, walk around the room, space, object, or person, fanning the smoke over its entirety while focusing on cleansing and clearing negative energy. (You can cleanse your own body as well as your babe's or partner – given it's safe to do so and they're not asthmatic, of course. If their skin starts tingling or

their eyes burn, it means they're a demon (lol, just kidding). Please only do it to others with their permission.

4. Once you've finished smudging and removed the negative energy, you can push positive energy into the space to maintain balance. To do this, declare your intention out loud or silently in your head, or you could simply invite new opportunities in.

You can cleanse your space anytime you feel drawn to; otherwise, here are some good options: before you go to bed after a long day being around people, before and after you've had guests in your home, when you move into a new home, before and after a healing session, before meditation, after any illness, or after you've had an argument or some kind of conflict. My favourite time to cleanse is after I've cleaned out my cupboards or have done a big clean or when I just feel like I need to press the reset button.

PART TWO
Control vs Surrender

My head is at ease knowing that what was meant for me
will never miss me, and that what misses me was never
meant for me.

Imam al-Shaf'i, *Source Unknown*

We need to wake ourselves up in the midst of this great
freaky game by savoring it, enjoying it, grieving exquisitely
for it, getting off on it, just like God does. When we do
this, we become lucid in the dream of waking life, capable
of executing marvels. We become undeniably, tangibly
aware of the divine presence, the spark of Godself within
us. We start to perceive our lives from the perspective of
the divine curiosity within us instead of from our grasping
egos.

Carolyn Elliott, *Existential Kink*

CHAPTER FIVE

Too Much Happiness

The greatest advantage of not having children must be that you can go on believing that you are a nice person. Once you have children, you realise how wars start.

Fay Weldon

The powerful, fierce feminine is very much a part of the psyche, but it is repressed; and when it is not acknowledged because it is threatening, it can become subversive and vengeful. But when it is acknowledged and honoured, it's an incredible source of power.

Lama Tsultrim Allione, *Wisdom Rising: Journey into the Mandala of the Empowered Feminine.*

Look at any high school yearbook, and you'll see that a decent proportion of teenagers list their life's aspiration as simply to be happy. In and of itself, that seems like a harmless and even admirable goal, doesn't it? In a sense, it reflects the lessons of the previous section of this book: no matter your job or life circumstances, you can choose to find happiness in the small moments.

But another, more sinister phenomenon has emerged from the emphasis our modern-day culture and society place on being happy. Many of us are uncomfortable if we're *not* happy all the time, and it leads us to pretend to be happy when we're not. I discovered all this when I studied positive psychology during my university years – ironically, a time in my life when I was still wrapped up in doing rather than being – but I really learned it in my bones once I became a mother.

I grew up in a household that valued education and modelled the power of personal development. My mum was always working on herself, and I knew that knowledge was power.

I was in a car accident when I was twenty years old. It scared the bejesus out of me and led me down a scary path of depression and anxiety. The logical, intelligent, and only way I knew I was going to pull myself out of this was to change the direction of my life and go to university to study the body and the brain. I wanted to understand what was happening with my thoughts and how I could change them. As I struggled to claw myself out of the black hole I felt I was stuck in, intelligence and brain power seemed like a rational and familiar way I could do it.

I moved to the city and started my degree, majoring in psychology and biology. My eyes began to open to the wonderful world of wellness and well-being. I started to learn to meditate, oil pull, and eat organic fruit and veg. Because I had such a shaky sense of self, I was clinging to any new craze of buzzwords in the health and wellness industry. I completed my thesis on positive psychology and strengths-based approaches and was a die-hard believer in gratitude. I practised it religiously and used positive affirmations like they were band-aids on any minor or major inconvenience I had. I didn't know it at the time, but I was suppressing anything negative that came up for me. I was divorcing myself from anger, aggression, and fear because I had labelled these emotions as 'bad'. I pushed away any desire I had that didn't meet the expectations of the 'happy' life. I knew how the brain worked; I knew I could train it to be happy and grateful. So if I had any subtle fears or doubts, I thought something was wrong – and I disconnected from those feelings and any parts of me that I didn't like. I'd lost touch with my body and my feelings, and I'd forgotten how to listen to the whispers of my soul because I had shut down any tender yearnings I had that didn't match this ideal, squeaky clean, happy life.

Interestingly, even though I was studying positive psychology, I was actually misinterpreting how to put it into practice. Whereas traditional psychology has been about studying what's wrong with a person and relieving human suffering, positive psychology flips traditional psychology on its head and views living well as more than just the absence of disease or suffering. Positive psychology is the study of what is *right* about a person and raising the bar for the human condition to get the most out of life – and, as it turns out, Martin Seligman, the father of positive psychology, actually wrote in his book *Flourish* that he despises the word *happiness*.

As Seligman conducted his research into what makes a satisfying life, he noticed a major flaw in the research methods being used. Life satisfaction was typically researched using a self-report measure that asked, on a scale of one to ten, how satisfied a person was with their life, from terrible (a score of one) to ideal (ten). It turns out, however, that how much life satisfaction people report is determined by how good they feel when asked the question. So it's the mood you are in that determines how satisfied you are. And as we know (perhaps a little too well, being mums), our mood fluctuates and changes more times than we have washing to fold or dishes to wash. The results, then, don't reveal how you judge or reflect on your life but how you feel in that moment, and satisfaction is disproportionately tied to mood. When people ask me how the boys are going, my answer will either be 'they're so cute and going so well, thank you' or 'oh my god, they're insane. Three-year-olds are harrrrrrrrrd', depending on my mood. Obviously, I still love them in both scenarios, but depending on my day, how much sleep I've had, what food I've eaten, and where I'm at in my cycle will determine how I assess my life in a given moment.

Hence, positive psychology came to envision the goal not as constant positive mood and life satisfaction but rather as a deeper sense of well-being and flourishing (as in the title of Dr Seligman's book). To flourish doesn't mean you are just happy and go around high-fiving everybody and wearing daisy chains around your head; it means you are living a meaningful, purposeful, and engaged life – independent of how you feel in any given moment.

Even though I focused on positive psychology in my studies, it took me some time to learn this. After I graduated, the popularity of movies like *The Secret*, the *Heal* documentary, and the work of Louise Hay only plunged me deeper into the shadow side of positive psychology. I was terrified of thinking a negative thought – scared that if I allowed those parts of me in, I would manifest a life I didn't want or create an illness that would knock my cotton socks right off (and not in a good way). I felt something was wrong with me if I wasn't feeling good all the time. I became so obsessed with the pursuit of happiness that I would be overly grateful for a cup of coffee, and I lacked the confidence to send it back if it was too cold.

Hashtags like #firstworldproblems cemented the idea that negative emotions were socially unacceptable. If someone posts a mild grievance on social media, it's not uncommon to see them get slammed in the comments for being ungrateful. With social media, we're in each other's faces all the time, and there is pressure to show only the parts we love about our lives and ourselves for fear of being labelled spoiled or privileged. Then when we see other people posting only the highlights, it further reinforces the idea that we shouldn't share anything that doesn't fit the pattern. While we don't want to be the annoying pain in the a** who complains about evanescent things, it seems like it's no longer okay to feel annoyed or frustrated anymore; experiencing negative emotions has become socially unacceptable.

Motherhood, however, doesn't provide us with the luxury of feeling positive all the time and excluding all other emotional states. Our children push us to such extremes; the trials of motherhood lead us into a relationship with the forgotten and disowned parts of ourselves. What we bury and hide, what we deem unacceptable, stays hidden until motherhood pushes us so far that those emotions are forced to the surface. It may feel enormously uncomfortable, but encountering those parts we'd rather not know about is a necessary step on the path of growth. Motherhood allows us the opportunity to redeem and reclaim these rejected parts of ourselves, and the depth of the love we have for our children powers us through the discomfort. This renewal, arising in such an unexpected place, can be wholly transformative. The desire to feel happy all of the time has resulted in social pressure to deny and demonise negative emotions. Still, the negative emotions and the parts of ourselves we wish we didn't have are the portals to individualisation, wholeness, and authenticity. Just like comparing ourselves with other mums leads to feelings of inadequacy, it's not the actual challenging emotions that are the problem – it's the fact that we're forcing ourselves to be happy when we're not. When we stop telling ourselves what we 'should' be feeling and, instead, notice and accept what we actually feel, the self-acceptance we experience in these moments can provide a deeper level of contentment than the superficial happiness we were chasing.

Now, this isn't to say we should fixate on the negative. My initial impulse to practise gratitude wasn't misguided – but its shadow side appeared in the form of my fear and resistance to anything that made gratitude challenging. Human beings have an innate negativity bias that is rooted in our survival instinct. (From an evolutionary perspective, it's important that our brains tell us it's more urgent to run away from the bear that's just appeared than to keep snacking on the juicy berries in front of us.) The primitive brain that developed even before we were human beings, per se, continues to look out for us, scanning the environment for threats. It has now been shown in a wide variety of studies that a regular practice of gratitude – commonly framed as calling to mind or writing down 'three good things' to help us override that negativity bias – has benefits including improved sleep, decreased stress levels and blood pressure, increased immunity, and improved emotional regulation. In other words, Bridget Jones probably would have smoked way fewer cigarettes and drunk way less wine if she had included a little more gratitude in her diaries.

The natural state of human beings and other mammals is to be somewhat on guard at all times. However, in order to feel emotionally close to another human being, we must let that guard down a bit. To reproduce, nurture, and play with our babies, the brain needs to turn off its natural vigilance. Think about it – can you relax and enjoy the moment if you're caught up in worst-case scenarios and fears about your relationship or your child's development? Not really. Gratitude, then, offers a way to soften ourselves and put our body and mind to rest in the comfort that we are safe and surrounded by pleasures. Gratitude is a useful tool that directs attention to positive experiences and helps to keep this negative bias and hypervigilant defence mechanism in check. Too easily, though, it can drift into the same kind of toxic positivity that led me not to ask for my coffee to be reheated. Because seriously, a mum *needs* and *deserves* a hot cup of coffee, for goodness sake.

Recall from the last section that we desire meaning and purpose. Human beings naturally seek meaning and purpose in life; we seek to belong to and serve something bigger than ourselves. When we choose to become mums, we're choosing a life that's not all about feeling good in the moment – and we shouldn't beat ourselves up for not feeling happy all the time.

Remember that distinction Martin Seligman made between happiness and flourishing? On days when we don't feel great in the moment, we can still recognise that, overall, we are flourishing. For example, I might listen to Baby Shark on repeat and read the same tractor book for the fifteenth excruciating time in a row, not because it makes me feel good, but because it's my parental duty and part of what gives my life meaning. Then, later, I might choose to sit and watch *Friends* while I have a cuppa and a choc biccy because *that* makes me feel good. I choose to do these activities for their own sake, not because they give my life more meaning or for any other reason. The activities that bring me happiness in the moment are not necessarily connected to my higher purpose – and that's just fine as long as I'm clear on the distinction.

Anger: embracing the dark side

As a new mum of two, I prided myself on being warm and patient and generally quite deliberate with my positive and peaceful approaches, thank you very much. There had been times when I was tested, for sure, but I generally felt like I was doing a good job. But one day, that changed for me. My husband had been working late that week, and my second son had been awake through the night teething. I'd wake up through the night, ears pricked, praying I didn't hear crying, to then wake at 5:00 a.m. with Zephyr demanding we start the day. Broken sleep and long days. Knox was also transitioning from two sleeps to one, so I had to be spot on with his nap times to ensure I had at least an hour to breathe myself full again. The boys had been fighting and irritating each other all day. Zephyr was playing with his trains, and Knox couldn't even look at them without copping his brother's wrath. I was thinking to myself, *I can barely hold them off each other* now; *what will I do when they get bigger and stronger?*

Slowly counting down the minutes until bedtime so I could match their sleep times, I thought about how I would fill in the day. It would be nice to go for a walk with someone else who had kids, but everyone was working. And wrestling two boys into the car and packing enough snacks to keep them manageable seemed like more than I could handle. At least if I stayed home, we could all stay in our PJs, and I could avoid the struggle of getting them dressed. So I opted for the TV to give myself a break. Feeling guilty that they watch too much, I felt self-doubt and worry trickle in. These emotions, mixed with desperation for bedtime, anxiety, and self-doubt, were all adding flames under the simmering pot of rage about to boil over.

Naptime finally came, and to my surprise and relief, Knox went down easily. Desperate to get Zephyr down as well so I could take solace in a cup of tea and some mindless TV myself, I sped-read through his naptime books, skipping pages and mumbling words. I threw the books back in the corner, said no to his requests for more stories, and got out of there as quickly as I could. And he stayed in there just long enough for me to boil the kettle, make myself a tea, and choose a Netflix special.

I sat down and took one sip of my peppermint tea, almost crying with gratitude and relieved by the sweet reprieve of naptime. Then I heard Zephyr's door open, and he tiptoed his way out to see me. Reluctantly, I put my tea down, and without saying a word, I walked him back to bed. He pleaded with me to stay and play with him, but I just repeated over and over, 'It's time for a sleep now. It's time for bed'. *Phew*. I snuck out of the room without too much kickback. Somehow, I'd managed to coax him back into bed and under his covers. I flopped back down onto the couch and staked another soul-soothing sip of my hot and rejuvenating tea.

Then my ears pricked, I got a shiver down my spine, and I sat still as a statue as I heard his bedroom door open once again. Having so much success with my last attempt, I used the same calm and repetitive technique to get him back into bed. But I didn't even make it back to the couch before he was up again. I was biting my lips, barely breathing as I hoped and prayed his pleas to stay out of bed didn't wake Knox. I felt like I would literally die if that happened. Then Zephyr started to do his blood-curdling scream that triggers me right down to my soul.

I continued this merry-go-round for fifty minutes, trying all my tricks, desperately trying to stay calm and just as desperately watching the clock and pleading that I'd get at least fifteen minutes for myself. It was complete agony as I felt the heat dissipating from my once-hot cup of heaven. Trying to stay calm, hoping to outlast or outwit him, I felt as if my ears were bleeding from his desperate cries – and I was about to join him.

With all this rage and impatience and sleep deprivation bubbling at the surface, I was no longer capable of any discernment. I was angry at myself for not just putting him on the couch half an hour ago – I'm sure he would have fallen asleep there with the TV on. When I heard Knox start to stir and Zephyr pulling on his door handle, the simmering pot boiled over. I stormed over to his door, my blood was spiked with stress, and rage and guilt surged in my veins. In a fury, I slammed open his door. Now he knew – I could see it in his face. I watched in slow motion as his face turned to confusion and fear. I stood over him, knowing how scary and big I must seem to him, and I bellowed, 'Stay in bed!'

The release felt good. His little body jerked with fear, and he ran back to his bed, terrified. He was still screaming but stayed in his bed, and I stormed out, slamming the door behind me. I stood there, listening to his screams as he lay in his bed. I'd gotten what I wanted, but in the moments after, all the anger was gone and just sadness remained. I went back into his room, held him tight, and apologised over and over again. It was when I finally got his little body to soften and his tears to stop that I heard Knox wake. I remember thinking at that moment, *I'm doing a terrible job.*

Remember Lisa Marchiano's analogy that motherhood is like being flung down a dark well? A fall like this will initially involve numerous losses, including a loss of freedom, a loss of control, and a loss of ourselves. Floundering around at the bottom in the darkness can be scary, and returning home can be harder for some than for others. Often, old and painful wounds will be brought to the surface again while we're down there, but if we don't shy away from them, we will have opportunities to heal ourselves.

Being open to your inner world and what you encounter and experience down the well, even though it can be painful, always offers the possibility of renewal. There is no doubt that this transformation can be painful, lonely, and even frightening, especially when it feels so dark that we can't see a way out. However, the difficult feelings you encounter while you're down there are not to be avoided. It is in this darkness that new things grow. It's the darkness that gives rise to transformation. We must meet whatever 'demons' we find down there with curiosity, humility, and open-heartedness if we are to return from the well with gifts of expansion, compassion, and wholeness.

It isn't helpful to spend our lives dangling our feet over the edge of the well, praying and hoping we don't fall in. All this energy spent on avoiding the well can leave us feeling depleted and exhausted, not to mention how excruciating it is to live out of alignment with who we are. We don't live a balanced and authentic life that way. We need to embrace the plunge and trust that whatever we experience down there, we can love it so hard that it transforms into something beautiful. I dangled on the edge of the well for so long, suppressing my rage like when I screamed at my son, that when I couldn't hold it any longer, it was like a destructive, wreckless force. The part of me that told me I was doing a terrible job was also the part of me that instigated change. So I love it for that.

Analytical psychologist Carl Jung called doing this work 'shadow work' or exploring our 'shadow self'. Fully exploring this concept would require stepping into the deepest portals of the psyche, and hey, that could be a whole other book. So in the interests of brevity, I will bring you up to speed with the basics of Jungian shadow work and how it influences how you show up for yourself and your children. In essence, the shadow self is the darker side of ourselves that we repress or ignore. It is the parts that scare the pants off us when we're at the bottom of the well: The anger, the resentment, the depression, the loneliness, the guilt, the parts that feel misunderstood and like we're being 'too much'. The parts that feel too scary for us even to face, let alone try to explain to someone else. But if we don't embrace the entirety of our being, including the parts we're confronted with at the very depth of our being, we can't live a full and unfettered life.

Confronting these parts can mean letting go of the ways this shadow side is secretly serving us – and perhaps finding more productive ways to meet the needs our maladaptive habits served. It's not an easy or pleasant process. But '... until you make the unconscious conscious, it will direct your life', Jung tendered, 'and you will call it fate'. Until we shed light on the darkness, it will continue to run our lives.

The idea of shadow work is acknowledging all parts of the psyche, effectively bringing what is dark into the light, where Jung said you will find 'ninety percent pure gold'. A shadow can lead to limiting beliefs, which may snowball into all manner of undesirable outcomes: self-sabotage, destructive ego and behaviour, and ruined relationships. Without doing this work, you can't live wholeheartedly or reach individualisation or authenticity. Shadow work actualises living a multifaceted life that incorporates the good, the bad, the beautiful, the ugly, the embarrassing, the uncertain – which encompasses all of the mothering experience. All of it. It's about learning to accept that we can still love our children, ourselves, and our lives when riding life's cycling energies.

All of us reach adulthood having sustained some injury to our sense of self – because, even if our parents encouraged us to embrace all parts of ourselves fully, greater society hasn't gotten that memo yet. Motherhood provides us with an opportunity for healing and transformation by pushing us to the brink. Our children so eloquently (and sometimes not so eloquently) evoke so much within us – parts we didn't even know were there, emotions we had buried deep within ourselves that pop their head again, and some brand new ones too. And, as we learn the lessons from our shadows, we can pass our learnings on to our children, providing our own evolution as an example *and* teaching them to recognise and embrace all parts of themselves.

All the shadow self wants is acceptance and acknowledgement. When the shadow is accepted and acknowledged, it can be seen for what it is – absolute golden nuggets of wisdom – and we can approach it with curiosity and pure love. By doing this, we grow more whole and come closer to who we really are at our core. Opening ourselves to these qualities may be painful, and our ego will try to defend them at all costs, but it will also result in our consciousness being fundamentally changed, and we transform.

Looking back on that day when my anger boiled over, I realised it had been suppressed for so long that it was just dying to get out. Somewhere along the line, I internalised the idea that anger was not okay; anger was to be hidden, shut down. That it was wrong. So I played by the rules and kept it inside until motherhood demanded that I become in touch with all of myself, just like when I first lost my temper with my son. Motherhood evoked my anger so I could be given the opportunity to build a healthy relationship with it, to hold more space for myself. To tenderly hold all of me with compassion and therefore have a deeper understanding and compassion for others' pain, too. Particularly my children's.

By doing this work, facing my shadow selves, I can be more authentic and whole. I can hold more space for myself, and over time, I begin to attune to my instincts and listen to their whispers before they have to scream at me. I am not possessed or consumed by my shadows. I don't lose myself to them. Or when I do (because I'm human), it's an invitation to spend some time connecting to myself. This healthy relationship I develop with them enables them to come to my table with their gifts of love and vitality rather than destruction and their iron fist. Motherhood may offer one of the few experiences in our lives where we most clearly see our own shadow because our children can push us to such extreme somatic states. And it allows us to choose a different way for ourselves and our children.

Our culture overvalues an idealised, unrealistic set of expectations about ourselves and our experience of motherhood. Our shadow side – dark, wild, and sometimes frightening but also filled with vitality and authenticity – is notably hidden in the public arena. So much of ourselves and the ways we experience motherhood are hidden. We idealise the notion of blissful unity and find it hard to admit that struggle and despair are also a part of the experience. The energies we have in our deep interior are very different from the part of ourselves we consciously show the world. So in light of sharing my unpolished, unfiltered self, I'll tell you that one time I got so exhausted and angry while mothering, I fucked up a wash basket. I threw it into the wall over and over again until it broke into tiny pieces. And fuck, it felt *good*. The painful part comes from judging ourselves for the anger even if we express it in a sacred way, which realistically is a completely justified emotion given our circumstances. Even if your children witness this anger, this inner lioness, don't be too hard on yourself. You're showing them that you have another level, that you're capable of great things, that you have an inner fire ready to ignite and light up the skies whenever your kids need it. And that if you're kids needed you to, you'd unleash the beast to keep them safe. I don't think that that's the worst thing. I've learned over time that anger isn't the enemy; it's how we express it that holds the weight. We can learn to consciously release it (which I'll show you how in a later chapter) rather than have it explode out of us unruly and unconsciously.

Many times, while doing my own shadow work, I have experienced my shadow selves coming to me while deep in a meditative state. This visualisation is like a dream, and in the dream, I arrive as my highest self, floating on air in my pure goddessness. When I invite these parts of myself in – the angry self, the resentful self, the mean self – I envision them as other versions of me. I invite them in, and we sit together at a round table. The round table symbolises a lot of things – inclusivity and equality. But more than that, I, as my highest self, ask the other parts of me what they need. I hold space for them, and I listen to them. I acknowledge what they need, and I give it to them. And when I do, my body relaxes, I relax, and they loosen their grip on my attention. They return to me and my highest self, and we merge together and make a more whole and expansive version of me. It's like I heal these parts. Ironically, I judge these parts of me. I judge them for being mean, selfish, and exclusive. But it's actually me who is being those things by not giving these parts a voice.

Have I lost you? If I don't let the mean, judgemental, and bitchy parts of me have a voice – but when you look closer, *I'm* being mean and judgemental by *not* giving them a voice. As soon as I validate and recognise what these parts of me need, without labelling them as good or bad, I set myself free. These parts don't fight so much for my attention. They don't have to haunt me anymore and no longer tug at my heels because they have been seen and heard – and that's all they ever wanted.

PARTS OF YOURSELF

WHAT PARTS OF YOURSELF HAS MOTHERHOOD EXPOSED THAT YOU WISH YOU DIDN'T HAVE? PERHAPS IT FELT UNCOMFORTABLE, SCARY, OR SURPRISING.

Envision this part of you breaking away from your being and standing right in front of you.

Take yourself back to the moment you discovered this shadow, and feel the sensations you felt within your body. For example, my angry self manifests as a tightness in my chest, my teeth gritting, and my face hot. Make these sensations very real for yourself; feel them within your body.

As your highest self, ask your shadow or that part of you, 'What do you need?' Give your shadow parts a voice, give them the microphone, and let them express everything they're feeling without holding back. For example, my angry shadow self just wants to be noticed, she wants more help, and she wants someone to tell her she's doing a good job.

Once you understand what your shadow needs, can you give it to her? Can you envision your highest self opening her arms and embracing your shadow? Give her everything she is asking for and tell her what she longs to hear.

Notice the sensations change within your body and, with curiosity, see what happens next.

I often see my two parts, my shadow and my highest self, merge together. And it's like my shadow lives in my heart, and every now and then, I'll bring her out and heal her by making her feel seen and heard and loved unconditionally.

Resentment: follow where it leads

As emotions go, anger is pretty straightforward. Resentment, however, is anger tangled up with feelings of injustice, sadness, guilt, and envy. It's emotional soup.

Let's break it down with an example. We might feel angry because we want the time and freedom others seem to have (particularly our husbands if your situation is similar to mine). We feel envious of the time they have to themselves, and it can feel unfair that we are constantly on 'kid duty'. (That twenty-minute car ride in solitude that he gets on his way to work? What a dream!) And then, to cap it off, we feel guilty that we feel this way and that we want time away from our kids.

This scenario played out when Zac informed me that he was going on a fishing trip with his cousins and uncles. The boys were just one and two years old at the time (aka a handful). While I would have preferred that he not go for so long, my higher self was happy for him. I knew he would be in his element, as it's one of his favourite things to do. Doing things that bring us joy and pleasure is something we all very much deserve and need. But what consumed me was feelings of resentment. I was resentful as hell. I was angry because I wanted a trip away and some 'me time'. I was green with envy because he could have time to himself, and I felt it was unfair that he got to relax and I had to be at home with the kids by myself. Then, to top it off, I felt guilty that I reacted this way because I 'shouldn't' want so much time away from my kids, and I was selfish and ungrateful.

It took some time for me to learn that I wasn't mad at him; I was mad at *myself* for not giving or creating for myself what I needed. You see, the resentment we feel toward others can be a wildly useful tool in helping us understand what we want for ourselves. Once I learned and felt this to be true, I felt a shift in how I was prioritising myself and my needs. It's hard, but after a while, it just started to make sense. It was easier and more familiar to blame Zac or to put being responsible for my resentment onto him or something outside of myself. Then it wasn't my fault. But in the process of pointing my righteous finger, I slowly, over time, began to notice the three fingers pointing back at me. It's hard to look in the mirror and face your resentment, but understanding it instead of wallowing in it has a much bigger payoff.

I wanted to feel okay with Zac leaving the house. I wanted to feel okay with Zac going to see his friends, play golf, or have a weekend camping and fishing. But in the beginning, I was just so consumed by feelings of resentment. Wasn't it enough that he got to leave the house to go to work every day while I stayed home? Wasn't it enough that he could leave the house whenever he wanted while I had to organise babysitters and sit on the breast pump for a week if I wanted to go anywhere? Wasn't it enough that his life seemed to seamlessly carry on while I was knitting back the pieces of my fragmented self? These were what were most triggering for me.

The question to ask yourself is: What do you resent the most? Is it the lack of freedom and control, like it is for me? Or perhaps it's something different? Whatever hits a nerve for you the most is what's worth fighting for and giving yourself. You might have to get creative.

Here's how Zac and I have solved the issue. At the beginning of the year, he and I go through our schedules and book monthly nights out, taking turns. When it's my turn, I like to go to the city to shop with friends or my sister, or visit wine country and get massages. Sometimes it's just a night out with some cocktails and BFFs. It doesn't really matter what I do, but that one night away every so often gives me a sense of freedom. It's me answering the call of my resentment and using it as a tool to understand my own needs. It's a need that I can meet. If we're so busy pushing our resentment down, we'll never notice the signals it is giving us about how to meet our own needs.

The dark feminine: the key to our instincts

Sleep with your baby; don't sleep with your baby.

Feed your baby to sleep; don't put your baby down asleep.

Follow their lead; follow a routine.

Use a dummy; don't use a dummy (or a pacifier for my U.S. sisters).

The earlier, the better with toilet training; the later, the better with toilet training.

Start feeding your baby fruit when they start solids; start your baby on bitter veggies when they start solids.

Like, seriously! No wonder we can doubt ourselves and get overwhelmed and have those moments when we feel we're doing it wrong. In a culture that values intelligence and rationality, there is no shortage of 'expert' opinions and advice out there. Even when we don't go looking for it, as new mothers, we are always facing pressure from mothers before us who are eager to share their tidbits of unwanted and unsolicited advice. But what works for one mother might not work for another.

A little bit of information is good and powerful, but too much can be confusing and overwhelming. Oh my goodness, I spent a whole day online researching and wading through all the information I could find about how to start babies on solids. When Zephyr was ready to start solids, I sold my soul to the internet and fell down the rabbit hole of research, leaving me floundering and in a tizz by the time Zac got home. It seemed like there was just as good an argument for starting your baby on fruits as there was for starting them on vegetables. I was overwhelmed, to say the least. What I wish I could go back and tell that version of myself is to start looking within for the answers I was seeking. Put the parenting books down, step away from the podcasts and mummy blogs. Tune out of the outside noise and tune into my inner wisdom – you'll always find the answer there.

The thing is, there are so many forces conspiring to encourage us to ignore this wisdom. There is a concept known as the 'dark feminine', similar to our shadow side but specific to women. It refers to the inner goddess we all have within us. The 'dark' part of it comes in when she's left in the shadows for too long, not listened to. That's when she becomes unruly and destructive. She's the part of us that screams and ruins everything in her path, and she's also the one who sets firm boundaries to keep us and our children safe. Society fears this inner wisdom (hence the 'dark' terminology), but when she is properly acknowledged, she uses her powers for good and not evil. If the monarch butterfly was on Instagram, she might get detached from her instincts to migrate because she's so consumed with what everyone else is doing. I can hear her doubting herself: 'Sally is flying north; should I be flying north?! The experts are suggesting I need to buy a GPS to make sure I'm going the right way – I've never not known where to go, but if the experts are saying my children's lives depend on it, shouldn't I do it?' Or a pregnant woman preparing for birth and being bombarded with information like, 'We'll induce you when you get to forty weeks' or 'A home birth is the best way to go'. We doubt ourselves when we innocently consume the copious stimuli out there that convince us that we need whatever it is they're selling. We forget that our instincts are powerful; in fact, sometimes we forget we have them at all. But no matter how much we neglect them, they're always there, lying dormant, ready to be activated.

We need to invoke this dark feminine when grappling with all of the outside influences trying to dictate how we parent – because you will always find conflicting ideas. I read a book by a scientist who wrote about how he struggled to get his research papers published for years because people just didn't want to hear about his findings. He said people can prove anything they want to. He said he could prove using research and science that Mars bars are good for you – he would test tired drivers at 3:00 a.m., but he wouldn't tell you that. Research is important, but if it draws conclusions based on faulty assumptions or hidden agendas, this can throw us off from listening to our innate wisdom.

Nothing can replace the innate wisdom you have within you. We have evolved over billions of years to know what we know and to do what only we can do. We are perfect because Mother Nature makes no mistakes. We need nothing except to remind ourselves that we have all the answers. Always look inward first because the answers will always be there.

Because I had years of practice silencing inner parts of myself, my inner voice and intuition had shrunk to a tiny whisper. But it's comforting to know instincts and inner wisdom don't go away. They never disappear, no matter how much we disown them. Instincts generally point us in the direction we must go, so getting cut off from them left me feeling overwhelmed and unsure of how to proceed. When cut off from our instinctual foundations, we doubt ourselves, we're easily moulded by what we think others want us to do and be, and we can't trust or rely on our own decisions. Mothering like this can be difficult. Dancing was one of my favourite ways that I began to get in touch with this inner wisdom. Dancing allows me to drop out of my head and into my body, where my intuition resides. I move to the music, *feeling* where I want my body to take me. And if I feel my mind creeping in, like worries about what I look like or what other people might think of me, or if my husband would think my moves are dorky or sexy, that's just a sign to keep dancing. Sitting in silence, without any distractions, is also how I create space for my true self and instincts to come through.

When we remain open to our inner life as we navigate the trials of mothering, we gain priceless wisdom. Engaging with our shadow selves enables us to get better in touch with our instincts and our mothers' knowing. Our inner prompting becomes louder, and we build self-trust that allows us to parent with confidence and wisdom. It also allows us to claim our inner authority.

By bringing the angry or resentful parts of me out of the shadows, I was able to be strong enough to set healthy and clear boundaries and say no when I wanted to. I was able to give constructive and honest feedback to my staff (in my yoga business, Lunar Yoga), and I was able to step up and claim my life. I was able not just to acknowledge my needs but was aggressive enough to ensure they were met in a respectful and compassionate way. Not having a healthy relationship with my inner 'dark side', I ran the risk of her running rampant. Keeping her in the shadows meant she either burst out of me in explosive moments of rage, like when I was trying to get Zephyr to nap, or turned inwards, and I ended up hating myself. You see, the anger has to go somewhere. And this powerful dark feminine (that we'll call Her) is not someone you want running wild. You want to harness Her gifts and utilise Her energy. Becoming comfortable with our own dark feminine means we also become comfortable accessing and claiming authority. We cannot stand in our knowing, trust our intuition, and follow our instincts without a healthy dose of ferocity. It serves your authenticity, and learning to access that side of yourself will serve you: in the constructive aggression with your children that enables you to say no to the third yoghurt pouch in thirty minutes, or even when you feel the pull to empty the dishwasher when all you really want is to sit on the couch with a cup of tea.

By the way, we not only teach our children but also learn from them on this one. Children are the perfect example of being in touch with their instincts and spiritual wisdom. It's either a full-body 'yes' or a full-body 'no' for children. And there are ways that we can and should enable the connection they have to their inner wisdom to foster self-trust. If they don't want to kiss Grandma goodbye, let's not force them to go against their instincts. We might think we are teaching them to be polite and well-mannered, but, on reflection, what are we really teaching them? To push against your own inner dialogue to make someone else happy, even if you feel uncomfortable? To please others before you trust and listen to yourself?

Just as we do, children have a right to feel feelings, no matter how big or small, no matter if we see them as socially acceptable or not. It's often because of our inability to sit with our uncomfortable emotions as they boil up within us that we might push our children into kissing Grandma when they don't want to. We've become so good at hiding our emotional baggage that it's triggering when our children express theirs so freely. We've learned to hide parts of ourselves to make others happy, and they should learn to do that too – so the logic goes. But at what cost? Indecision, mistrust, lack of boundaries, low levels of confidence, second-guessing who they are. No. 'Grandma is here. How do you want to say hello? She's here when you're ready'. 'You're making Grandma feel sad' when children don't meet social norms doesn't sit right with me. Shaming and guilting them and crossing their boundaries perpetuates that people-pleasing business, which, as you will see, has taken me years to unlearn. As uncomfortable as it can be, allowing them to feel their full-body noes and yeses will get them in touch with who they are and build a strong sense of self.

EMBRACING YOUR MAYBE

Of course, in life, there are going to be times when we don't feel either a full-body 'yes' or a full-body 'no'. And putting pressure on ourselves to always know the answers doesn't give much room for flow. The more we let go and surrender control, the more our life will flow. To embrace our maybes and accept that, in life, there are sometimes going to be some grey areas we can surrender. Again, I like to dance, to meditate, to sit in stillness, to do my moon rituals. Sometimes, just a simple act of repeating 'let go' to myself while I unclench my teeth and relax my shoulders is enough. It's with this space that there is room for decisions to be made.

Own the angry parts of you, the fiery parts of you, the dark parts that you've been too scared to bring out of the shadows. These parts call us to be the person we were meant to be. And when we get out of the way, our parenting can allow our children's authenticity to unfold. Motherhood is an invitation to claim our inner wisdom in all its forms and to stand strong in our knowing, even against self-doubt and the criticisms from others. A healthy relationship with anger and resentment helps us do that. And once we do, we are set free to pursue our authentic path to individualisation.

It's not about seeking perfection, but authenticity

Managing our emotions is not about being perfect. It's not about never making mistakes or never letting our emotions control us every now and then. Honouring your emotions is about living an authentic life in which you are true to yourself and love yourself in all of your forms. We are human: we make mistakes, and we learn from them (sometimes more than once), and with practice, we get better and managing emotions becomes easier. But that doesn't mean it's not hard and we can't feel overwhelmed with it all sometimes. It's certainly the case that living an authentic life might be more challenging as it requires us to take personal responsibility for our emotions. Even though there are moments of 'you made me feel upset ...' 'or 'you make me so happy' when people trigger us, we have the power and authority to decide what we do with this incoming information. Whether it's good or bad feelings, people will influence how we feel – but it's up to us to decide where the power lies. Is it with them, or is it with us?

For example, let's say your child is having a meltdown in the supermarket – not too hard for any of us to imagine. If you get upset and flustered and perhaps start to bribe your child with treats if they will only stop, they are intrinsically learning that their behaviour influences you to change yours. Yes, their actions impact others, but you can still show this and maintain your emotional regulation. You can notice the triggering emotions arising for you and still choose to stay calm and not gauge your self-worth or how good of a mum you are by the way your children behave in the supermarket. It shows real emotional maturity when a parent can regulate themselves and understand that the measure of a conscious parent isn't how you control your child's emotions but how you take charge of your own. Children who are shown this don't grow up to be adults who manipulate other people's emotions and behaviour with theirs. They know that their own and other people's lives are their responsibility.

Taking responsibility takes work – it's much more familiar to us to blame someone else or a situation. But, we can only be in the state of a 'creator' – liberated and happy – when we are being ourselves. We can create our own happiness. We can create our own power and freedom. We can choose how we respond and react to the outside world because other people and situations are just incoming information – it's up to us to interpret that and create our reality. Not to say that others won't trigger you or cause a reaction. For example, if you had an abusive father, a male who is yelling and being aggressive will most likely trigger you. It's not the trigger we have control over; it's the choice to heal that part of ourselves by offering understanding and self-compassion or being sure enough of yourself to set a clear boundary to limit it from happening again.

Having a perfect mother or father or a perfect brother or sister sets unrealistic expectations of how life looks. It's so important to our children and those around us that we are vulnerable and still have to work on and wrestle with our emotions from time to time. To say sorry. To admit that we are wrong and to cry when we are sad. Normalising emotions and talking about them makes it okay for others to talk about theirs. We don't want to hurt, and we don't want our children to hurt.

But we also want them to do more than simply get through their difficult times; we want them to grow from their troubles and evolve as human beings. When we share our own feelings and troubles, our kids learn to think about what's happening within others and themselves and grow in their ability to understand and respond to what's happening within and around them. By simply drawing your kids' attention to either your own feelings or other people's emotions when you're out and about, you can open up new levels of compassion within them and exercise their wise minds. You are building your child's ability to feel empathy.

If you're still working on your own authenticity, start by commenting on emotions you see in people at cafés or on the TV. Things like, 'He looks sad because …' or 'It's good that he's crying! He's letting his emotions out'. This is particularly relevant for your stereotypical male, who has had years of conditioning to feel that crying is weak, unmanly or you've got no balls. By practising authenticity and steering well clear of seeking perfection, we implicitly encourage our children and people we love to come to us for help when they need it. Normalising and accepting that life has ups and downs is how we embrace life and love it to the fullest.

I can't help but think of a teenager needing help here, someone you would want to come to you for support, no matter what pickle they were in. Say, they're at a party, and their ride home has had too much to drink. Instead of being worried they will be in trouble for drinking and getting into a car with a drunk driver, they know they can call on you for help without being judged; in fact, you'd probably express how proud you are that they made that choice. A valuable opportunity for growth here, that's for sure. This doesn't come from them thinking that you are perfect and wouldn't understand because you've never had hardships. It comes from openness, talking naturally about 'failures' and fixing mistakes when they come. Giving the impression that we are perfect and always in control says to ourselves and others that if you have struggles, something is wrong with you, which is far from the truth.

Using simple questions like 'Are you okay?' instead of the statement 'You're okay' (which may not be true in the child's perception) is a good place to start. Encourage those emotions to surface; don't always look for the quick fix when a tantrum arrives (full permission to do this when you're about to lose your mind!). Uncomfortable feelings are not bad; they are useful. And when the people around us have them, we love them anyway, which is a nice segue to loving ourselves in all our glory.

CHAPTER SIX

Understanding How We're Wired

Everyone is born creative; everyone is given a box of crayons in kindergarten. Then when you hit puberty, they take the crayons away and replace them with dry, uninspiring books on algebra, history, etc. Being suddenly hit years later with the 'creative bug' is just a wee voice telling you, 'I'd like my crayons back, please'.

Hugh MacLeod, *Ignore Everybody: And 39 Other Keys to Creativity*

The parent-child connection is the most powerful mental health intervention known to mankind.

Bessel van der Kolk, *The Body Keeps the Score*

If there is anything that we wish to change in our children, we should first examine it and see whether it is not something that could be better changed in ourselves.

C. G. Jung, *Collected Works, Vol. 17*

Zephyr started to display a broad spectrum of emotions when he was about two and a half years old that, quite frankly, had me googling if he was possessed by the devil. This was triggering for me since it was activating the parts of my being I'd been keeping in the shadows. Lifelong learner that I am, I eagerly put on my student cap and went to work; much of what I learned I'll be sharing with you in this chapter.

When I was learning about childhood development and little bodies, I remember feeling this profound sense of confusion. With everything I was learning about how to hold space for my children, I was thinking: *I need this. Most adults need this.*

Ironically, I was learning how to manage my toddler's wide array of emotions before I even knew how to do that for myself. I was going into this new learning blindly thinking it was for my children's sake, when really it was my inner world reactions that led me there.

If I knew how to hold myself completely in all my forms, I wouldn't have had to do so much learning on how to do that for my children. But I wasn't motivated enough to do that for myself; it came much more naturally to spend my energy adding value to someone else and putting the needs of my children before my own.

The ways our children trigger us are no accident. They're more like invitations to heal and reclaim hidden parts of ourselves. As mothers, it's easier to be motivated by our children's psychological growth than by our own. This is how we flip the paradigm and see that our children aren't doing things *to us* but *for us*. This creates the space for us to self-reflect. And with this space and self-observation, we can begin turning hardships and moments of emotional chaos from feeling like complete inconveniences into psychological growth.

Two brains are better than one

You probably already know that the brain is split into two hemispheres. The two hemispheres are not just anatomically separate, but they also have two very different personalities, each side with a mind of its own (pun intended). The left hemisphere (which we'll call the 'left mind' from now on for simplicity's sake) loves order, logic, reason, linguistics (it likes words), and literal thinking. Literally. Think about the part of you that loves to make lists and enjoys colour coordinating your highlighters with your pens. (No? Just me?) On the other hand, the right hemisphere (or right mind) is non-verbal, holistic, and creative. It includes emotions and personal memories and big-picture thinking. Such things as facial expressions, eye contact, tone of voice, posture, etc., are the right mind's bread and butter (mmm, butter.) Think of it this way: Your left mind is linguistic, logical, and linear and loves that these all start with the letter 'L'. The right mind is non-verbal, emotional, and creative and doesn't give a boob that they start with all different letters.

Little children are right-mind dominant, particularly in their first three years. Young children have yet to master the ability to use logic and words to express their feelings, which is why our little ones have tantrums. They don't have verbal skills just yet, so they communicate with their little bodies and behaviour. Children are the perfect example of what it's like to be connected to intuition and spiritual self-knowledge. They speak from their souls through their physiology. They have tremendous freedom in expressing their true selves, not caught up in worrying about what they look like or what others will think of them. They demand their needs be met because they're so clear on what those needs are. Even when it's 'Pick me up! No, wait, put me back down. Actually, pick me up again!' They are one hundred percent connected to their bodies and honour what they feel. They act on their instincts and intuition, and most of the time, they don't need words to do it. In a sense, then, tantrums are a gift, allowing us to see a pure display of emotion without any filters screening out what might be considered inappropriate to express.

Instead of encouraging our children to suppress their emotions, we can speak to them about their feelings. We can help give them words to express their emotions so the physical manifestation no longer needs to be so dramatic. By doing this, we help them develop their emotional intelligence and understand their own and others' feelings more fully. And by allowing them to stay connected to their bodies and intuition, we lay the foundations for self-trust. Conversely, if we deny them their reality of what they are feeling or force them to go against or reject their intuition, they learn they can't trust themselves, and that inner intuitive voice withdraws, becoming harder and harder for them to hear. If we refuse to play a role in driving these parts into the shadows, we save our children from having to do so much shadow work later. By teaching our children to trust their 'gut feelings', we can help them feel confident to express their unique identity and not look to others to shape their reality.

When a toddler starts to ask 'Why?' all the time, you know that the left mind is starting to kick into gear, grasping cause-and-effect relationships in the world and beginning to use language to express logic. But until that happens, when a child is upset or experiencing big emotions, logic won't work until we have responded to the right mind's emotional needs. We must connect to their emotions first before we can do anything else.

When a child is having big feelings, saying something like 'Don't be silly' or 'It's just a pencil' dismisses their concerns, feelings, and reality. To the child, it feels as though their version of reality is irrelevant or unimportant, just because our adult perspective doesn't understand it. 'What's the difference between a blue cup and a red cup?' you find yourself asking while your child is dying on the floor because you gave them the wrong one. This issue feels serious to a child. But even if we can't understand on a logical level the reasons for the emotional response they're having, we know what it's like to feel dismissed. When we don't feel understood or heard, it doesn't exactly evoke our best behaviour. When we feel seen and heard and loved, our ability to see problems through a different lens and our ability to be rational is increased. Phrases like 'Uh huh', 'Go on', and 'It sounds like you're feeling …' create a sense of connection, as opposed to 'That doesn't make sense' or attempts to solve the problem or relate it to the listener's past experience. It helps to have our feelings validated, even if they're not rational.

We can keep this in mind when dealing with our children's big feelings. It's tempting to jump in with solutions or try to stop the behaviour altogether. It's our job, instead, to support them in solving their own problems, and we're just here to love them through it. That's where the connect bit comes in before we redirect. In other words, we've used our right mind to connect to our children's right mind. Then we can start to bring in the logic, or left mind. For example, your child wants another chocolate biscuit (shocking). Connecting to the emotional mind would be, 'I know you want another chocolate biscuit. You're feeling so sad and upset! (cue empathetic tone of voice and gentle touch). Wouldn't it be wonderful if we could eat chocolate *all* day?!' Then, the logical mind, once they feel seen and heard, 'You've already had a chocolate biscuit, we can have some more tomorrow'.

For older children (and adults), logical reasoning is much easier to understand, and issues can be handled with a more rational approach. Daniel Siegel and Tina Payne Bryson put it beautifully in their book *The Whole-Brain Child*, likening the parent to a lifeguard who rescues a drowning child. You wouldn't tell your child not to swim out so far next time while they're still struggling to keep their head above water; you would guide them back to shore and ensure their safety before giving this advice. In the same way, when your child is drowning in a right-brain emotional flood, you'd do well to help them out of that state before discussing guiding their behaviour. The authors write: 'This approach can be a life preserver that holds your child's head above water and keeps you from being pulled under along with it'.

Research shows that assigning a name or label to what we are feeling calms down the activity of the emotional circuitry in the right hemisphere. This is the same science that explains why journalling is so powerful in helping us heal and develop emotionally. We are giving our children an enormous gift when we teach them to name their feelings – and because so many of us never learned this lesson as kids, when we finally do learn it, it can dramatically change how we parent.

When we as parents connect our left and right mind, we can approach parenting from both a grounded, rational place where we can make important decisions and solve problems that honour boundaries as well as a place that takes into account our child's feelings and connects on an emotional level so that we can lovingly respond to our child's needs. What's the difference between supporting our children's emotional intelligence and our own? The answer: not much, really.

The anatomy of emotions: give yourself permission and then let go

When it comes to parenting, we are extremely patient, resilient, compassionate, and forgiving. We know the difference between a tired cry and an emotional cry, we know that a temperature over 37°C is a fever, we know our kids are psycho when they're hungry, and we know green snot is worse than clear snot.

My biggest challenge has been knowing the answers to the following questions about myself. What are my emotions telling me? What is my body telling me? Can I be aware of and nurture my own emotional and physical health just like I do my children's? Early on, this wasn't even on my radar. I was just focused on surviving and getting through the day. But just like we want more for our children, that starts with wanting more than mere survival for ourselves. Just like resentment is a clue, other emotions also teach us about ourselves and our needs. You learned the importance of accepting all emotions – not just happiness – in the last chapter, but if we're going to accept our emotions, first, we need to know what they are.

So, how do we connect to our emotions? My favourite way of thinking about this takes us back to high-school physics. You would have heard of atoms before; when I think of them, I get taken back to my physics teacher telling me that everything is just vibrational energy. I remember laughing and thinking he was just some loopy hippie science teacher; now, as it turns out, I'm the loop. But with age and maturity and more of an open mind and basic understanding of the universe, I know that just because I can't see something doesn't mean it doesn't exist. We are more than just our physical bodies.

At its most basic level, your body, the chair you sit on or the bed you lie in, the clock on the wall – and, in fact, all matter in the living and non-living world – is made up of tiny units called atoms. Atoms are not solid but rather little balls of mostly empty space, with some miniscule particles whizzing around and taking on and emitting waves of energy. So, everything in the universe is energy and vibrating at particular frequencies. These are the basic principles of quantum physics. Everything in the universe emits a vibration – and the higher the vibration, the more power it has. Because they are also energy, emotions also emit vibrations. There are really cool experiments showing that even the growth of bacteria is affected by human emotions and that plants register reactions to our emotional state.

I have a beautiful friend whose little unit is filled with more plants than I've changed wet nappies. She's recently started her own business, but before she had the courage to quit her job that she wasn't loving, she was in a transition state. She was umming and ahhing and feeling a little bit lost in fear before she took the plunge to quit her secure job and take the risk of starting out on her own. During this time, all her plants drooped. She was emitting this energy, and her house was filled with her fear. It wasn't until she faced her fears and started to kick butt again that they stood up straight and healthy again.

This isn't the first time I've heard of this happening. I bought a peace lily for a girlfriend for her birthday. She had a really tough year, and it didn't flower at all. Then, the year after, she met the love of her life and was on cloud nine – and, yep, the flower blossomed right alongside her. Because all living things are connected on vibrational energy levels, our basic emotional state is picked up and reacted to by all life forms around us.

Gulp. That's a lot of responsibility, having children around us all day, every day. These little beings are picking up everything that we're feeling.

The good news is, we can pick up on theirs. And *this* is how I'd suggest connecting to your emotions if that skill is a little rusty for you. I'm sure you've completely lost yourself in your newborn's tiny little face, little tiny nose, and the little baby hair on their little ears. Totally innocent and peaceful. We can feel that too. Or a toddler lying on the floor mesmerised by pushing a truck or car up and down, watching its wheels turn over. A moment of pure joy and being present. And it's like you can literally see their little minds ticking and thinking about nothing else than what they are doing in the present moment. Not a worry in the world. Just totally immersed in the moment. We can lose ourselves in their glorious, playful, lighthearted energy.

The basic rule is: we have to let go. What I mean by that is to let go of the resistance we have around them. We can have feelings, absolutely. And they can be extremely pivotal in accessing and expressing our true selves. Letting go refers to dropping the judgement around having certain feelings without putting them into boxes such as 'good feeling' and 'bad feeling'. Because this leads to us feeling like we are bad for having the bad feelings, and we should avoid them at all costs, the same way we should relentlessly chase the good ones. We can be stuck behind a slow car that's completely driving us bonkers as we're late for work. We can be frustrated, sure! But that frustration doesn't have to be labelled as a bad thing. In fact, it's a totally normal response when stuck behind someone driving who you can only assume is 157 years old. It's just a feeling. And we're allowed to have them.

A feeling that is not resisted will disappear as the energy behind it dissipates. It's resistance that keeps the feeling going. Sometimes our reaction to the feeling is worse than the actual feeling. For example, a dog is barking when you finally get the opportunity to sleep in. 'How effing annoying. What are the chances you finally get a day to lay in, and you're kept up by this insanely whiney yap yapping next door'. But it's just a dog barking. Our expectation that we wanted to lay in without any noise amplifies the problem. Our resistance to and frustration with the barking blows up, and we have a harder time with our feelings about the dog than the actual event. The inner war becomes bigger than the external one.

To surrender our feelings and let them go, we foster a mindset of 'It's okay if it happens, and it's okay if it doesn't'. We let go of any attachments to what we think should happen and how we should feel, and we're free. Feelings then come and go, and we realise that we are not our feelings, but the real you is just witnessing them. The you that is observing them is always the same. Each time you acknowledge and embrace your feelings, rather than suppress them or distract yourself from them, you get closer and closer to your real self. You become aware that feelings are a valuable inner compass that can direct us towards a path that feels more aligned with who we truly are and less about denying our reality and experience. You aren't a victim of them, they're not something to avoid at all costs, and you know the truth about yourself and who you are. The real self is that space between our thoughts and our feelings.

The only difference between children and adults managing their emotions is that young people are yet to develop the part of the brain responsible for reasoning and logic. There is no difference between a young boy lashing out at his brother because he won't share his toy truck and an adult man using violence against his partner when things get too much to handle. Both don't have the tools to manage their uncomfortable emotions and self-regulate. Children learn to self-regulate by picking up cues from the people around them (more on this in this chapter). It's called co-regulation, and it happens outside of our conscious awareness. Adults, on the other hand, have the ability to use logic and reasoning to self-reflect and self-analyse *within* the realm of conscious awareness. We can be aware of our awareness, so to speak. We can bring logic to an emotional situation, whether before, during, or after the episode, deciphering and making sense of what happened and if we would do anything different next time.

Lashing out with our words or violent behaviour is sometimes the only tool in our repertoire until we either nurture and learn it ourselves or teach it to our children. That energy has to go somewhere, right? And if it doesn't come out with intent, it will explode recklessly and dangerously. We know that we have to connect with our children's right minds when transforming big emotions into learning opportunities and creating connections; the same goes for us big kids. And where do we feel our emotions? That's right, in our bodies.

When emotions are high and we're on the peak of the emotional wave, logic is out the window, which can be kindling to a flame of an argument with your spouse. (Unfortunately, I have some experience in this area.) Perhaps your partner tries to offer some logical and rational words of advice, something along the lines of, 'Calm down; we have plenty of time' when you're feeling stressed about whether you've packed everything you need when leaving the house for a holiday. To which I, of course, immediately feel more calm and lovingly respond, 'Oh my gosh, you're right, babe. This is such useful feedback. What else can I do to make your day better?' Um, no. Never in the history of calming down has anyone ever calmed down by being told to calm down. Whether it's totally warranted or not. Situations like these get my mind racing on overdrive, and I can easily board the train and let this emotion take me on a wild ride. My body feels tense; my mind is foggy; my jaw is clenched. What started as an insensitive comment that evoked an uncomfortable feeling weaves an ambiguous narrative, and suddenly, I see my future where I'm living alone with seven dogs and three birds. We need to let go of any expectations of how and when we should feel certain things so we can take inconvenient feelings to psychological growth.

Letting go of our feelings doesn't mean they hold no significance and we want to get rid of them. The letting go I'm referring to is the expectation that we should feel certain things at certain times. Like when I found out I was pregnant with my second son, Knox, way sooner than when I was ready. A lot of the pain I felt with that was feeling my first reaction should not have been shock, but gratitude. It's letting go of this judgement and giving ourselves full permission to be guided by our feelings and less so about the narrative our mind gives them. Our minds are amazing tools that, when used correctly, can be imperative in creating our dream lives and manifesting our deepest desires. Letting go of judging our experiences creates room for self-compassion, self-awareness, and curiosity. To let go, it is helpful to understand what the mind does. Our mind likes to judge our experiences, puts them into boxes like 'good' or 'bad', and creates narratives around them so we can make sense of the world happening around and within us. The thing is, the narratives are often where pain is created.

If I had given myself full permission to think thoughts of guilt for not being overwhelmed by joy when I found out I was pregnant round two, they would have flowed through me a lot more freely. It's the judgement and resistance to them that makes them hang around. Observe your thoughts, observe your feelings. Understand that you have the ability to self-reflect and consciously ponder how you might or might not react differently next time. Understand that your thoughts and feelings will not always be rational; initially, they will always seem the opposite. Know that by embracing this turbulence and accepting what is, you can always bring logic into it later. But for now, let it go

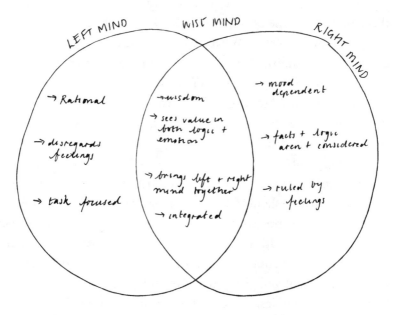

LEFT MIND   WISE MIND   RIGHT MIND

→ Rational

→ disregards
   feelings

→ task focused

→ wisdom

→ sees value in
   both logic +
   emotion

→ brings left + right
   mind together

→ integrated

→ mood
   dependent

→ facts + logic
   aren't considered

→ ruled by
   feelings

Sure, a brain is good — but have you heard of the nervous system?

Russian psychologist Ivan Pavlov made conditioning therapy famous in the late 1800s. Pavlov would ring a bell and then feed his dogs. After repeating this exercise several times, the dogs learned that when the bell rang, food was coming. Their mouths would salivate in preparation for the food. Then Pavlov changed his procedure. Instead of offering food after he rang the bell, he presented nothing. The dogs, however, continued to salivate. They had been conditioned to associate the sound of the bell with eating.

This experiment has been repeated thousands of times with different animals and even human beings and cells to support this conditioning theory. Conditioning is the mechanism by which our prehistoric ancestors and even the very first single-celled organisms on the planet learned things, protected themselves, and survived. Note that salivating is not a conscious decision. Our bodies automatically and subconsciously learn to prime ourselves for our environment without our conscious awareness. The thing is, though, after long enough, our bodies are conditioned to respond in the same way when we perceive something happening as they do when that experience is *actually* happening. When I'm tidying the lounge room and pick up the TV remote, my youngest son will see the remote in my hand and automatically go and sit himself up on the couch, expecting me to turn it on. Even when I don't turn it on, he still preempts the notion and takes his seat accordingly. (My kids watch too much TV.)

This type of conditioning is why the stress of modern life has such a detrimental effect on our health. Our nervous systems are conditioned to respond to threats in our environment – and sometimes this is still useful. (For example, when we've just mindlessly stepped off the curb without looking both ways and our peripheral vision catches sight of a car approaching – quick reflexes and adrenaline flooding our system serve us well in this situation.) However, most modern stressors are not life-or-death situations but more like stress at work, conflict within our relationships, or feelings of vulnerability when posting on social media. Our nervous systems and bodies still react the same way to stress, uniformly treating it as a life-threatening situation – but by understanding our nervous systems, we can learn to interrupt this response. We can react to stress with a more thoughtful and measured approach. We are no longer the dogs salivating at the sound of the bell, regardless of whether food is present.

We are so much more than our conscious minds. We have a heart, a soul, a spirit. And what I'm going to talk about now, is the ancient, intelligent tool with powers beyond our comprehension just waiting to be unleashed: our nervous system. It's common to be unaware of what is bothering us on a cognitive level, but there is usually no hiding from our bodily reactions, such as an increase in heart rate, pounding of the chest, or sweating. That's our inner wisdom coming through our physiology.

In our culture, we place high importance on rational thinking and the power of our brains and minds. However, despite this enhanced level of intelligence, we have become ignorant about what our bodies need to feel good. Our bodies are generally overlooked. We tend to put a higher value on our thoughts than on our feelings. There is a bit of a bias emphasising mental processes and minimising feelings emanating from our bodies. We have to ask ourselves, is the goal of our parenting to educate our children, or is it to make them better human beings able to reciprocally interact and regulate themselves and others to feel good and live fulfilled lives full of connection and love?

With my background in psychology and love for the brain, combined with our culture's high importance placed on intellect and rationality, the power of the nervous system and body is something I overlooked when building my emotional fitness muscles. Mindset and growth mindset have been buzzwords in this field for good reason, and changing your mindset can change your life. But do you know what can have an even bigger impact on your life? That's right, your nervous system. And when this landed for me, everything changed. My motto shifted from 'change your mindset, change your life' to 'change your nervous system, change your life'.

It's our mindset that is being created *through* our nervous system responses. Our nervous system is four times stronger than our minds. That is to say, we have four times the number of neurons sending messages from our body to our brain than the other way around.

Let that land for a moment.

We can use our energy and resources to train our brain, understand how it works, and cultivate a wise mind and parent with the brain in mind. However, if we don't incorporate or invite our nervous system to the party, we are missing out on opportunities to heal ourselves and shape our desired reality.

You would have experienced the power of your nervous system directly. You take a strong cup of coffee – it elevates cortisol and changes your nervous system's state. Imagine yourself driving in your car, you've had little to no sleep, you're stressed about meeting work deadlines, you have unhappy kids in the back seat, and you're going home to a messy house and copious amounts of washing, and to top it off you had a fight with your spouse this morning. Fair to say, you're feeling stressed to your eyeballs, and your mind is not a pleasant place to be. The next thing you know, your favourite song comes on the radio, and you instantly feel a shift in your energy. You turn the music up, you start to dance, and all of a sudden you're not thinking about your problems. And when the song finishes, this shift in energy changes the way you feel, and you start to think differently.

Same with when you are triggered by something. Can you think of a time recently where that's happened? It's because your body and nervous system are having a response. And when you change your nervous system's state, you change your mindset. You have a different feeling in your body and, therefore, different thoughts. You can't always use your mind to convince your body to feel something different. But we can lean into our bodies' sensations and change our physiology to change how we feel and experience the world. Imagine trying to solve your problem from *that* place rather than the stressed and burnt out place we often find ourselves in when facing challenges. You literally see things differently.

The brain-to-body conversation is called a top-down process. Top-down processes recruit your brain to guide your body onto your desired path and state. An example of this is meditation, which is an act of training your attention and mind to regulate your nervous system's responses. You can use language like 'I am calm, I am relaxed' in your mind to then filter down and change the feelings in your body to match what you're creating in your mind.

The opposite of this is the bottom-up process, where you can use your body's power to affect your mind. Breathwork, physical aspects of yoga, and cold therapy, like Mr Wim Hof, aka The Iceman, who is famous for putting his body under extreme pressure (freezing water), to develop mastery of our nervous systems is how to do this work. We have the power to consciously choose specific interventions that actively decrease our stress levels, building tolerance and our ability to shape whatever reality we desire. You would probably already know how taking a few rounds of deep breaths calms your body, and then your mind follows suit, as opposed to the other way around. Calming a wild and out-of-control mind can be harder than lassoing a runaway bull or chasing a toddler who's taken off when you asked what's in their mouth. Using the strength of our nervous system to influence our mind has been, in my experience, a more powerful way to create longer-lasting effects on my emotional state. Yes, meditation and thinking calm thoughts or whatever thoughts I need have been helpful. Putting a guided meditation on when I feel dysregulated within my body – tight chest, clenched jaw, anxious heart – has certainly helped me regulate my physiology. I had these tools and skills before I became a mother. But when I was faced with the extreme emotional waves and pressure of mothering, I needed more than my mind to help me. Mindset work wasn't enough. I needed my body and my nervous system's help, too. Nervous system work is how I bridged the gap between my intelligence – what I was *thinking* – and what I was *feeling* within my body. For example, I could feel lonely or sad or depressed, thinking in my head about all the people that love me, but *feel* completely unloved within my body. When feeling stressed or overwhelmed now, instead of trying to convince myself within my mind that everything will be okay, I use my nervous system as well. I can say my mantras in my head and also take deep breaths to calm my nervous system.

Raising children is an emotionally charged space to be in. Being able to regulate our emotions means we can experience an emotion, either intensely or mildly, and allow the sensations to pass through the body by breathing through it – as opposed to distracting ourselves from it with TV, social media, food, or alcohol. We then identify it: 'I am feeling overwhelmed right now' or 'I am feeling sad'. The practice of emotional regulation enables us to remain calm and centred through the various stresses presented as we mother, so we are able to return to a psychological baseline.

During the early stages of my motherhood journey, my coping mechanism when anything felt too hard or I was under pressure was to withdraw. I would never initiate a conversation about how I was feeling. If anyone started this conversation for me, I would quickly shut it down or walk away from it and retreat to my bedroom. I understood that I was stressed out, though I felt confused about why I seemed to cut myself off from connection when it was what I was so deeply craving.

Later, when I started learning about the work of Dr Stephen Porges, the psychiatrist who revolutionised the way we see trauma and the body's stress response, I discovered why I always felt the need to make myself small. Porges' polyvagal theory helped me understand how our body remembers everything, how it stores every memory and continues to shape our reality.

The term polyvagal refers to the vagus nerve, which connects every organ to the brain through many branches of sensory fibres that run throughout the rest of the body – from the brain stem to the heart, lungs, genitals, the lot. When you think about it, we're able to respond so quickly to stress because of the location and function of these nerves. It's why our heart rate increases when our child begins to tantrum in public, why we might start to shallow breathe when we feel panicked, and why our bodies want to shut down and withdraw from any social interaction.

When things are going well for us and we feel regulated, the vagus nerve acts as a brake, keeping us open and calm, ready to socialise. When the vagus nerve is activated and it enters its defensive system, fight-or-flight responses kick in almost immediately.

A great analogy to understand this missing piece to our nervous system is to think of it as driving a car. The accelerator, or the gas pedal, is the sympathetic nervous system. And the brake, the shutdown, is the parasympathetic nervous system. Then we have the ventral vagal, which is like the view, the music, the company, the conversation. It's the experience as a whole. Ultimately that's where we want to be. We want to be in the driver's seat; we want to enjoy the view, the music, the holistic experience, the anticipation for the journey ahead, and gratitude for where we've been, with control and awareness of the accelerator and the brakes so we can access life as fully as we possibly can. And more importantly, be able to connect with all of ourselves and engage as our highest, most conscious selves.

Most of us mother in the near-constant fight-or-flight mode. We're always on the go, we're always tired, and we're always standing on tiny bits of Lego that have us crawling out of our skin and on a constant lookout for the next piece that's about to pierce our souls (or soles). The stress response is an automatic function controlled by the same system that regulates involuntary functions like our heartbeat, breathing, and digestion. It's our autonomic nervous system, and it's always working to allocate our body's resources. It's constantly scanning our environment for more Lego pieces, more choking hazards, trip hazards, you name it.

When it comes to identifying with our environment, from an adaptive survival perspective, the 'wisdom' resides in our body and the structures of our nervous system. Which is why we need more than just our mindsets. It operates outside of our conscious awareness, and as we mother, it's often left 'on' even when it doesn't need to be. When our autonomic nervous system puts a situation into the safe category, our vagus nerve tells our bodies to relax. When you drop your kids off at their babysitter's house for the first time, you scan the environment, check the closets for skeletons, check for sharp corners, and notice no real dangers here. This place is 'safe', and you can go off to your appointment knowing everything is okay.

This is when our parasympathetic nervous system has its turn in the sun, something that people call the 'rest and digest' system. The vagus nerve sends signals to our body. It can spend energy digesting our food, our heart rate slows down, and we can take longer, deeper breaths. What a treat for our bodies and our minds when we're in this calm state! From this state, we enter what is called the social engagement mode (ventral vagal), where we feel safe, secure, and ready to connect with others. When we're in this social engagement mode, we even look more friendly, we smile (the vagus nerve connects to the muscles of the face), our voice sounds friendly and rhythmic (the vagus nerve also connects to our voice box), and we can hear better. Our vagus nerve connects to muscles in the middle ear, which open in this state so we are more attuned to other human voices. Even our saliva glands are stimulated during this time so we can use our mouths to communicate and connect to those around us. *Impressive.*

In this state, we aren't consumed with the hypervigilance of our defence systems, and the focus shifts from survival to creation and connection mode. Our resources can be allocated to higher executive functions of the brain that enable us to self-motivate, connect with others, regulate our emotions, problem-solve, or plan for the future. We are more likely to learn from our mistakes, and we are more likely to get up when we fall. We are more likely to hold space for our children when they tantrum, we are more likely to problem-solve how we are going to get through the day until nap time, and we are more likely to be able to see how we can make a meal out of dry pasta and a potato. We feel more joy, compassion, and love. We are flexible, open, peaceful, calm, and curious.

The yang to this yin is the fight-or-flight response. When we feel threatened, the sympathetic nervous system activates our body. As we've explored earlier, we perceive the world differently in this state. (Remember, we don't perceive things as *they* are, we perceive them as *we* are.) And it's important to know that we enter this state completely subconsciously. It's our bodies' instinctual and involuntary wisdom; it is not a deliberate choice. We cannot blame ourselves or shame ourselves as bad mothers when we lash out, any more than we can blame someone for sweating too much when they exercise. The same obviously goes for our children. There is no such thing as a 'bad child', just one that has been triggered, and their subconscious programming has put them into defence mode. We just need to do a little more work to help them regulate their nervous systems.

The piece of the stress response that doesn't get as much of the limelight is the 'freeze' part. We know about the fight-flight, but the 'freeze' often gets left off at the end. Our friend Dr Porges pointed out just how important this piece is.

Our vagus nerve has two pathways. Social activation and engagement mode is one pathway. The second pathway is more primitive, and when it's activated, we become immobilised. Our whole body shuts down. Our heart rate and all other bodily processes slow to a crawl. This happens when our body can neither fight nor flee. It is activated because our body sees no other way to survive.

Justin Sunseri, a polyvagal-informed therapist, describes immobilisation in a way that makes total sense: 'If you see a bear, your mobilisation mode may be activated, as your body primes you to either run or fight. But if the bear is already on top of you, your body might just give up and play dead'. This is dissociation mode. The degree of this dissociation shows up for people differently. Some people might leave their bodies psychologically, appearing to interact with others but not present. For me, the disconnection was showing up in the way that I craved intimacy and connection with my husband but couldn't seem to cultivate it.

Diving into this work with my nervous system and polyvagal theory, I realised that the inability to connect wasn't because something was wrong with me; it was a measure of my nervous system's response to my environment. And I could pin it back to my car accident. You see, I was trapped in a car and wasn't physically able to fight or flee, so my body froze. While the car was rolling, my body immobilised to keep me safe and alive, as it was my only option. This explained so much. You can't recover from this state quickly once you've entered this mode, which explains why it was so hard for me to disengage from this detached state even years later, and why my default coping mechanism was to withdraw and say nothing. The phrase *The Body Keeps The Score* (the title of an excellent book by Bessel van der Kolk) never rang truer than when I connected the dots with my car accident and how I was living my life. Those of you who have experienced trauma or were raised in a household where your feelings were invalidated or taught to be kept in the shadows might recognise this disconnect.

Imagine, for a moment, you're attending a new mothers' group. You might obsess over what to wear, plan in advance what you're going to say or how you'll introduce yourself, worry about how your baby will behave, or you might feel totally neutral about attending the group. Either way, none of it matters once you enter the room and join the circle. Suddenly, your baby starts crying, and you feel all eyes are on you. Your face grows hot and red. Even if you know rationally that this is not a hostile place, that no one is looking at you or judging you (and if they are, who cares?), it's nearly impossible to shake this feeling once you're consumed by it as you're comforting your baby. That's because your subconscious perceives a threat in a non-threatening environment (the mother's group) and has activated your body, putting you into a state of fight (you disagree and retaliate against anyone else's opinions or views), flight (leave the group), or freeze (say nothing). The fear of being cast out of the herd triggers our survival instincts, even if our rational mind understands there is no real threat to our survival. Unfortunately, once this state is activated, it's hard to get out of it. Even if you see a friendly face or a smile, you will ignore this in favour of things that confirm your belief that something is off. Social cues you would normally perceive as friendly when in the social engagement mode are misinterpreted or ignored.

We need to feel connected to others to survive. But with our nervous systems constantly on edge, we are least able to connect socially precisely when we need it the most. And if we are going to make it through motherhood alive in an emotionally charged and anxiety-ridden world as we tend to our babies' needs and keep them alive, we must learn to regulate our nervous systems.

As you will see in the pages that follow, there are ways to improve our nervous systems' ability to shift between sympathetic and para-sympathetic activation in response to the daily stress and trials motherhood offers. By doing this work, we can become less reactive to our environment and strengthen our ability to regulate our own emotions. We can bring ourselves back down easily when we are heightened or activated, and we can engage and lift in times when we have withdrawn, returning to a psychological baseline.

The calming of our physiological state enables us to create safe and trusting relationships with our children. When we parent within our social engagement mode, we signal and coordinate safety cues to our children through our gestures and tone of voice. Our children subconsciously pick up on this, and we downregulate their little defence systems so they can also enter their own social engagement mode.

Learning how to harness the power of the vagus nerve was the most influential in my journey because I learned that my reactions to stress or whenever I felt big emotions was normal; *it made sense*. Even though, on a cognitive level, I couldn't understand why I wanted to avoid deep conversations like the plague, why I silenced myself and just cried whenever things got too hard, this was my body's subconscious and automatic response. Immobilisation was my default coping mechanism that worked for me before (car accident), but now I had the understanding and compassion it took to update my programming. And this time, it could come from a place of loving appreciation for my body and my reactions rather than doing the work because I felt something was wrong with me and I needed fixing.

Our default coping mechanisms don't always come from severe trauma or traumatic events. Trauma is not something that can be measured or labelled as 'big' or 'small'. An insensitive comment can hit as hard as the emotional and physical pain of being in an abusive relationship. Trauma can come from how we were raised or what might have seemed insignificant life events that perhaps you don't even remember. There are ways to tap into this by doing inner child work, which is what I facilitate with my clients. We go back in time in meditative states and pinpoint times when we had a nervous system response. From there, we learn to hold ourselves and gain tremendous compassion and love to then gently move forward. It's important to know that there is no bad response, just a learned response, and we do have the power and ability to update our responses. Remember that next time you lose your cool with your kids or slam the door walking away from a difficult conversation. You're always doing your best, and at the same time, you can do something about it to update your reality.

I hope the tools I'm about to share with you are as helpful for you as they have been for me.

CHAPTER SEVEN

Emotional First Aid

The carry-over of the practice is just as important as the formal practice itself. The time you need the petrol is not at the petrol pump.

Tibetan Lama Choedak

The body's story can be better understood by following the impulses, internal sensations, breathing patterns, voluntary and involuntary movement patterns, and restriction of muscular tension, and it is through this awareness that one may be able to open themselves to missing pieces of an experience.

Keira Cristobal

When it comes to noticing and allowing our feelings, you might understand the importance of it but have no idea how to *embody* it. This chapter is about your 'emotional first aid' toolkit, bringing together the best tools I've run across while working with these issues. From my psychology studies to my science teaching to my wellness coaching and trauma release therapy, I've encountered some great practices, and I'm sharing them all with you here.

Just keep in mind that it's still important not to get caught up in 'doing' mode. The idea is to *be* with these practices and spend time with them. Maybe bookmark this chapter to come back to over and over. With practice, you can move from the old paradigm of trying to control your emotions and keep them under wraps so they're not visible to anybody else into the new paradigm of surrendering to your emotions.

This toolkit combines top-down and bottom-up processes to support you on your journey to emotional freedom. Whether you're having trouble letting anger go from when your in-laws were late to pick up the kids and you missed your chiropractic appointment, or you have guilt churning inside of you for screaming at your kids for walking raspberry jam into your new rug. Sometimes you have such a buildup of emotions that it seems too hard to move on to integrating your left mind, and your right mind is in complete control. You don't know how to name it because you have so many thoughts and emotions in your body that it's hard to catch one before the next one arrives. It's too much and you can't seem to give it any space to breathe, and you're suffocating. And you can forget about trying to meditate because sitting alone and still with your thoughts and feelings seems like your worst nightmare right now. I've been there, sister. And I still visit this place from time to time. I've tried many things along the way and sometimes failed, but I'll just give you the good bits.

Think of it like this: if I told you that I'd give you a million dollars if you made a basketball shot from the centre of the court one month from now, when would you start practising? A week before the shot? An hour before the shot? The obvious answer is: right now. Start loving yourself *now*. Start these practices *now* so that when we need them, you're ready to go. You're not developing these skills at the time you need them, but you're already a seasoned campaigner for yourself. You start to know yourself, you start to trust yourself, and you understand that you've got your own back and know exactly how to care for yourself in any given moment.

Name it to tame it: identify your feelings

In the scenario from the last chapter, when I first found out I was pregnant with my second son, Knox, it sent me into an emotional tailspin because I judged myself so harshly on what I thought I should be feeling. It put me into a heightened state because I felt like I was a terrible mum. In that emotionally flooded state, I lost access to the rational part of my mind that knows I'm doing the best I can in each moment with the tools and skills that I have. Our right mind can be quite dramatic and likes to make big generalisations and assumptions and elaborate narratives about what sensations we feel within our bodies.

When we start to practise naming our emotions, we are like the toddler who starts asking 'why' every two seconds. We are developing our ability to integrate the left mind to allow us to make well-rounded, logical but meaningful emotional connections and decisions. If the right mind has one hand on the steering wheel but the left mind is there to balance it, there's less chance of veering off the road. Bringing the same amount of curiosity to our own emotional states as the toddler asking 'why' a thousand times puts less pressure on our relationship, not just with ourselves but those closest to us, and allows us to have more self-compassion.

The fact that we create our own reality becomes even more clear when we consider the way identical circumstances can affect us differently on different days. For example, when my husband can't sleep, he goes to watch some television or meditate for a while in the spare bedroom. Sometimes it's actually my idea because him being restless next to me both (a) drives me crazy and (b) makes me worry about him. Sometimes I'm like, 'Yes, just go, babe. Seriously, I don't care'. Other times I say I don't care, but I actually do because I'm worried one of the babies will wake up and I'm left here to manage it myself, or my feet will get cold without him to keep me warm.

The lens I'm looking through in any given moment will determine how I respond – even when faced with the exact same scenario, my reaction will be different. The mind's narrative will be different. Just like the flaw that Martin Seligman identified when measuring life satisfaction, it will be mood-dependent. It's also like a good pigeon pose in yoga. You know, the one where you have one leg extended behind you and the other folded up under you, and you lean into the folded leg in front of you. Some days it's bomb; other days it's excruciating. The situation hasn't changed; we are the constant. Bringing a certain amount of curiosity to our reactions and triggers gives us a little more space and breathing room. Our internal states determine our external realities – so it pays to be curious about what lens you are looking at the world through. When we're struggling with a big emotion, taking a step back to evaluate how our brain is working and the state of our nervous system – what lens we are looking through and what mind we are predominantly using – we can get a clearer picture of what's happening and make better decisions. It's easier to let go of the negative dialogue that spits venom and blame and neutralise it so we can have productive conversations and connections with ourselves and others. When we feel life is getting hectic, there are three questions you can ask yourself to feel more grounded and integrate both mind and body. (1) What's going on inside your body? Notice the sensations you can feel and what's alive for you in the present moment. (2) What do you know about this response? Now that you understand trauma and how your past shapes your present, you can bring more compassion and understanding to your response. And (3) with your hand on your heart, ask yourself, What does this part of me need right now? Maybe some words of encouragement, maybe some time out. Then, can you give yourself that? You bring that to the table, and you're unstoppable.

By the way, it's not that the right mind is inferior to the left mind. We need both. I've found that during parenthood, my right mind is often dominant, probably because our children bring out so many emotions in us and they, too, have lots of big emotions. But every now and then, I let logic take over and forget to feel compassion and empathy. We don't want to veer off the road in either direction. We need balance.

Picture this: your toddler is screaming that they can't find their favourite Lightning McQueen car, and you're running late to go see Grandma. Your younger toddler is already in the car, waiting for you, and you're agitated by the holdup. You have three choices: (1) Tell your toddler 'too bad, too sad'. You don't have time to find Lightning, and you force him into the car because it's your way or the highway. (2) You sit and cry with him and empathise so hard that your toddler waiting in the car is now an old man with grey hair googling what to do with his superannuation on the phone he was watching Baby Shark on. (3) You find middle ground. 'I know you want your car; it's your favourite! You're very sad that we can't find him', using understanding and empathetic facial expressions, body language, and tone of voice. Then, you crack your toddler's heart open (in a good way where they feel safe with you to be soft and vulnerable, rather than closed off and not wanting to connect with you), 'Come here, you little rascal! I'm going to race you to the car and be as fast as Lightning McQueen! I'm going to beat you!' Then you tickle them and wrestle them and get them into the car seat with lighthearted playfulness.

If you choose option one, you might feel like a bully and uncontrollably cry yourself to sleep that night. And if you choose option two, you never, ever, ever, ever, get to Grandma's. Which leaves option three. It might take a bit longer and require a bit more of your patience, but in the long term, you are building trust and connection between you and your children. And that feels good. You're not pushing his already stretched and heightened nervous system over the edge. And when mum feels good, babies feel good.

Notice that option one is left mind only – it's only thinking of the logical response: we're running late to Grandma's; get in the car as quickly as possible. Emotions aren't important or considered with this option. Even though it's the quickest way to get to Grandma's, mistrust, disregarding your children's emotions, and invalidating their reality are the by-products. It's toxic for your children and, later on, for you because it doesn't feel good to you. Option two is the other end of the spectrum. There's nothing wrong with empathising and expressing compassion for your children in their times of need, but we know as mums that if we did that every time a toy got misplaced, we would never get anywhere. This is the right mind in action. Option three, you would have already noticed, is the wise (balanced) mind in play. You successfully integrated the right mind by connecting to your toddler's emotional state: 'I know you're feeling sad'. Your empathetic tone and body language make your toddler feel seen and heard, and their heart cracks open enough for them to relax a little and get into the car. They're then in a place where they are receptive to what needs to be done, and the left, logical mind has room to wiggle in. Whether dealing with our children or ourselves, naming emotions creates just enough distance to bring a calmer approach.

Movement

When I refer to movement in my toolbox, I'm not referring to hour-long runs or sweat sessions at the gym, although when we can create that opportunity, it can certainly help. As mothers, we can't often drop everything and care for our emotional state in real-time. When a toddler hits you in the head with a metal toy car in the bath and you need an emotional release, you can't exactly leave them in there to go for a quick run around the block. You can schedule a time to do it later, or you could do ten quick star jumps. You could stand up if you were sitting, do a quick sun salute or a little booty shake. Move to a different part of the room or house or even just to the other end of the couch. Just *move*. Get that energy moving through you physically, and help clear the path for the emotions to follow. Open your body and create a channel for those emotions to flow through instead of resting stagnant on your shoulders, weighing you down.

You may have already experienced this directly with your children. When they're getting a little stir-crazy – hitting their siblings, recklessly throwing their toys, losing their tempers quicker than usual – a common response is to go: 'Right! We're getting out of the house! Let's go for a walk and go to the park!' You intuitively know it's time to mix things up a bit, change the scenery, and get new energy flowing.

Conscious movement like dancing or walking with the intention to move energy through you takes courage and may bring up a lot of emotions for you. You might cry; you might feel strong emotions. You might then have another urge to run or keep moving. When we start to acknowledge what comes up for us, that's the beginning of healing. If you feel like you need a safe place with privacy, organise a time for you to move at a time when you're not responsible for your children so you can completely be there for yourself. Breathe, and keep breathing.

This type of movement is a very different thing from exhausting ourselves physically as a way to ignore or suppress our emotions. This is known as *emotional recycling* – when we feel an emotion over and over again without actually releasing it. We can go for a run or a walk whenever we feel stagnant or like we need a release. Still, if we never actually let it go and surrender to it, we will continue to hold it within our bodies and emotionally recycle it. Here's what I recommend for this: while you're moving, match your breath with the mantra 'let' as you breathe in and 'go' as you breathe out. Or perhaps the words 'surrender' or 'I trust' or 'I am safe' land with you better. Visualise that energy that isn't serving you, whatever it is, leaving your body as you move. You could even imagine yourself with a big pair of scissors 'cutting cords' and releasing you. Acknowledge that it's there, love it, wrap loving arms around it, kiss it on its forehead, and then send it on its merry way.

Dancing is the perfect way to use our bodies to change our physiological state. You know, when you're in a funk, consumed by thoughts, and your body feels heavy, your favourite song comes on the radio, and your body makes an instantaneous shift. That's what I'm talking about. Put your fav jam on, close your eyes, and just feel into your body. Lean into your body's natural movements, and let that change your mindset.

On a biological level, when we move, the neurotransmitter dopamine is released into the body, and you start to feel better and full of new life and energy. On an emotional level, when we move, emotions have the opportunity to move through us. Simply by moving, you've created a vibrational shift. Because the body evolved for locomotion, we can experience a sweet relief as stuck or stagnant energy that vibrates at a low frequency is released. Out with the old and in with the new.

As Peter Levine writes in *Waking the Tiger: Healing Trauma*, movement is part of how animals discharge fight-or-flight energy from a stressful situation after the danger has passed. If you've ever seen a dog get spooked or shrink into a cowering freeze state, when the animal feels safe and relaxes, it often engages in shaking behaviour to literally 'shake off' the fear. What's actually happening here is that the hormones and neurotransmitters released as part of the fear response (sympathetic nervous system activation) take some time (ten to twenty minutes for human beings) to dissipate in our systems if we're simply sitting still. But if we engage in relaxed movement instead of staying at rest, this shifts us into a ventral vagal state – in motion but calm instead of fearful. When it comes to stress, animals get it right. We humans tend to sit and stew in our stress. And when we keep adding more without shaking it off, it just builds and builds.

You see, it's not stress that's the enemy. It's how we perceive it and react to it. Psychologist Kelly McGonigal does an amazing TED talk called 'How to make stress your friend' and explains that stress only has negative effects on your body if you perceive stress as being bad for you. Things like heart disease, high blood pressure, asthma, insomnia, headaches, back pain, digestion problems, and decreased immune function are heightened when you stay in these stressed states for long periods of time because you can't move forward in constructive ways.

Remember that stress serves a very valid purpose and doesn't need to have a detrimental effect on our lives if we know how to discharge it properly after it's served its purpose. On a recent trip to Lake Eppalock, my kids and I went for a spontaneous dip. It wasn't a planned outing, so I didn't have the regular sunscreen or life jackets. I stripped them off, and they played in the shallows, throwing rocks and splashing in the water. Because of the no-life-jacket situation, I was a bit stressed, so my body was on high alert. When my youngest fell over in the water, not knowing how to swim yet, I could spring to his aid like lightning because I was anxiously awaiting danger. I helped him up and out of the water within seconds, and he carried on playing, oblivious to the danger he'd just been in. I could feel the physical signs of my hypervigilant, stressed state – rapid heart rate, eyes wide open and not blinking, muscles at the ready to jump in and help him. It was a great thing that my body was able to get into that state. This stress response exists for a specific purpose and is something to be moved through and discharged, not a state to spend time in indefinitely. The narrative of my mind in that situation was not that something was wrong with my rapid heart rate and tension in my chest from being hypervigilant – it actually served me well. Afterwards, because I didn't label my bodily sensations or response as 'bad' or that it was so uncomfortable that it shouldn't be there, it was easier to shake off compared with if I was judging what I felt as a bad thing. To let go of this response and get it out of my body, letting go of the narrative was helpful, and then moving my body, playing with the boys, and literally shaking my body was helpful.

When we make stress the enemy, we actually stress ourselves out *more*. If we tie ourselves up in knots with worry that poor health is an inevitable result of the stress we're under, we're choosing to perceive the stress as a bigger problem than it is. It's like winding up a spinning top and then never letting it unwind. Or pulling a spring back and expecting it to return to normal without letting it go and unleash. Or expecting to have to jump to your children's aid playing around water and then just expecting that energy to release on its own.

Next time you feel stressed or anxious in your body, honour it and nurture it without putting energy into changing it or wrestling it away. Let go of the narrative. Stress is a part of life. We can't avoid it. It's about learning to surrender, to surf through the waves, and to shake it off when it's over.

We can use movement as a tool to help our children, too. We know that children who are hitting or kicking or stomping their feet in the middle of a tantrum are caught up in a stress response. Their body has prepared them for action, and we are asking a lot of them to either stop or calm down immediately without allowing them to release that energy from their body. When we notice hitting or kicking or movement that is less desirable, we can redirect them to conscious movement that is acceptable. Like jumping on the trampoline or throwing a pillow or kicking a ball or lifting something heavy. Something along the lines of, 'I notice you want to use your hands right now; let's go and play in the sand pit'. Or, if you have less time, grab a ball if they start kicking. Resist the urge to go against biology and nature's way of letting the energy out. Of course, have boundaries; this doesn't mean you have to volunteer to be your child's punching bag. You can stop them from hurting you, themselves, or their poor little brother by using 'I won't let you hit Mum/Dad/Brother/insert victim here' while redirecting them.

THE AMYGDALA HIJACK

To get all technical and give you more insight into how important and useful it is to move when we feel big emotions arise in our body and why we can feel so overwhelmed by them sometimes: there is a reason our emotions take charge of us and consume us, and we sometimes find it difficult to see logic and reason. It's because the sympathetic nervous system was designed to act quickly. We had to decide in a hurry whether we were going to run or stay and fight because our lives depended on it. There is a structure in our brain called the hippocampus that perceives threats and potential threats. When it does, the amygdala processes this emotion and immediately sounds the alarm, causing the master gland, the hypothalamus, to signal to the pituitary, which sends neurochemical signals through the bloodstream to the adrenal glands above our kidneys, flooding our body with adrenaline and profoundly altering our entire physiology. Our heart rate and blood pressure increase, breathing gets faster, palms are sweaty (knees weak, arms are heavy, vomit on his sweater already), blood flow is directed and distributed to our big skeletal muscles to prepare us for action. Our pupils dilate so we can see if there is a threat on the horizon, and our shoulders and legs get tense in preparation. We are on super high alert! This all happens within milliseconds deep inside our mammalian brain, the limbic system, long before our newer and slower neocortex, the more rational, thinking part of the brain, or the left mind, can even wake up and smell the coffee. Our emotions have to be first, so know that you are human when you can't seem to escape them or insert logic into the game just yet. That's what makes you normal, that's what gives you a healthy brain, and that's what has kept us alive for so long and thriving as a species. What we do have to remember, though, is that our amygdala is super efficient and can jump in when we are not in life-threatening situations. In modern life, this can be triggered by exams, traffic, broccoli thrown on the floor, or peanut butter on your new jumper. When we notice these emotions rising in us, know the amygdala and brain are just doing their job, even though it may feel uncomfortable in your body. There is nothing wrong with you. If you feel your mind start to creep in with narratives like, 'There is something wrong with me. Why won't this feeling stop?' correct it by telling yourself that you are safe, you are not in a life-threatening situation, you can let go of the panic narrative. Get moving, get that blood moving through you, and let that rubber band go.

Meditation

Viktor Frankl was an Austrian neurologist and psychiatrist as well as a Holocaust survivor. His book *Man's Search for Meaning* is truly a mind-blowing story about human resilience. He famously said that 'between stimulus and response, there is space'. He means that even when it comes to acts as barbaric as confining millions of people in death camps, there is space for us to choose how we respond to the way others behave towards us. If Frankl could find this perspective, even in his situation, surely we can do it when the babysitter bails two minutes before you're about to leave the house. You could respond by writing an angry text back and then lose yourself in the emotions of life being unfair, or you might just *witness* that that is what you're wanting to do without actually doing it. Then, with time and space, you can respond in a way that is more aligned with your values.

When it comes to our emotions, we can create space by noticing when they surface. We can become aware that some incoming information has triggered us and just observe it for a moment before deciding how to process this emotion. This is part of surrender: we can't choose how to respond if we don't first notice our feelings, and we can't notice our feelings if we don't accept and allow them.

When we experience a negative emotion, though, it's not as easy as it sounds to observe it – we automatically want to snap back, react, or let it take us over. Like when your toddler pinches you or throws a wooden block at your face, it's almost like a knee-jerk reaction to get mad. By creating a bit more space for our emotions, we tend not to be driven by them so much. We can make deliberate decisions about what to do about them rather than letting them own us. It just takes time and practice to train our body and nervous system to be less reactive.

Enter meditation. My definition of meditation is observing one's thoughts without judgement or criticism. It can be done with just one conscious breath in and one conscious breath out. I think the biggest misconception about meditation is that it's about controlling or stopping your thoughts. That's impossible, and attempting to do so is a lot of hard work. Thinking is what the mind does. But what meditation does is create more space between our thoughts and feelings. It can give us bigger gaps of silence and relief between each one, giving us more time, patience, and understanding when deciding how to respond consciously rather than reacting without much thought. With meditation, we learn that we are not our thoughts and feelings; we are the observer, and we can choose which ones we pay attention to and which ones we let come and go like clouds floating by.

Make yourself say 'hello' right now in your head. Now make yourself *shout* 'hello' in your head. Now ask yourself, was I the one speaking or the one listening to that hello? When meditating and creating space for our emotions, we are the listener. We can observe instead of being caught in experiencing. The more we practice meditation, the easier it gets and the longer the gaps between our thoughts and feelings get, and we can gradually feel more okay with big emotions being there. We learn to be okay with uncomfortable emotions, and we get more integrated and whole. Loving and accepting all parts of us that are easy and hard becomes fathomable. We start to be more accepting of everything we experience, and when we interact with the outside world, we aren't triggered so much by what we see, hear, or feel. We can be with more of a range of human emotions and know that it is okay without being triggered and reacting so much. We train our nervous system to feel safe and that it's okay to switch off. We are more at peace. We are fulfilled.

You are probably already aware of the amazing health benefits of meditating. Study after study shows how meditation reduces stress, increases focus, improves sleep, lowers blood pressure, increases physical performance and brain concentration, enhances our immune system and metabolism, and reduces feelings of depression and anxiety, to name a few, and has been found to work more efficiently than medication. Pretty impressive! We live in a world now where we can no longer deny the benefits of practices like meditation and gratitude, and it's uneducated to label them as 'woo woo' or 'fluff'. Many well-known celebrities and highly successful people have openly spoken about their meditation practices and how it's been pivotal and an invaluable part of their lives. One of my favourites is the famous tennis champion Novak Djokovic. Imagine being in an arena filled with hundreds of thousands of people watching you and yelling at you. How is one supposed to concentrate and play the type of tennis that wins you countless grand slams? The answer is that he meditates because meditation sharpens your attention muscle and enables you to have the laser-sharp focus needed to be a champion.

There are many types of meditation, but generally speaking, you can divide them into two main categories: guided and individual. *Guided meditation* is listening to someone else's voice instruct you and guide your thoughts, focus, and awareness. *Individual meditation* is where you do this yourself, without assistance from anyone. Guided is my favourite, but when I'm pressed for time or don't have a spare minute and need a moment of clarity, a few deep and conscious breaths do it for me.

Deep breathing stimulates the parasympathetic nervous system, the 'rest and digest' part of the nervous system that's active when we are relaxed. Our bodies constantly shift between parasympathetic and sympathetic activation in a complex dance of balancing and rebalancing our bodies according to how we perceive our inner and outer experiences. We need both systems to survive; we need to be able to gear up and ready ourselves for bath time, and we need to be able to rebalance, rest and recover, reconnect and heal, or we won't last very long. The hormone oxytocin is the key player in the parasympathetic nervous system. Oxytocin (the cuddle hormone) is associated with trust, healing, contentment, and positive social interaction and emotions. Stimulating the parasympathetic response helps us to feel peaceful, calm, relaxed, open, trusting, and harmonious.

Sometimes, these moments happen by themselves, but we can create more of them. Whether we're time-poor or have a rare twenty minutes up our sleeve, this is what our breath can do for us and our bodies. The best part? Our breath is with us at every moment of every day; it's an amazing tool to have with us to centre ourselves and create space between our thoughts and emotions, particularly when big ones start to overflow. If you like, you can take a few deep breaths now and see how you feel. Gently close your eyes and perhaps put one hand on your chest and one on your belly. Take a deep breath in through your nose, envisioning that breath going deep into your belly, feeling your belly rise, then filling your ribs and all the way up to the tops of your shoulders. Then take a long, even, slow exhalation out through your mouth, squeezing out all of that stale air to make room for your next deep breath in. You can't do that ten times and not feel relaxed. There is no one way to do this, and some days you might find it relaxing, or on other days you might need to take forty or fifty deep breaths before you start to calm your body, mind, and nervous system or feel any of the benefits.

Meditation is a personal practice, and there is no single right way to do it. I know I find it particularly challenging on some days compared with others. It takes consistent practice to really master it, but you don't have to be a master to reap the benefits. You can still feel calmer and create space with just a few short breaths.

You might already have a practice you love or be a seasoned

meditator, and if you are, feel free to speed read over this section like Kath from Kath and Kim. If not, here are some helpful hints and some practices you can give a go.

Counting breaths

You can sit or lie down in any comfortable position to count your breaths. To begin, you start by breathing deeply in through your nose, filling your belly, chest, and tops of your shoulders, filling your whole lungs with air. Then you release out of your nose or mouth all the way out until there is no air left in your lungs. You continue this, counting one as you breathe in, two as you breathe out. You continue until you get to ten before you start again. You can return your breathing to normal when you feel like it, and when you notice your mind wandering, gently bring it back to focusing on counting your breath.

Box breathing

Box breathing is the idea that you breathe in for four counts, hold for four counts, exhale for four counts and hold for four counts before repeating. Visualise a box as you do it. And again, whenever the mind wonders, you can watch to see where it goes before gently bringing it back to your breath.

Guided meditation

If guided meditation is more your thing or a silent practice is a bit too tricky to begin with, I recommend downloading a guided meditation. I've made a few for you, and you can access them by following the links on my website at emilyeast.com.au.

There are also heaps of meditation apps out there, but my favourite and probably the biggest one to date is called Insight Timer. You can search meditations by length if you have a short time or a long time or by a theme that matches the mood you're in. There are meditations for pregnancy, for falling asleep, for visualising and manifesting, for when you feel angry, lonely, or even unwell. There's something for everybody in any mood. You can also add friends so you can see what other people have been listening to for inspo. Find me there. And you can see what I love doing.

Work on just a few breaths, then work your way up to five minutes and then twenty. If I've been pressed for time or don't feel like meditating, that's when I need it the most and make it a priority, at least just before I go to sleep. I might put my feet up against the wall and lay there just for a few breaths before swinging my feet around and catching some z's. Whatever it is that works for you, experiment until you find it. But remember, it only takes one percent effort. Don't beat yourself up if you've never tried it before, and don't make it longer than two minutes. Persist, commit, and know that a little effort now will add up and pay you back tenfold.

Breathwork

We know that our autonomic nervous system is automatic, meaning it functions outside of our awareness. Though parts of our body's systems are under our conscious control, we can't tell our heart rate to beat slower or our liver to detox our body quicker, but we can deepen and slow our breath and slow our heart rate that way. We can draw in more air, oxygenating all of our cells and calming our minds. And we can also do the reverse: we can take in short and frequent breaths to awaken our sympathetic response. We can escalate or de-escalate, all with the power of our breath. Doing breath work engages the autonomic nervous system, which strengthens our vagus nerve.

Try it when you've got some time alone, preferably first thing in the morning (I do this lying in bed, just as I wake up; it's also better to do it on an empty stomach).

Draw a breath in from the bottom of your stomach and once you can't breathe in anymore, hold your breath here for a few moments.

Exhale slowly.

Take one breath here – in and out normally.

Repeat

Journalling

Journalling helps us integrate our left and right minds to help bring the balanced perspective of the wise mind. And again, there is no right or wrong way to do this – you already know how, so don't feel you need to follow a fancy instruction list for it to work. Trust your instincts. But, in case you're curious how my practice of journalling looks, I like to take my time in buying a really flash notebook and pen, something that I'm excited to use and feels special to me.

Gratitude journalling. Over the years, I've been a gratitude journaller, meaning that I list the things I am grateful for at the end of each day before going to sleep. You could start with writing three, then work up to ten. You'll soon find that it's hard to stop once you start looking for what makes you feel grateful.

Guided journalling. If you feel like you need some more guidance when it comes to journalling, I'm a fan of astrology and working with the seasons of life. What I've found really helpful is working with a beautiful woman named Christina Luna. She creates an Astrological Transits and Guidance Map, which includes journal questions for almost every day that align with the major transits. It's given me channelled guidance and has taken me deep into my inner wisdom, with specific questions for tapping into my soul's knowing. You can get it in your hot little hands over at her website at lunation.live/shop.

Letter writing. A handful of times, when I've felt overwhelmed with emotions, I write a letter, either to myself or someone who has triggered something in me that I'm upset or angry about. It releases all my emotions, and I feel such a sense of letting go afterwards. Then, I go back over it and read it a few days later, and I always seem to have such a different perspective. You might choose to give the letter to the person who triggered your emotions. However, I find that the act of writing it gives me the release that I need, and I haven't actually needed to take the extra step of giving it away. Writing the letter helps neutralise your feelings and allows you to have more constructive conversations about them rather than unloading your emotional mind on that person.

Letting emotions fly can easily be misconstrued for blame and attacking, which, in my experience, leads to more emotional turmoil. The letter has been a saviour for me a number of times.

Music

When I used to teach primary school kids, I would often play music during my lessons to inspire, motivate, and help set the tone of the classroom and learning space. When I wanted kids to have a quick re-en-ergising break or get them to do something where I wanted them to have lots of (or more than usual) energy, I would play upbeat hip-hop. But when I wanted them to be still and quiet and working independently, I would play slow and soft classical music. I used to use the same strategy with my voice. If I spoke quietly and softly, it changed the tone and feel of the whole room, but if I was loud and energetic, the kids seemed to follow suit.

The same goes for our own energy. I'm sure you have a song that lifts you up, and you can't help but dance to it and just want to hit the clubs asap with your friends. For me, it's 'Crazy in Love' by Beyonce. Actually, it's anything by Beyonce, really. And if I want to feel a little sexy and slow my nervous system a little bit, I love Sinead Harnett. The rhythm within you matches what you hear and process. There are slow ballads that could bring you to tears or lullabies that make you want to close your eyes. You wouldn't put Metallica on as white noise for your babies if you wanted them to be calm and go to sleep. So experiment with which music makes you feel certain ways and tap into that resource. Even a song that makes you feel sad or angry can bring those emotions to the surface. Music is so activating.

You might also be interested to hear how singing along to your favourite jams can help, too. A high-pitched sound made with a tight throat and tight mouth is a sound we make when we are afraid or in some sort of distress, think, trying to hit that high note in Adele's 'Rolling in the Deep'. However, when the mouth is relaxed, the jaw is soft, and the throat is open, we can have a very different singing experience, one that contributes to a sense of relaxation. See what happens when you sing and elongate your out-breath when you do. It may help you let go and go even more fully into the parasympathetic nervous system. For example, nail the 'hello' in the opening line of another Adele hit, 'Hello'. (My whole body melts listening to it.) And since the vagus nerve connects to your vocal cords, making sounds stimulates the nerve and increases our heart-rate variability and vagal tone. Plus, I bet you would sound *great*. So why not?

Whatever emotion you're experiencing, music can help you connect with it fully, surrender, and allow it to move through you – and it doesn't matter what music you like. Turns out, whether it's a bit of Miley Cyrus, The Beatles, Adele, or Beethoven, the grey matter in your brain prefers the same music as you do. For a while, researchers thought it was just classical music that increased brain activity, a phenomenon called the Mozart effect. It was Dr Stephen Porges who dove into how music cues vagal regulation – and not just classical music. Porges' interventions engage the neural regulation of the middle ear muscles by exaggerating the processing of voices in the music. That feeds back as a cue to your nervous system that you are in a safe place, which then changes the vagal regulation of the heart. Pretty impressive how listening to music (particularly in Porges' work, vocal music) can change our whole physiology to safe mode. And we know that when we feel safe, our social engagement system is stimulated, and we can relax, let our guard down, connect, and be ourselves. Porges writes about his interventions in *The Pocket Guide to the Polyvagal Theory: The Transformative Power of Feeling Safe*. So get jamming, and you get extra points for dancing and moving along with it.

Know your hormone seasons

I swear I'm like clockwork. Literally, six days before I start menstruating, Zac starts pissing me off. I have way more head noise than usual, I go to war with myself and my feelings, and I withdraw from Zac. It's a little hard for the ego to hear because it likes to have someone to blame (aka Zac) when I'm feeling like this. It feels a little too comfortable to withdraw and go into the little cave that I like to call my bedroom, which has more crystals than I've had hot dinners and salt lamps to boot. I feel the pull to withdraw into the space of familiarity more often when I'm at this stage in my cycle and need to pay extra attention to my thoughts and feelings. Whenever I'm feeling this extra pull, I like to look at my period tracker app on my phone, and more often than not, I'm in that same stage in my cycle.

Understanding the magic of menstruation has allowed me to give myself more permission to feel whatever it is that comes up for me. I give myself extra space and allowance because I understand that it's a normal part of being a woman and our cycles are complex. Our bodies, moods, metabolism, and hormones fluctuate throughout the month, and it's normal to have different feelings and emotions arise at different stages. We are anything but linear. Knowing the internal processes happening within me gives me more space to be compassionate and understanding of myself and my emotions. It's easier to give myself permission to feel whatever it is that I'm feeling. Eckhart Tolle wrote about women being more likely to feel and become spiritually enlightened because our bodies physically release and shed each month. I love that. Its symbolism of releasing and shedding the parts of us that are no longer serving us and physically letting go and surrendering to what it means to be human really landed with me. I've learned to embrace the magic of my cycle. Instead of trying to pretend we have energy levels that stay the same throughout the month, we can surrender to the ebb and flow of our cycle. We can make the most of those high-energy days and take it a little more slow and gentle at other times instead of forcing ourselves to push through. It's all about learning how to best leverage our energy.

The menstrual cycle can be compared to the natural seasons of Mother Earth. The phases of the moon and the weather seasons move in ebbs and flows like the menstrual cycle, and it can be a helpful tool to align them together. It not only creates a helpful visual but connects us with nature and reminds us of our roots – we are all a part of this beautiful universe. And when we rhythmically align with it and match its vibrational frequency, we step into our power and our highest selves.

The divine feminine energy of the moon and Mother Earth herself, it doesn't get more badass than that. How can we not feel more empowered and free when we tap into that same divine feminine energy that lives within us all? The divine feminine energy that lives within the moon and Mother Earth also lives within you. It's like a divine inner compass that we share with the mothers of all mothers. Looking at our menstrual cycle in this way brings forward and lights up the same part of ourselves that is also a part of what makes the moon shine and the seasons dance. It's magical, and when I looked into this more, pennies started dropping for me all over the place. Here's a framework I like to use to understand the energy of each part of our cycle, mapping that cycle to Mother Nature's four seasons.

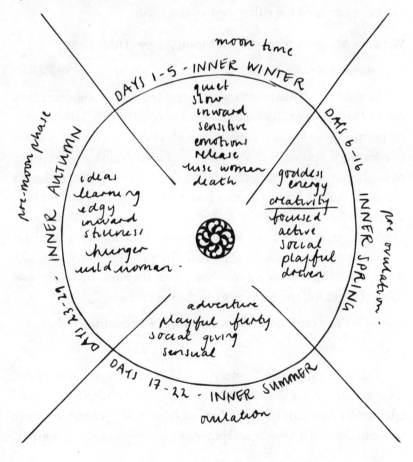

It's important to note that when we mother, we can do the same things with a completely different energy. In the Winter phase of your cycle, when things are feeling slow, you could swap the park date for some chill TV or colouring time at home. Or, if you do get out or have appointments to meet, take your time. Be intentional. This framework isn't only about mapping your calendar to suit your inner seasons. It can also be about keeping your diary the same but bringing a different energy to your daily tasks. I like to keep track of my inner seasons in my diary, so I know what type of energy I'll be bringing to the week. It helps me decide when to run workshops or say yes to interviews, when to organise play dates, and when I know I'll be feeling slow and want to stay home. Doing this, I feel like I'm flowing *with* the river and natural rhythms of life rather than against them.

Winter – Menstruation – Dark Moon / Low Tide

Approximately days 1–6 in our cycle.

Menstruation, this is when we're actually bleeding, approximately day 1 to 6 in our cycle. It's a time to rest, listen, and clarify. To hibernate. It's normal to feel low in energy as our body undertakes the massive task of releasing the previous cycle through our blood. It's like a 'dying phase' of our bodies, literally releasing what we don't need and what no longer serves us. We're reborn. This time is all about the relationship we have with ourselves. It's a time to slow down, rest and recharge. Biologically speaking, our hormones are at rock bottom, so up the self-care in this phase. Enjoy some alone time. Journal. Sip warm tea. Use heat packs. Snuggle in. Whatever floats your boat. Plant the seeds of self-love so you feel super full and ready to go in the next phase.

Spring – Pre-Ovulation – Waxing Moon / Incoming Tide

Approximately days 6–13.

This is the yang to the Winter yin and is our most masculine season. It's time to take big active steps towards our goals. We often feel renewed after winter and ready to step out of our cocoon. Our energy levels are up – emotionally, spiritually, and physically. It's time to inspire, motivate, and plan. This is when the seeds of self-love that you planted in winter start to sprout.

Summer – Ovulation + Post Ovulation – Full Moon / High Tide

Approximately day 14–21.

In this time, we can tap into the parts of ourselves that are playful, social, and extroverted. This phase is all about our relationships. Host a dinner party, organise to meet up with some friends for dinner and drinks. We feel more tolerant and patient in this phase. Create, commit, and achieve, sister. Reap the benefits of all your work. Those little self-love seedlings are flowering, and they may even bear fruit that you can give and share with others.

Autumn – Post Ovulation + Pre Menstruation – Waning Moon / Outgoing Tide

Approximately day 22-28.

Our hormones drop just like the leaves falling off trees. We feel less tolerant and more irritable than in summer, so it's important to say no when we feel we need to or be aware of the energy we will be bringing when we say yes. It's a good time to reflect on what worked and what didn't in this past month. Analyse and refine, be truthful. Prune back the trees and get ready to plant new seeds, girl.

HOW YOU CAN BE WITH THESE CONCEPTS

My good friend Dr Russell Kennedy, author of an excellent book called *Anxiety Rx*, told me something that pierced my heart (and made me laugh at the same time): 'There is no parenting without guilt', he said, 'unless you're a psychopath'. Our feelings are not wrong; they don't mean *we've* done anything wrong. Emotional releases are just a part of it. If you want to be a calmer parent, it might seem like you get there by having fewer feelings – but the truth is that we get there by allowing our feelings, surrendering to them, and surfing the waves. We get calm by being aware first. Aware of the moments that we're *not* calm, love them, release them, and understand that feeling angry and frustrated are just a part of it. This 'it happens' attitude *is* the path to being the calm, serene, and radiant mother. When our children make mistakes, we want their reactions to be 'I need to call my mum', not 'Mum is going to kill me'. Or perhaps we do a bit of both – but that's the point. We can wash the day away in the shower and desperately scrub the poo from under our nails *and*, at the same time, not feel sad about our sadness or guilty about our guiltiness. Opening our hearts and allowing emotions to flow through us is how we become a vortex and suck all the good things life can offer towards us. It's just physics.

Now that you know the importance of allowing our feelings and making space for them so they don't steer the car off the road, here are some ways to integrate the concepts into your being.

CONSCIOUS ANGER RELEASE (CAR) TECHNIQUE

Our partner makes an insensitive comment, works late, leaves the lid off the Vegemite (again), snores or eats too loudly. Our children don't listen; they fight, break shit, whine and nag and hit each other. Family life presents so much potential to spend chunks of time in a state of anger. And because anger is such a tough one for so many of us, we'll spend a little more time on it in this section.

Sometimes, it's a mild form of anger, a mere irritation or annoyance. It makes us snap at our kids or bicker with our partner. Other times, the sheer volume of work that family life demands of us and its inconsistency and lack of opportunity to attend to our own needs is overwhelming. Our thoughts turn scary, and we lose ourselves in a state of rage. You might even destroy an innocent wash basket.

Many of us haven't learned how to express anger. For most of us, it's been pushed down within ourselves or shut down. We see so much untamed anger in the media and our society that when we feel it ourselves, it can invite a lot of shame. Even more so if we are mums. We want to shut it down because we see it as being bad (often for good reason). It can be dangerous without a healthy relationship with how to express or master it. We can blow up, like my nap story, or it will slowly seep out of us through comments here and there. Even worse, we turn that anger inward and have an overly aggressive inner voice. Angry energy has to go somewhere.

The healthy way of expressing anger comes from being allowed to feel it. As children, if we are given permission and a safe container to express ourselves, we learn how to release the anger in a healthy way. We might be given permission to yell, throw pillows on the floor, or even punch a mattress. As parents, we can hold space for this and redirect our children to let that energy out in an acceptable way. We can show them that feeling anger doesn't make them 'bad'. We can give them space to release it from their little bodies. We can teach them that it's okay if they feel this and there's a way to be aggressive without hurting themselves or hurting others. Think about it, have you ever taught your child to push? You may have redirected them to say stop instead of pushing, but being able to embody a push and the pushing movements is an in-built, basic developmental movement. When a child is taught that they aren't allowed to push, they aren't allowed to say no, or their boundaries and reality are constantly overridden, they're unable to form healthy boundaries and grow up as people-pleasers with low self-esteem, among other things. Bonnie Bainbridge Cohen is the pioneer of this work. She teaches the influence of human movements on our physical, perceptual, emotional, and cognitive functioning. She shows how basic movements like pushing or surrendering the body, like when a child is being held, shape how we bond, defend, learn, organise, and sequence information and how we relate to others, ourselves, and the world.

So what do we do as mothers who feel angry? Maybe we weren't given the space to feel anger in our own childhood, or maybe we've been conditioned over time to see anger as being bad. What do we do then? What do we do if we feel ourselves blow up, lose our cool, lose our temper, yell, or make rude comments under our breath to our partner? How can we 'parent' ourselves and give ourselves the same space and container we provide our children? How do we give ourselves the skill set to manage anger so that we can assert our boundaries and needs and stay in tune with our inner wisdom? When we master this, we can show up more fully in life. The next time you're feeling angry, try this:

Find a safe place like your bedroom, the shower, or your car, and then set the scene. You might like to play some music that really gets you revved up so you can feel the anger. You can even schedule a time in your calendar when you're going to do this. Motherhood makes it easy for me to access this emotion.

Ride the emotional angry wave. Bring to mind what you're angry about. Replay the details and feel all the feels. Where do you feel the anger in your body? Let your jaw clench, your face contort, your fists tighten. Whatever anger looks and feels like, fully embody it. You might scream into a pillow or punch the mattress. And just like a wave has a peak, ride it all the way to shore.

Come back to regulation. Feel your body settle again as you ride the wave to shore. Relax your jaw again, pay attention to your body.

Do something nourishing, then relaxing. We can easily get 'stuck' in this emotion. Nourishing ourselves, making ourselves a smoothie or wrapping a warm dressing gown around ourselves, for example, can help move us through it. It's also a beautiful reward to relax afterwards and remind ourselves that we are doing amazing work. Think about it, what do your children want after they've calmed down from a tanti? A warm hug from mum. So mother yourself here a bit, too.

Some other helpful hints: be sure to set an intention so you're not just expressing anger for no reason, then go through the process intuitively. Imagine yourself riding the wave of emotion, and eventually, when you are ready and feel it releasing from your body, you can ease off and ride it in to shore. It will take practice. If you've started with a song that expresses anger, once you've ridden the wave, change your music to something more relaxing and soothing to make coming back into regulation easier. We've been in a heightened state, activated our sympathetic nervous system, and now we want to regulate and bring ourselves back down into a ventral vagal state to feel connected, grounded, and safe.

I can't tell you how many times I've done this, only to laugh out loud at myself for how ridiculous I must have looked: screaming into a pillow, punching the air to 'Zombie' by the Cranberries. My drug of choice is the shower because I feel safe there and like that it provides full privacy (minus when the kids join). With practice, I've come to loosen up and give myself full permission to show up and not hold back. It took me some time, but how it's enabled me to stop recycling my anger has been super powerful. The nourishment and relaxation piece at the end has been the cherry on top of the pie when it comes to fully moving out of the emotional state and loving ourselves back to life.

More ideas for being with the concepts from this section:

- Make a list of things you can do in real-time to up-regulate yourself when you are feeling disconnected and a list of things you can do to down-regulate when you are feeling heightened and activated. For example, you could have a hot drink when you are activated and need to come back into regulation. And vice versa – if you notice you are dissociating, make yourself a cold drink to up-regulate, the same way upbeat or fast-paced music might lift you up and classical, low-tone music helps calm you down.

- Visit my website emilyeast.com.au and follow the prompts to download the free 'Activating Your Inner Wisdom Meditation'. It's designed to elevate your intuition and get it firing.

- Visit my website emilyeast.com.au and download the free nervous system training called 'Divine Resilience.' It dives into creating flexibility for our nervous systems and moving through varying emotional states.

- Journal questions: What are you most proud of? Do you have a specific moment? What were you doing? Why were you doing it? How did you feel at the moment? Was that an easy moment or a hard moment? How do you feel about the way you showed up?

- Next time you are triggered by something, try the three questions to feel more grounded: What sensations do you feel in your body right now? What do you know about this response? What is this part of you needing right now, in this moment?

- The next time you experience a tantrum (your own or your child's), notice how you react. Do you try to distract yourself or your child? Do you try to steer yourself or your child away from their emotions? Become the observer of your patterns and 'go-to' management strategies.

- What are your common ways of handling big emotions? And then what does that look like for you? Some examples are withdrawing and going to your room, yelling, procrastinating, social media, and alcohol. Awareness is key. Next time you feel those feelings and behaviour patterns pull at you, train your body and brain to do something different. Release these emotions in a different way from how they've been showing up in your life up to this point. For example, my knee-jerk reaction is to pull away from my feelings and my loved ones. When I feel the pull to withdraw, I can acknowledge it, permit myself to feel it, and then instead of going to my room to be alone, I can stay and sit with the feelings, talk about them, and release them from my body using one of the tools in the emotional toolkit outlined in this section. Like movement or music. See how it feels to go against what feels familiar to you. Shake things up a bit and allow the emotional recycling a new way to release from the body.

- Download a period tracker app on your phone and jot in when your period starts and ends. Then, the next time you start to feel the pull of fear or anxiety or overwhelming emotions, you can make note of where you are in your cycle. You might soon see some patterns emerging for which you can allow yourself more space and permission to feel whatever it is that you experience.

Journal prompts to help you get more clarity around your thoughts and feelings:

For self-reflection:

What activities set your soul on fire?
Who do you look up to and why?
What distractions are hindering your productivity?
What actions can you take today that can simplify your life?
What do you know to be true today that you didn't know a year ago?

For self-love:

What are ten things you love about yourself? Why?
How would your best friend describe you?
What parts of your life are you in love with?
What are your favourite things to do to treat yourself? Why? How do they make you feel?
What have you achieved that you are proud of?

Gratitude:

What made you smile today?
What is your favourite memory and why?
What is your favourite quote and why?
What ten things are you grateful for in life?
What activities/people bring joy into your life?

PART THREE
Judgement vs Acceptance

Grace is not hard. Grace is not something you go after as much as it is something you allow. You just let it become. You may want it to come like thunder, lightning, or a big train so you know it is there – you know, with lots of noise and drama. It comes in naturally, however, like breathing, and you may not even know it is happening.

John-Roger

CHAPTER EIGHT

Challenge Is Good (Easy Sucks)

The size of the problem determines the size of the person. You can gauge the limitations of a person's life by the size of the problems that get him or her down. You can measure the impact a person's life has by the size of the problems he or she solves.

Jeff Olsen, *The Slight Edge: Turning Simple Disciplines into Massive Success and Happiness*

Being a parent is like jumping out of a plane with a bunch of people who don't know how to open their chutes. So you fly around doing it for them. And then you hit the ground. But you don't die. You get your arse up and cook dinner.

Unknown

I've spent sleepless nights with Zephyr lying on my chest because he was teething or unsettled. I've kinked my neck on holidays cuddling him to sleep because I didn't want to move or wake him. I've legit pooped my pants nursing because I didn't want to interrupt or stop Zephyr from feeding. Having to explain to my husband why I showered at three in the morning 'just because I felt like it' doesn't exactly make me the poster girl for honesty in that situation. (Is there anything more demoralising than shitting your pants as a grown lady? Asking for a friend.)

Which brings me to how hard I've had to work on myself and my relationships. The shift in my identity was huge for me, and navigating and regulating these huge emotions left me feeling lonely and resentful. I've had moments crying in bed and, ironically, telling my husband I was scared he was going to leave me because I cry all the time, then the very next day seriously loathing him and his existence. I love him one day and curse his penis the next. I love motherhood one day and am desperate to ship my kids off to daycare the next. I love myself one day, meditating and moving my body, then eat twenty choc chip cookies the next. I told you – *big* emotions. *Big* pendulum swings.

But let me tell you something about these moments of hardship and worry: these are the moments that build our self-esteem and confidence. It seems counterintuitive, I know, but spending time with my difficult emotions just gave me more skills in knowing how to move out of the next one with a little more grace and be less up and down like a yo-yo. I've spent nights cramped in my son's cot thinking he was never going to go to sleep, then eventually climbing out of the cot like a night ninja so as not to wake him and then climbing into my own bed with the biggest smile on my face thinking, *I did it.* These are not enjoyable moments. They're a downright shit fight. But when we look back on them, they are the moments that build our confidence. These moments let us know what we're made of and what we are capable of.

It's not a matter of *if it doesn't make you, it will break you* because these moments can definitely leave you feeling broken. But being mums gives us the superpowers to get up and keep going, no matter what. We find that second wind when we need to. Which is why it can be so easy to burn out and run ourselves into the ground. But with practice and awareness, we take these challenging moments and hold them in a lighter way. We don't see them as failures; we see them as confidence builders.

Grandma had a point to what she used to call 'character building'. Something we can add to the resume under 'Skills': can cook dinner with no hands, with one infant on hip and another a trip hazard underfoot.

I'm not endorsing pushing on, or 'soldiering on' as Lemsip (the lemon drink that's meant to cure your cold or flu), the cold and flu 'experts', would have you believe (cue eye roll – I have never heard of something so ludicrous as 'soldiering on' or 'I don't have time for a headache', which is their slogan). You're not a hero if you still have sick days left at the end of the working year. I'm just suggesting that knowing there is some good that will come out of the hard times is a helpful way to keep our sanity.

It's the same reason over three million people have voluntarily signed up for Tough Mudder events worldwide. You know, the obstacle courses that play on common fears like water, electricity, fire, and heights (not that different to parenting – #lol). You crawl through mud, walk planks and everything, all designed to test you mentally and physically. So why do people sign up for these brutal events? Because people love to overcome challenges. It makes them feel good.

We can use these parenting moments to make us feel good, too, if we look back on them with pride and a sense of awe for ourselves rather than questioning our abilities. We are mothers, and we can do anything. I have this image of my eldest sister super preg with her second child. We were at the park, and her eldest son, Macklin (who was then just two years old), needed a nappy change. So she laid him on the slide and changed him there. I remember it distinctly because we were laughing, and she said to me, 'It's about surviving, not thriving!'

Remember how we established this all the way back in the Introduction: some days, surviving *is* thriving. Although this situation warranted a good lol, my initial thought was, *'You are thriving, sis.'* Even when circumstances are less than desirable, we get ourselves out of potential sticky situations because that's what we do. We're pretty good problem solvers. My sister did the job that needed doing and then kept playing. We have no sleep, and still get up to make the kids breakfast and go to work.

When you look back on your tough moments as a mother, I suggest taking the attitude we can assume Christina Aguilera does when she thinks back on the time she thought wearing assless chaps was a good idea, '*How did I pull that off?*' Because these moments contribute significantly to our overall well-being. These moments are not enjoyable or fun, but it's where we grow and evolve the most. It's how we become the amazing mothers we are today.

Speaking of stress, when the endocrinologist Hans Selye began investigating the human stress response in 1936, he found that almost everything we do in our lives causes stress to some extent. So many things are stressful: conflict with a partner, illness, or even a tense game involving your fav sports team – even if your team wins. From the perspective of the stress response, the intensity is the same whether you are falling in love or breaking up. It's partly because of Selye's extensive research that we know it's not possible to avoid stress. He was a bit obsessed with finding ways to avoid stress – he published forty books and 1,700 articles on it. Ultimately, he concluded that the answer was that there *is* no answer; we can't avoid stress, and the best thing to do is manage it.

It would seem that Selye answered the question once and for all, yet we still haven't learned the lesson nearly a century later. We seem to think it's possible to avoid stress; we fight it away like it shouldn't be there or get angry at it for showing up. Just like our difficult emotions, the problem with stress isn't the fact that it's there; we make it worse when we fight it or deny it or judge ourselves for the fact that it's there.

The universe doesn't gift beautiful endings to those who simply have talent, confidence, faith, or wisdom; it grants them to those who are brave enough to claim what they really want and be who they're really meant to be. When we mourn the loss of our old lives after having children, each of us is gifted with a new one. With any rite of passage and ending, it can be painful, lonely, and a little scary – but what's needed to move through it and out the other side with gifts of psychological growth to share is only the belief that you are enough to begin with. You don't need to be totally 'there' yet to know that you are worthy, loved, and whole. Just put one foot in front of the other. There's no need to try everything at once or push yourself so far out of your comfort zone that you can't breathe. The rite of passage from maiden to mother isn't smooth sailing, but the payoff is that it brings out gifts in you that you never knew you had and shows you your endless pit of resourcefulness.

Having said that, we don't want to feel overwhelmed with challenges all of the time. It's one thing to be anxious and overwhelmed all day, every day; that's not okay. But leaning into that uncomfortable feeling and knowing you can rise to the occasion is another. If feelings of overwhelm, stress, burnout, and anxiety are consuming your experience, I hope this book gives you some relief or guidance on how to change that. Otherwise, there are places you can go. For me, that's when I hired my first coach and started buying into group coaching containers and e-courses. I want to say to you very directly, imagine my hands are on your two shoulders right now, looking into your eyes – *reach out*. Reach out to me online, share with me as much as you feel safe to, and I will endeavour to share my medicine, whether that's working closer with me or pointing you in a direction that feels aligned with you. There is no shortage of help and support out there, and you don't deserve to live a mediocre life. You were made for something bigger. There's no 'self help' anymore, it's all about that 'team help.'

The other day, I watched a mother play with her daughter at the same park where Zephyr first learned to climb stairs. Her daughter was about five years old, and she was climbing up the wobbly rope ladder wall. Her mother was two inches behind her every step of the way, chanting words of encouragement like, 'I've got you, I'm right here, I'm not going anywhere, I'm just behind you if you need me'. This might have been a great approach to help her daughter feel secure on the first try, but eventually, Mama will need to step back and let her daughter do it on her own – even if she falls.

It got me thinking about how it was the perfect metaphor for life because, inevitably, there will be times when we are not there for our children. We can't always watch their every step, and if we can and attempt to, how do you plan on catching a thirty-six-year-old eighty-eight-kilo man when you're getting older and frail? You can't. As hard as it is, they have to learn to make their own decisions and manage their own risks. To build self-esteem, they need to know they can do hard things, learn and grow from every mistake we hope they make, and not shy away when things get a little tough. It's our natural instinct to protect our children at all costs. But if our children don't grow up doing hard things, then easy things become too difficult.

When Zephyr first started to walk, I have this memory of him climbing the stairs up to the top of the slide at the park around the corner from our house. He's crawling up, one knee and leg after the other, wobbly and unstable. He slipped a couple of times, hitting his head in the process, but it seemed to faze me more than it did him. It took every ounce of my being not to take him off the steps or to pick him up and put him at the top of the slide myself, but in my head, I heard Maggie Dent's voice saying 'risk management, risk management, risk management' over and over. (For those who don't know Maggie, she's a fabulous author and boy mum advocate – basically the mum of all Australians.) As for Zephyr, he did make it to the top, and I had chewed off all of my fingernails in the process. But I tell you, the look on his face was priceless. A look of astonishment, pride, and amazement all in one. He had done it.

It's time to surrender and let go of our obsessive need to control everything, as excruciating as it is, even when we don't know the outcome. Children need opportunities to learn the capabilities of their little bodies and how to make good decisions. They also learn how to make good decisions by practising making decisions. (Shocking, right?) Kids also need to know the consequences of risky behaviour.

You might be thinking, how can you afford to let your children engage in risky behaviours? My answer: how can we afford *not* to? When variables come into play that we as parents can't control (aka life), if we've shielded our children from all adversity, they'll have no strategies, problem-solving skills, or resilience to cope with failure or negative experiences or emotions. We don't want to throw our kids in the deep end of the pool and shout 'I'm just building your resilience and self-esteem, sweetie!' But sometimes you have to take their life vest off and let them know you're there to rescue them if they need it, to give them the opportunity to see if they can swim.

Meeting our own needs

One of the hidden gifts of challenging moments is that they can high-light our own needs for us – and only once we recognise our own needs can we learn to meet them (including, at times, asking for others' help in meeting them).

As mothers, it's easy to meet the needs of everyone around us before our own. And I am all too familiar with the dance between questioning how much responsibility I take for meeting my own needs and how much I can give to others. On an intellectual level, I think that my needs are my responsibility. But the confusion comes in when I think about the people around us who love us. Particularly being married, isn't it part of Zac's responsibility to help lift me up when I don't feel capable? He is literally witnessing my life; I have chosen to live this life with him. Isn't there some power and responsibility for him to care for me and turn the light on to illuminate the path leading back home to myself? Is there a fine line between meeting my own needs and craving the feeling of being totally taken care of? He can't make me drink, but why can't I expect him to lead me to the water every now and then? I have struggled with my mind believing my needs are my own responsibility, but my body yearns to share that responsibility with the person and people that I choose to live my life with.

The penny dropped for me when I came across a video on Rick William's Instagram page (@iamrickwilliam). He's a purpose and emotional freedom coach (and later became *my* coach), and he spoke about how we have the capacity to meet our own needs and then get 'topped up' by those we love. Even though I felt like I'd heard this before, the way he delivered it really landed with me. It bridged the gap between what my mind was telling me and what my body was feeling. I finally gave myself permission to lean on someone else. I finally gave myself permission to hold space for myself and my emotions.

A profound exercise that I now do when I notice I'm feeling big emotions or I've disconnected from either myself or my loved ones is to put my hand on my heart, close my eyes, and give myself whatever it is I'm needing in that moment. For me (and it will be different for you), it's that I need to feel seen and heard. So I put my hand on my chest, and I say these words to myself: 'I see you. I hear you. You are not invisible. You are doing a good job'. Whatever it is I feel I need, I give to myself. And even if I've identified that what I need is something *from someone else*, at least I've identified it so I can take steps to get it. For example, I might need Zac to go to the grocery store tonight, as I'm feeling like it's too much to get there myself. So I can call him and make these things happen. Asking for support from Zac is my responsibility and what I often do to get my needs met.

By the way, this is very different from the dynamic of a codependent relationship. In that dynamic, I would make Zac responsible for my happiness. I would expect him to read my mind and just know that I need him to stop at the grocery store. Do you see the difference? In a healthy dynamic, I take responsibility for my part (asking for what I want and need). A codependent relationship also denies the other person's needs – so in the scenario above, Zac also has a choice. If I ask him to stop at the store, he can say no, that he's had an unusually stressful day and is exhausted. I then get to choose *my* response: codependent (flying off the handle because how *dare* he have needs too) or a healthy dynamic that recognises his autonomy (and then I weigh my choices given the circumstances – either go to the store myself or maybe find a third option, such as ordering delivery or making do with what we have at home until tomorrow). It's too easy to slip into a codependent dynamic if we're unaware of our own needs. When we're out of touch with our own emotions and needs, we default to meeting the needs of others (especially in the traditionally nurturing role of a mum) – and resentment starts to build beneath the surface. Once we learn that we are the ones responsible for getting our own needs met, we feel empowered to lean on others in a healthy way that honours everyone's boundaries.

I used to crave these things from external factors; I used to need to hear the right words from Zac. And sometimes, I still do, but when I give myself what I need first and hold space for myself, I'm less demanding of those around me and less emotionally dysregulated. I make more requests than demands. I need less validation from the outside world because I feel more connected within. I feel valued because I've given myself validation and love. Needing that from others before we give it to ourselves can lead to resentment because we work so hard at making sure everyone else's needs are met without feeling ours being met in return. We have the power and the ability to give ourselves what we need – and challenging moments build that capacity. When it comes to mothering, we also learn that it is not our job to make our children happy, and we can't control *their* emotional state any more than we can our partner's. It's our role to support our children to create their own realities, to love them through their problems, and to love them regardless of whether they are happy or sad, and know that our self-worth doesn't solely rest on how our children feel at any given moment.

The first step is to identify what it is that we need. So, what is a need that you have that is not being met by others or that you are not meeting yourself? Do you feel like you need more love and care and attention? What is it that you need emotionally or physically? Identify that. Your work in the previous section of the book to identify your feelings will hopefully be helpful when integrating this work.

Now, give that support to yourself. Take responsibility for it. Whether the need is big or small, determine how you can give it to yourself and then do it – and as you do, let it land. Feel it in your body on a cellular level. Let it permeate down to your very bones. Put your hand on your chest or wherever you feel this act of self-care landing in your body. Remind yourself that you have the power to connect to yourself and meet your own needs. Do that over and over again.

The second part is to identify a need that you'd like *someone else* to meet. We are social creatures; we thrive when we feel connected to others, so it's only natural to ask the people we feel safe with to do this. For example, you might want to be taken out for a nice meal. Ask a girlfriend to take you out to dinner. Whatever it is, if it's something that gets your needs met while respecting the boundaries and capabilities of someone else, you've found gold. Breathe *that* in, and remind yourself that there *are* people out there who want to be there for you. I recently experienced this myself when it came to Zephyr's health. I needed help, not just to give myself a break when managing his health but also, if the operation was to happen, to help care for Knox and help me manage the household so I could be there for Zeph. At the time, my sister who lives closest to me was about to have her third baby. She made her boundaries clear; she couldn't be around to help me with the kids. She was great at bringing me coffee in the morning or taking me out for ice-cream at the end of the day when kids were finally sleeping. She was doing everything she could to help me within her boundaries. But where our lines crossed was that even though those things were helpful, they weren't what I was really wanting or needing. I needed someone to care for Knox so I could take Zephyr to his appointments. I wanted someone to take the kids for a walk so that I could do the household jobs and cooking. Our loved ones might see that we need something and lovingly take the initiative to fill the void, but it's very hard for everyone if we haven't identified and communicated our needs. We're left feeling unreceptive to their help, and they get confused and resentful. They might give and give, but if it's not the help we need or want from them, both parties are left feeling resentful and wanting. It's like watching one of those Rom Com movies where a painfully simple and frustrating misunderstanding keeps them apart, even though you know they are meant for each other.

The flip side of this, which I have also experienced, is to assume that no one is able or willing to meet our needs, and we can only rely on ourselves. In the situation above, that would look like me disconnecting from Jane – not returning her texts or calls, feeling resentful that she's not doing anything to help me – even though, in her eyes, she is doing everything she can. From my point of view, this does not feel good. It's like I'm giving the whole world the finger and claiming, *I don't need you anymore! I can do it myself! Fuck you!* As it turns out, I *can't* do it myself, and I know now that this is a trauma response. I *want* to connect with other people. And it all starts with first knowing what I need, communicating that, giving it to myself, and being able to ask for it from others. Sometimes it can take some trial and error when working on this within a relationship, but it's always worth it. You might have to get creative, but when your needs are met, you breathe that shit in. You let it land in your body, and you feel it within your nervous system. You remind your nervous system that you are taken care of. You can ask for help, and there will be a way to get it. You have the authority to make it happen.

Here again, we can learn from our children. When we give birth, our babies are these tiny, vulnerable things that rely on us to meet their needs. They need our warmth, our nourishment, and our love. And when they need something, they ask for it. When a baby is hungry, they cry. When a baby is cold, they cry. When a baby is tired, they cry. They instinctively reach out for things they want, a toy or food. That doesn't make them wrong (tiring at times, yes, but wrong, no). And they don't feel shame or judge themselves for asking for what they need.

Just imagine if you expected an infant to meet its own needs and not depend on anyone else. Ridiculous, right? Well, it's just as ridiculous to expect yourself not to need anything from anybody else. Infants are needier beings owing to their stage of development, but there isn't a human being alive who doesn't have needs beyond what they can do for themselves. We are interdependent beings. We are innately social and have basic needs for love and connection. Taking responsibility for meeting your own needs does not mean never relying on anyone. It means asking for help when and where you need it and honouring the other person's answer – whether yes or no – depending on their ability and desire to meet that need. Taking responsibility for meeting your own needs does not mean being all on your own in the world. It means opening ourselves up to friendship and love – because, after all, those are basic needs we all have – while also recognising that the other people in these relationships have their own freedom of choice about whether they will be the ones to fulfil these needs for us or if we'll have to look elsewhere.

Remember from Chapter Seven, when we were exploring why it's important to be allowed to feel our feelings – even the messy ones like anger and resentment – I introduced you to the work of a wise woman named Bonnie Bainbridge Cohen. It's not just pushing when we are angry that is an instinctive, developmentally in-built movement. There are many others, and one of those is allowing ourselves to surrender and be held. You never explicitly teach your child to surrender and trust you, but when you hold them, they learn that they can let go, soften their tiny bodies and relax in your arms. If a child surrenders and is not held and supported – or, in the opposite extreme, is controlled and dominated – they learn a different lesson. They learn they can't surrender because they can't trust what will happen. The patterns Bonnie has found usually emerge and ideally integrate in infancy, but revisiting these patterns and exploring them as adults can be eye-opening and transformational.

Once we start to look at the ways others are meeting our needs, examples are everywhere – whether it be a postman who delivers your mail or a nail technician who gets your nail art spot-on each time, the pizza man delivering your margherita pizza at two o'clock in the morning or your lover who knows what turns you on intimately. We can choose to see ourselves as constantly being disappointed and let down, or we can choose to notice the people who *do* show up for us (even if we find, at the same time, that we would like to cultivate more friendship or love in our lives). When we open ourselves to seeing it, there are people meeting our needs all around us.

Once we've learned to identify our emotions, it can be easier to identify what we need from moment to moment – and communicating that to others becomes *so* much easier, which leads, in turn, to us experiencing more success in getting our needs met. For example, you might need someone to listen to you or to hug you or to take you on a night out. It's easier for our needs to be met when we can actually identify what they are.

When you get a need met – either by yourself or by another person – let that land in your body. Feel it. Embrace it. Remind yourself that it is safe for you to receive. Reaffirm to yourself and feel it within you: 'People are willing to meet my needs. But I'm also able to meet my own. I can fill up my own cup *and* have it topped up by others'. With this comes freedom. It's not one way or another – I meet my own needs or someone else can meet them – it's both. Meet your own needs in co-regulation with others. That's where it's at.

CHAPTER NINE

Open Your Heart to Start Receiving

The goal of individualisation is not perfection; it's wholeness.

Carl Jung

We are weaving a new way, Stitching revolutions together, Spinning new worlds from our Wombs, Dreaming back the wild edges of our souls, Calling forth that which has been lost.

Azra and Seren Bertrand, *Womb Awakening: Initiatory Wisdom from the Creatrix of All Life*

In the spring of 1964, Robert Rosenthal and Lenore Jacobson carried out an experiment in a U.S. public school, giving all 500 children in grades one through five a test they called the 'Harvard Test of Inflected Acquisition' – a pretty spicy title. Teachers were told that the test 'predicts the likelihood that a child will show a learning spurt within the near future'. The test was multiple choice and was scored by two assessors who didn't know the identity of the children. The teachers administered the test and were allowed to see the results of the tests but were told they couldn't discuss the results with the children or their parents.

A year later, the children completed the exact same test, which was again marked by the same independent assessors. The students that Rosenthal and Jacobson had originally scored in the top twenty percent for 'learning-spurt potential' improved in English, Maths, and even IQ significantly more than the other students. The funny thing was that the Harvard Test of Inflected Acquisition was actually just a standard IQ test. Rosenthal and Jacobson did not *choose* the top twenty percent of students based on their results; they chose twenty percent at *random!* The reason these students 'spurted' was not because they had the most potential but because the teachers believed in them. A teacher, believing that a student was ready to 'spurt', might pay special attention to that student. The additional attention received could easily translate into accelerated rates of improvement.

The researchers named their experiment after the Greek mythological figure Pygmalion, who sculpts an ivory statue, Galatea, that comes to life after he lavishes it with love and attention. That story, and the study, show the power of someone's belief in us.

I saw this firsthand in my teaching days. There are always the students who try hard and do well and the students who just don't care. (Case in point: the pair I actually caught playing UNO cards during class – that was how little they cared about psychology! Either that or my teaching was incredibly boring, which can't be it.) But then there are the students who don't try, not because they don't care, but because they think they *can't* do well. When a student lacks self-belief, a teacher can make all the difference. A young boy in the same psychology class as the UNO kids was so clever and capable but rarely saw the point in applying himself. So, I'd go out of my way to encourage him, leave encouraging comments on his work, pull him aside and show him where he was doing well, and make it clear I saw his potential. If he really did want to drop out of psychology, I didn't want him to do it because he thought he wasn't good enough or capable. The Pygmalion effect came to life when, in response to my open and explicit belief in him, he went from failing and wanting to drop out to passing all of his assessments.

Someone else's belief in us has incredible power to motivate us when we lack belief in ourselves – but the thing is, we can give ourselves this same gift. Like Pygmalion sculpting Galatea, we can bring ourselves to life through unconditional love. This is part of moving into our full power and self-actualisation. What's more, when we *don't* accept ourselves and love ourselves as we are, we block ourselves from receiving all the beautiful gifts the universe has in store for us because we don't believe we deserve them.

Know your worth

Searching outside of ourselves for validation can lead us to make compromises like living according to other people's values rather than our own (as we saw in Part One). When we know we're worthy, we not only stop searching but also start to receive more love. When we don't feel worthy, we block ourselves from really feeling the love that surrounds us because we believe we don't deserve it and it will be taken from us at any moment (like the bank deposit that's mistakenly credited to your account – best not spend it because it's likely to be reversed when the bank realises the error).

Worthiness allows us to absorb this love that surrounds us without any sense of having to earn it or work to keep it. It's just out there, swirling around us and seeping into our pores. The vulnerability and shame researcher Brené Brown says the only difference between people who feel loved and connected and those who don't isn't determined by how many people love them but by their own sense of worthiness. It boils down to whether or not we believe we are worthy of love – whether we accept ourselves as we are or believe we need to change ourselves to become lovable.

This is why the relationship with ourselves is the foundation for all other relationships – including the ones with our partner and our children. We are hardwired for connection, but when we don't feel worthy, we don't receive or accept the love that's on offer. Then we run ourselves into the ground in search of it from others and external factors when it needs to come from within. Only when we know our worth will we start to embrace it from those around us. I'm sorry to say there are no quick fixes, and it sure is more familiar to blame others or place the responsibility in someone else's hands, but it's simply not the case. We have to instil a sense of worthiness and value within ourselves and believe we are deserving and worthy of love and connection. But even though I knew this on an intellectual level, I still found it hard.

When we don't give ourselves the love we need or allow ourselves to take that love in, we start looking for it in external factors. We start to make demands of other people, we drink, we mindlessly scroll through social media to get that dopamine hit. I know from experience that I can get stuck in this playback loop that just repeats itself over and over again, leaving me feeling more frustrated and empty. I ask Zac to meet my needs, and he asks me to meet his. But because we feel like our needs have to be met before we can start to give to each other, we just go around in circles. I demand he gives me what I need first so that then I have more energy for him. But if he is feeling the exact same way, where do we land? In this toxic place where we are making demands and have expectations of each other that are one-sided, it can be so hard. That's why it is so important to take responsibility for ourselves and meet our own needs first. The idea I'll repeat is that we fill our own cup, then get topped up by others. When feeling so depleted, it's my responsibility to get to a place where I can give from the overflow rather than scraping the bottom of the barrel to see if there is anything left for Zac. I practise identifying what I need, giving it to myself, and then asking for more from Zac rather than putting all responsibility and depending only on Zac to meet my needs.

If you're not sure how to start believing in your own worthiness, there are lots of suggestions coming up in the remainder of this section. For now, just know that this is absolutely worth focusing on until you really feel it through and through. It's one of the keys to having the freedom to live according to the values *you* choose and not what other people think you should do.

If it feels hard to do, that just means it will be worth more in the end. If it's hard to get up and give your partner a kiss when they first come home, get out of your own way and use the frustration and emptiness you feel as motivation to swim upstream. If you feel safe, do something different to get different results. Go against the grain and see how it feels. But until you do – until you learn and until you start to hold space for and care for and love yourself like Kanye loves Kanye – then remember this: I will hold space for you. You don't have to learn to love yourself before you are loved. You are loved now; you always have been and always will be. You've got this, and I'm rooting for you.

Motivation: are we setting each other up to fail?

I was mopping the floors at home while thirty-eight weeks pregnant, and Zephyr was having his nap. I was obsessed with the feeling of having mopped floors. It was nesting at its finest. It just felt so good – and even if the rest of the house was untidy, having clean floors just makes a world of difference to me. I sat down feeling totally puffed and relished in my clean floors and just how awesome I was for doing it.

After they were dry, I started to put the chairs back onto the floor from being up on the bench – but something stopped me. I thought if I left the chairs up on the table and bench, Zac would know that I'd mopped. He probably won't notice otherwise, but if I leave a big clue out, he'll tell me how amazing I am and just worship the ground I walk on for being so superhuman. Thirty-eight weeks pregnant and mopping floors. 'What an amazing human you are, babe', he would say! And only then would I feel amazing.

I left the chairs up for most of the day until I had another thought: I was forgetting why I'd mopped in the first place – because it felt good. I felt like I'd accomplished something, and I was proud of myself. It felt good to relax with clean floors. I didn't do it for praise from Zac.

I was putting too much ownership and pressure on Zac to make me happy. What if he didn't notice or say all those wonderful things about me? In leaving the chairs up so he'd praise me, I was making happiness completely dependent on him. I had given up all my power. It's not fair for me to put that load onto Zac. Because if he neglected to say anything, he'd unknowingly piss me off a hundredth of a second after walking in the door.

So I took my power back. I put down all the chairs, put the mop bucket away, and hid the evidence that I'd been awesome that day. I reminded myself how good it felt *for me* to mop the floors. Then when Zac came home, I told him. I told him that I'd mopped the floors and how awesome it felt, and he said all those wonderful things I wanted him to say – because I was open, honest, and crystal-clear about what I wanted from him. I met my own needs first, and then he topped me up. And you know what? His praise didn't even mean that much to me. It was lovely what he had said, but I was feeling good about myself anyway, and his reaction was just a bonus.

Consider the other ways this could have gone down:

'Didn't you notice I mopped the floors?'

'Don't you care about what I do at home?'

'Don't you know how hard it is to mop when you're the size of a whale?'

'You don't appreciate anything I do!'

For me, this dialogue would have been internal (complete with smouldering resentment). My mind would be going crazy and making a mountain out of a molehill. For others, shouting would be the preferred option. Either way, it doesn't lead anywhere good. It's much more helpful to stop and ask ourselves: why am I really doing the washing?

When I'm thinking about how underappreciated I am when doing household chores, it makes them harder to do. So now, when I find myself in that headspace, I simply stop. I wait until I'm in a place where the task in question feels good for me. Sometimes the washing or the dishes will sit there for a few days, but that's okay. I do them when it feels good – and if it doesn't, I don't.

You might find yourself wondering: do things ever get done? You bet they do. Because the more I practise associating positive emotions and physiological states with cleaning the house, the easier it is to get into the zone of keeping a tidy and well-cared-for home for my own sense of satisfaction. It became more important for me to lean into the energy I'm bringing and who I'm being than it is to get things done. So if I'm huffing and puffing around the house, angry and resentful but determined to get things done, it's more important to me to recognise that this isn't fun and not who I want to be. So I'll sacrifice my productivity for deeper meaning and self-preservation. I think that if the ultimate goal is to live meaningful and joyful lives, then productivity and being efficient aren't the primary metrics we should be using or relying on when we evaluate the use of our time. When I started to honour this part of myself, I found that the more I operate in a high-vibe place, the more I surrender into my being, and the productivity is actually a by-product. I have more energy for things like housework, and instead of it being a chore, it turns into feeling satisfied, good about myself and a time to shift my focus on my energy. I'd be lying if I said I didn't stop to do a saucy dance on my kitchen floor midway through the dishes to lighten my mood.

By the way, this is also a lesson we can teach our children (and can do so more effectively if it's one we've learned ourselves). Do I want my children to be motivated only by how others react? Not really. Do I want my children to be focused on validation from others rather than doing things that make them feel good? Not really. I want them to do things they care about – not what other people care about. I want them to be clear on their own values and beliefs – not dictated by those of others. And if this is how I want my children to live, I had better lead by example.

Intrinsic motivation means we are motivated to do something or behave in a certain way because it feels good for us. It's driven by our needs and what we think and feel internally. As opposed to *extrinsic motivation*, which is when we are motivated to act in a certain way because of external factors like what other people will think or do or how they will react. A big example of extrinsic motivation is rewards and praise (think your sticker chart at school – or my student with low self-esteem who had no motivation until I created it for him).

Extrinsic praise, or external praise coming from someone or something else, is fleeting. Feeling good about myself from within, or intrinsically, is longer lasting. If I'm intrinsically motivated, it means

I'm more committed in the long run to behave in ways I see as desirable because of the way they make me feel within and about myself.

Let's imagine for a moment that I did get the praise I was after from Zac when I mopped the floors. Or I got it whenever I did something helpful or useful around the house. I'd be satisfied with the praise he gave me in that moment. But what happens when he's not there to praise me when I do something good? He's not going to be there every single time. So eventually, I'll become less and less interested in doing those things around the house because I'm not getting the satisfaction I need from him each time to stay motivated. But if I were doing them for myself or for intrinsic satisfaction, I would be more likely to keep behaving this way. By depending on external praise from Zac, I can start to doubt myself when I don't get what I need from him to feel good. Then I start questioning my self-worth and asking myself if I am doing enough. Do you see how, especially in a relationship where praise is rarely given, this attitude can send someone off in a spiral of trying to do more and more to earn the praise that never comes? If I, instead, learn to motivate myself intrinsically, I can still listen to Zac's needs and requests of me, but I'll no longer depend on his validation to prop up my self-esteem.

This is one area where I think common parenting approaches are off balance – teaching children to rely too much on extrinsic motivation. Don't get me wrong – I'd be lying if I said I hadn't used it before. But it only leads to temporary compliance. For example, when your toddler is too shy to use the toilet at your Aunty's house and, this time, you opt to offer a choc bicci in exchange for him sitting on the toilet because you don't have the materials or energy to change shitty pants. Fostering intrinsic motivation in this scenario is bringing awareness to how good it feels *not* to have a full nappy. It's actually not the best feeling walking around with shit in your pants (speaking from experience). Additionally, I know my sons have actually been motivated to use the toilet because it's just like Mum and Dad do. For example, 'Notice that Mum and Dad use the big toilet!' or 'You went to the toilet all by yourself. How does that feel?' Whatever it is that you notice sparks joy or interest or curiosity with your children, use that. Foster that. Use it as a tool to grow that intrinsic motivation bigger while you're using it to guide them towards the behaviour you want to see (aka poop in the toilet).

When we think about the goal for our children, it's for them to be fulfilled and have a strong sense of self-worth. We can give them a say in what they are doing so they can learn to develop self-awareness around what they like to do and their capabilities without us deciding for them and judging them each time. Kids learn to make good decisions by making decisions, not by following our instructions – but we are teaching them the opposite every time we tell them 'good job' after they jump through our hoops.

Instead, let's show them we love them for who they are, not for what they do – and that when they screw up or fall short, we don't stop caring and loving. Praise comes naturally to us when they do something exciting, new, or desired, like eating their string beans, and they can feel our love in these moments. But what about when they've hit their brother or thrown food on the floor for the billionth time? Of course, we still love them then. But do they know that? We haven't given them any positive attention or enthusiasm. The message is confusing. Praise teaches our children that only when they do something that we decide is good will they get our attention – I don't notice you or respond otherwise. But our love isn't something that they earn. They have it, always. Learning that we love them unconditionally will pave the way for them to love themselves unconditionally, too.

Of the 'new paradigm' suggestions in this book, this one may be especially tough to implement. Our culture is hyper-focused on telling children how clever they are, how athletic they are, and how good their painting is when they take two seconds to do a couple of purple dots on a crumpled-up piece of paper. It's easy to love and accept our children when they act in ways we approve of. It is much – *much* – harder to create a warm, caring, and accepting attitude of who they are regardless of their behaviour. But until they experience our love in moments when they're going psycho, our praise holds little value.

I'm not saying don't praise your kids. If you want to go crazy over a half-torn piece of paper with three scribbles on it that they brought home from daycare, go nuts. Frame it, by all means. But practising unconditional love toward your child means showing them 'I care about you. Not because you fulfilled my expectations of sharing, staying regulated, getting good grades – but I care about you and accept you simply because of who you are'.

When your child hits or says hurtful things to you or their siblings or throws their food on the floor that you put so much love into preparing, I'm not saying to praise that behaviour. I'm asking you to look past it, beyond what's happening on the outside, and use your incredible mama wisdom to understand what's happening for them on the inside. Maybe they're hitting because they didn't get to go on the swing, or they're throwing food because they're tired and have a bellyache. Look beneath the behaviour to see the goodness in them. (Sometimes, you'll have to look *reeeeallly* hard.) Then use that insight to connect with them. Ask a question that shows you understand or are trying to: 'Are you sad because you didn't get to go on the swing?' Instead of getting caught up in what they shouldn't be doing, guide them toward what you'd like them to do: 'Food is for eating. Put the food on the table', or my favourite go-to, 'It looks like you're sad. What do you need?'

Love in the new paradigm is unconditional, not based on efforts to control behaviour. And it's hard to give that kind of love to our children when we haven't yet given it to ourselves – which is why working on that foundation is so important.

Older children often bring you their work and ask what you think of it (looking for extrinsic motivation). An easy way to flip this to encourage intrinsic motivation is to ask them what they think of their work themselves. Because really, who am I to judge? How do I know if they were doing their best work or not? Only they can really tell. When you get answers like, 'I think I could have done this bit a little better, but I'm really happy with how I did this part', I've encouraged them to self-evaluate and decide for themselves. My feedback? It's always more descriptive. Instead of praise (which would encourage extrinsic motivation), I like to ask questions about what they've created and are showing me. Attention in this form builds connection and further encourages self-evaluation and awareness.

When Zephyr throws a ball or does his cute little run, what comes most naturally is 'Woah! Fast running!' or 'Wow, big throw!' When you think about it, aren't I limiting him? How do I know if that throw was as big as he could do? By telling him that was a big throw, am I limiting him to think he can't throw even farther? He might not have even been trying to run fast, but if I tell him it's fast, he might not try to run any faster. Instead, I like to say, 'You threw the ball!' or 'You were running! How does that feel? Is that fun?'

I developed this method during my time as a classroom teacher, but we all have an innate knowledge of how to connect with intrinsic motivation – it's just that it's been socialised out of us. Have you ever noticed that younger children don't really care what you think? They might show you the pictures they drew at daycare, but it's because they're proud of what they made. It's not about gaining your approval. Somewhere along the lines, we start to care what other people think – which isn't all bad until it starts to be prioritised over our own opinions and thoughts. We can start when our babies are little to care more about how they feel and what they think and what they enjoy or don't enjoy themselves rather than looking outside for the answers and be moulded into whatever shape the world wants them to form. (By the way, this means we have to accept that our children's preferences for their own lives may be different from what we would have chosen for them! I think this is one of the reasons parents don't teach their children to rely on intrinsic motivation more frequently – but it's also one of the biggest ways we can set our children up for satisfaction and fulfilment in life.)

No carrots, no sticks.

When Zephyr first went down his slide on his own, I was so excited I clapped and cheered and carried on like a pork chop. I did this over and over until I noticed something that reminded me of what I know about brain development and emotional intelligence – I decided to add some more detail to my cheering. Because after Zephyr went down the slide, he would look at me for reinforcement or to get the praise I was dishing out. I realised that he was going down the slide, not for his own enjoyment but because he wanted praise from me. It got me thinking about the habits I want to instil in him early. Like doing things because they make *him* feel good, for his own sense of accomplishment and satisfaction – not the approval of others – not even me. Because these habits grow into succumbing to peer pressure as a teenager or striving for other people's approval instead of finding inner peace. So instead, I changed my cheering to descriptive feedback to develop not only his vocabulary but his emotional intelligence as well. Now he goes down the slide because he loves it, not because he thinks I want him to. My goal is to build his emotional awareness and confidence in himself and his decisions and capabilities.

Descriptive Feedback:

'You went down the slide!'
'How does that feel?'
'Is that fun?'
'Does that make you happy?'

Instead of:

'Good boy!'
'Yay!'
'Well done!'

Even people with strong self-worth sometimes need a little encouragement to take a leap of faith. Someone to cheer us on when we're a little hesitant to step forward ourselves. Just that little friendly push with a loving hand on our backs lets us know we've got this. This belief turns into self-confidence and grows within us. We then start to have that confidence ourselves. It's such a magical thing. Can you picture someone who's given you that gift? Even if it wasn't a parent, I hope you've had the experience of having at least one person believe in you. Once you've experienced it, you can call to mind that feeling when you're grappling with self-doubt. Know that this is a feeling you can return to anytime you want.

The people who love us know we don't do everything picture-perfect. If we are honest with ourselves, we mess up more often than we get it right. Probably by a lot. More than once, I've got it wrong. But we don't need someone shouting at us that we've fallen short or got it wrong because, most of the time, we already know that. Most of us don't need more instructions; we simply need someone who believes in us. Because when we make those mistakes, we know we are loved either way. We know we have someone who cares for us and knows we'll get on with it and be better next time. Someone who knows we can be better, not that they don't love us for who we are now, but someone who wants for us to break through the ceiling and live life the way it's meant to be lived. With a full heart and a brave spirit. Find that person for you; be that person for someone else.

Without the secure knowledge that we are loved no matter what and accepted even when we make mistakes or disagree, we cannot learn who we genuinely are and what truly matters to us. We find it unbearably uncomfortable to experience conflict or anger with a loved one and find ourselves subject to the tyranny of others' needs, wishes, and demands. We are not armed with the ability to say no or assert our needs. And that's not really what we want for our children, either.

We want them to know that we believe in them. We don't need to give them endless instructions. Our silence is engagement. If you want to go down the slide, Zephyr, you go for it. I believe in you. And if you hurt yourself, I'll still be proud. Because that's better than looking at the slide *wishing* you could go down it. With my encouragement and watchful eye, Zephyr will take these healthy risks that perhaps he wouldn't if I wasn't there to let him know he's got this. Without risk, we don't grow. I'm not promising him a safe life. I can't promise him anything in life except that I will love him eternally. But I can lead the way in living a daring, courageous, and purposeful one.

Mothers aren't here to solve all our children's problems. We're here to love them as they solve their own. We're here to back them up and give them loving support to go out in the world and discover their mysterious gifts they were inherently born to share with the world. When we say 'I believe in you' to our children, we give them wings.

CHAPTER TEN

The Seasons of Self-Care

You can't help someone get up a hill without getting closer to the top yourself.

General H. Norman Schwarzkopf, Jr.

The one thing you can control is how you treat yourself. And that one thing can change everything.

Leeana Tankersley

When my younger son, Knox, was about twelve months old, I got deathly skinny. Not like a 'lost the baby weight' cool kind of skinny, a 'she needs help' Amy Winehouse kind of skinny. I resembled a skeleton, and that's exactly how I felt – like a lifeless, empty vessel.

In the process of making sure the boys were fed, bathed, wearing clean clothes, and doing fun activities they enjoyed, and just alive in general, I myself wasn't getting fed. I definitely wasn't wearing clean clothes, and I also wasn't doing anything fun that was just for me. I'd nibble on the boys' leftover food or not even think about food until late afternoon when I'd realise I hadn't eaten all day. I was knee-deep in 'doing' mode, ploughing through the day doing everything for everybody else.

Intellectually, I knew I needed to care for myself to give my best to my children. But as I like to say, common sense is not common action. Did you know that over eighty percent of doctors are overweight? Even though they might have all the knowledge of what constitutes a healthy lifestyle, putting that knowledge into action is a completely different thing. I knew all about the importance of self-care, but once I became a mother, it felt like prioritising my own needs would take away from my kids. Plus, I just didn't have the energy.

During this time, I went to see a gorgeous reiki healer named Narelle. As I lay there like a corpse on her therapy table, she told me I was so depleted that my aura was within an inch of my body rather than being an arm's width like a healthy one is. She spoke of the nutrients I was missing and what I needed to do to start caring for myself, physically and mentally.

That appointment was a turning point for me. I understood that constantly operating in 'doing' mode wasn't working for me. I needed to take the time to nurture myself and my body. Shortly after that, appointments with my doctor and naturopath repeated what Narelle had told me. I was severely underweight, and if I kept going the way I was or lost any more, I'd probably find myself in hospital. I needed to eat more. For me, this wasn't about body image; it was about learning to see myself as important. I just didn't have an appetite for my life, and it was showing up in my relationship with food.

With the opinions of these trusted healers pointing me in the same direction, I decided I was going to change my life. I took a break from social media. I bought all the vitamins and started taking them. I ate fewer processed foods. I was determined that *this time*, these changes and healthy habits that I knew were good for me would stick.

However, in a few short weeks (cough, days), mental resistance crept back in. I was no longer taking my vitamins or taking the time to fix myself a nourishing lunch. At the time, I wasn't aware of the underlying belief that I wasn't worth taking care of. What I was aware of was my mind telling me, 'You can't do this'. It was then that I made the decision to hire a coach for the first time. Together, we dove into healing my nervous system. Through the inner child work we did together, I began to see how working on myself would impact how I was showing up for my kids and Zac as well as myself.

Six months later, when I returned to the healers for a tune-up, although I still wasn't meeting my own needs fully, I had made progress. What's more, I felt like the healers' words finally landed and got through to me. I finally 'got it'. I had to hear the same message multiple times from multiple different people before I could really feel it in my bones – but suddenly, these a-ha moments were all around me. As the saying goes, when the student is ready, the teacher appears.

Suddenly, I understood with complete clarity how my actions were setting an example for my children. I was implicitly teaching them that when you love someone, your own needs don't matter. I was showing them that they needed to do things to earn their worthiness instead of worthiness residing innately within them. This was not the legacy I wanted to leave behind.

The irony of it is that I wasn't living up to my potential as the mother, wife, and woman I could be – precisely because I was so wrapped up in doing instead of being. I had to step out of the cycle of constantly trying to do more. Because who I was at that moment in time was a grumpy, overworked, lethargic, lifeless, and disconnected human doing. To be all that I could be, I had to accept myself as I was and shift my attention from what I was doing to who I was being and becoming.

Since then, I have committed to making food no longer an afterthought, and I put as much love into creating my food as I do eating it. For me, it was never about the food. It was a by-product of how I saw myself – as unimportant, with needs that didn't matter. Food, for me, has been a medium for mixing up this belief and turning it around.

With my head and heart finally in full alignment, I was able to prioritise my own needs. I finally understood that this was the foundation everything else was coming from – that my physical needs were just as important as my emotional and spiritual needs because my ability to channel my emotions and energy comes through my physical temple. Each of us is like the receiver and transmitter on a power line. We can bring in all the good vibes, but if the transmitter can't handle them, it will all just blow up.

This, dear sister, is the importance of self-care. As a new mum, when you suddenly find yourself responsible for another being who is one hundred percent dependent on you in almost every way, the mum-guilt can come on hard and fast when you start to confront balancing your own needs with those of your child. True self-care will make you uncomfortable. It's not always an indulgent act that makes you feel good. It might look like removing yourself from relationships that are draining you or that require you to deny parts of yourself, or getting up thirty minutes earlier to journal, or grabbing your book when you really just want to grab the remote for the TV, or spending time in meditation even when your mind disagrees with you. For many of us, self-care will evoke guilt-based emotions, but the key to self-care and developing self-worth is to honour these needs of yours – even when it feels uncomfortable or it doesn't get you approval from others. True self-care can be thought of as giving up the need to be liked or validated by others in order to love, respect, and honour yourself. That's why this chapter is all about self-care and how we need to reframe it once we become mothers. Healthy relationships with others (including our children) rest on the foundation of a healthy relationship with yourself.

There isn't a modern wellness dictionary out there that doesn't include self-care. The concept of retreating to yourself to calm your body and mind is simple and profound, but for some reason, whenever I hear it, my eyes roll. Over the years, and particularly now being a mother, it feels more like a clever marketing slogan used to sell us things from soaps and oils to spa sessions and self-help books.

As a new mother, I knew self-care would help with my postpartum blues. I knew it was the way to breathe myself full again and connect with myself. I knew I needed to fill my cup up so I had something to give. I wasn't stupid. But as much as I knew I needed to do this – it felt impossible.

This is probably the case for everyone who doesn't sufficiently engage in self-care. I'd venture to guess that there's not a person out there who *doesn't* know how important meditation or moving your body is and how much new energy and new life it can give you. But just because we know these things on an intellectual level, doesn't mean we know how to put them into action. It's not a matter of not being smart enough. We're intelligent women, thank you very much. But even if our minds are on board, as we've learned, if our body is a no, it's a no.

Almost every new mother has undoubtedly pondered the question: how do you care for and love yourself dearly when you have another human being (or human beings) so dependent on you for everything – the liquid gold you supply (also known as breastmilk), your touch, your soothing voice, the ability to use a stove and boil a kettle, how you know just what books to read and what songs to sing, your ability to translate and comprehend toddler dribble, and all else that accompanies parenting?

Even if you know perfectly well what filled your cup up and how you cared for yourself *before* becoming a mother, quite often, after becoming a mum, you find that (a) those things don't bring you joy anymore, (b) you can't do them anymore, or (c) you don't have the time or the energy to do them. For example, I used to play netball pre-babies. It meant training once or twice a week and then game days. It was an outlet for my competitive nature, it was social, and it was guaranteed exercise. But once I had children, my body had been through so much that I couldn't just pick up where I'd left off, fitness-wise. I didn't have the time or mental focus required to excel at it the way I used to. And once I did start to get back into it, I found that mum-guilt was seriously hindering my ability to enjoy my time on the court.

It can be helpful to think of self-care in terms of seasons of life. Just like our babies grow out of clothing, our needs for rejuvenation and mental recalibration change, too. In the ebbs and flows of life, we are the constant. Life itself is constantly in flux; our identity and what fills us up is never really fixed. Our interests will mature and change, thank God. Some friendships become treasured memories as we create new ones, and our careers and hobbies evolve as we do and mirror our growing intelligence and soul's expansion. When you think about it, not being able to do the things that brought us joy once upon a time is almost a good thing. It means we've grown, evolved, and taken huge steps forward. We can still touch base with those practices, and if it still feels good, we can work them back into our daily. But it's also an amazing opportunity for growth and development. We get this new chance to discover other aspects that bring us joy.

Let's take my netball example and unpack it a little. What did I actually enjoy about it? What was it that made me feel good and connected to it? What do I miss so much about it, and why am I grieving this part of my 'old life' so much? I can narrow it down to three things: it was social, I could fully be myself, and it was physically challenging. These have now become my new criteria for choosing a new self-care practice. There are tonnes of other things I can do that fit these criteria. Let's take yoga. It's social when I go with someone, teach a class, or go to a class with a friend. It provides me with opportunities to be myself in that I can push myself physically some days or fully soften and surrender on others. I can bring my aggressive and competitive self to a class, or I can bring my calm and gentle self to class. And I'm always challenged, whether it be with a crow pose or a mental challenge trying to switch off during savasana or accepting that what I could do last week in class just isn't happening for me today. All my boxes are ticked. I'm getting the same fulfilment out of something that looks completely different. Just like our identity, our self-care routine transforms once we become mums. We'll be much happier (and actually *have* a self-care routine) if we accept that instead of trying to fit a square peg into a round hole.

If I tried to replace my exercise with going for a run or a walk by myself just because it's convenient, it wouldn't last long and motivation would dwindle. I don't have to get into the car to drive anywhere when I go for a run; I can do it by myself, and it doesn't chew up too much of my time. But running isn't going to tick those three boxes for me. I'm not going to get out of it what I need to keep me going. I might push through for a week or so, but it will be damn hard to keep me disciplined and motivated to do it. On the other hand, the Couch to 5K app? *That* got me going. It meets all three of my criteria: it was social in that other people could do the course as well; I could express and bring to it whatever I felt in the moment, whether that was to push myself and go faster than the day before, or soften into my running rhythm and just focus on my breath and putting one foot in front of the other; and it was certainly challenging.

The point I'm trying to make here is, take a closer look at what you used to do for self-care and unpack it to its bones. Ask yourself some questions and get to the bottom of what it was about it that brought you so much joy, passion, and purpose. Or whatever emotion it evoked for you that you want more of. You're then more likely to find a replacement that suits you. Just as our identity can be flexible, our go-to methods of self-care can be flexible. It can sometimes feel sad to notice that what we once enjoyed isn't quite as practical for us anymore, but remember that humans are not meant to go through the motions of the same routine every day for the rest of our lives. We are meant to evolve; we are meant to change and adapt. Otherwise, we're just passing the time until we find ourselves at the pearly white gates of heaven. Take becoming a mother as a catalyst for new opportunities to arise. See it as your chance to return from the bottom of the well with new gifts to share.

In helping me not to miss the hobbies and pastimes I'd left behind so much, I found the following analogy helpful: you wouldn't buy a new couch if you didn't have anywhere to put it, would you? Or at least you wouldn't stuff it into your living room along with the old couch and all your remaining furniture. You'd have to get rid of something to make space for the new. But holding on to all the trappings of our life before motherhood is like trying to stuff the couch into the room along with all the furniture that was already there. Sometimes being open to the gift of new experiences means letting go of some old familiar things, at least for a while. Trying desperately to hold onto all the pieces of the old puzzle is just depressing. We're allowed to miss things. This can even be a good driving force to try to integrate these things back into our lives. But we make room for new experiences and opportunities by softening ourselves. Hold those things you used to do to care for yourself a little looser and thank them for their lessons without saying goodbye. Loosen your grip on them and move your gaze from the rearview mirror and onto the horizon. Good things are coming. I promise.

Getting to a place where self-care is possible

When I was battling some postpartum blues, Zac and my sister Jane would encourage me and say to me, 'Go and do something for yourself! What do you love doing? Go and do it, for crying out loud!' My answer to that: 'If it were that easy, I would. And if I could be doing those things, then we wouldn't have a problem, now would we?'

In that moment, what was stopping me was a combination of mum-guilt for leaving or doing something for myself, the idea that I wasn't worthy of pampering, and not knowing what on Earth I could actually do to feel better (since I didn't even know what self-care looked like for me anymore). Plus, I had a thousand other things on my to-do list – I couldn't possibly add anything else. Add in breastfeeding, and it can feel like whenever you have a short window to do anything, it's more likely to be spent washing or cooking – or watching TV and trying to rest and then feeling bad for not doing said washing and cooking.

In that season of life, I didn't even know what I needed, let alone have the capacity to give it to myself. I felt that people who would tell me to care for myself or take time out for myself just didn't get it. They didn't understand that I already knew that it was common sense (but not common action).

So, how do you get to a place where self-care seems possible? When things are going well, it's easy, but what do we do when things aren't going so well? When we don't have the energy or know how to get ourselves out of a slump, we can use the people around us to get things going for us. It doesn't mean we don't take responsibility for ourselves, but there are some simple steps we can do to feed off the energy of those around us to then get to a place where we can start to practise self-care – which is the foundation of being able to care for others.

This can be especially hard for single mums and those still building their support system. Or perhaps for those mothers who have well-established support systems but feel like they're failing or incapable if they ask for help. Sometimes the first step in making self-care possible is simply acknowledging that it's *really freaking hard* right now. If we can stop judging ourselves for not doing better, for not doing more, then we can hold the whole situation a little more lightly. Baby steps become accomplishments when we can see them for what they are – steps in the right direction – instead of comparing ourselves to some impossible standard and judging ourselves for not moving forward faster. When you don't have a ton of resources, asking for help becomes especially important, as does surrounding yourself with a caring community – and seeking those people out if they're not in your life already.

During those times when you can't identify what you're needing, when you don't have the energy to lift yourself up, here are three suggestions for where to start.

1. Surround yourself with high-vibe people

At one point or another, we've all connected with someone who felt like they were on the same 'wavelength' or have had the feeling of being drained or 'brought down' by the mere presence of a particular person. In conversation, we automatically assume the body language or posture of the other person. We start to talk or use the same sort of slang as our close friends or housemates; we unconsciously sync our footsteps and start to clap in time when we're cheering. When my dad calls up his favourite Japanese restaurant, he imitates and absorbs their accent when ordering his spicy pork. When we bought my first car from a lovely Indian man, he took on his accent as well. Embarrassing but logical. We all know that person in your life who has a contagious smile or laugh (I bet someone's smile just came to mind, and you gave a little smile just thinking about it – that's the magic I'm talking about). These people are worth their weight in gold. As we learned about the social engagement system and how our nervous system states are transferable, we absorb the energy of those around us. Mirror neurons make this possible. A mirror neuron is almost exactly as it sounds. Mirror neurons are fired exactly the same in our brains whether we are watching something happening or doing it ourselves. You could be watching your dad crack open a peanut, and at the same time, the neurons in his brain mirror yours as you watch, even though you're not the one performing the task.

A surefire way to boost our energy and frequency when we don't have the know-how or just can't get out of our own way is to go and be with these people. Absorb their energy, and let them do the hard work until you can take over. Literally use them as a mirror and take advantage of our neurological biology (but maybe for something more fun than cracking open peanuts).

That's what I mean by surrounding yourself with high-vibe people. Source people that are operating on a frequency that you want to be at, and be near them, soak them up, buy them coffee, go through their rubbish. Breathe them in and let their energy radiate into your very being. These people might be friends, they might be family, or they might be friends of friends. You might not even know some of these people, but with the potential to connect with anyone at any time through social media, you can find some. One of my mum friends now was once a stranger to me before she reached out on Instagram. I had never met her before, but she had children roughly the same age as mine. It was very out of the blue, but she messaged me on Insty and asked if I would like to go for a walk and a play date. Even though I didn't know her (yet), it's the perfect example of how we can put ourselves out there and interact to find our high-vibe. We went for a walk together, chewed each other's ears off, and have been friends ever since. She's a little bit younger than I am and told me that most of her friends don't have children yet, so she was wanting to fill in her days with other mums and get her children meeting new people, too. I thought to myself, *Wow, you are so brave reaching out to a stranger and putting yourself out there; you're also a GENIUS!* And she rocks, so I'm so grateful she did.

There's a common belief that a person needs to be a big empath or quite sensitive to become 'in tune' with other people's energy, or vibrations, or pick up on how others are feeling. But what I'm about to share with you is that we *automatically* pick up on other people's vibes without any conscious effort on our behalf, just as subconsciously as our lungs breathe and our hearts beat. It applies to every single one of us. We capture the energy of those we surround ourselves with and are prone to picking up others' wavelengths, which is the natural tendency to *synchronise* or *co-regulate*. This co-regulation is a part of our inbuilt, biological nature. We were born inclined to tune into other people's vibrations and auric waves, not just in ways we can see, like picking up people's accents or walking in time with them, but emotionally, cognitively, and physiologically as well. It's mind-blowing to know that this synchronisation means activity in the body over which we have no conscious control. Things like brainwaves, heart rate, sweating, and pupil dilation coordinate between people around each other. For example, our hearts literally will beat in time with those we love and spend time with. When you cuddle up to your partner at the end of a long day, you'll notice that your hearts connect. When I'm feeling anxious or overwhelmed or my mind is running away from me at night time, I like to roll over and put my hand or head on Zac's chest. I feel into his heartbeat, and mine eventually starts to match his. This has a natural way of slowing down my heart rate, making me feel more connected and grounded. But it doesn't have to be someone we have a connection with or even know very well. When you're talking to someone, anyone, every time you make a specific sound, a tiny area in the prefrontal cortex in your brain is activated. The same area will light up in the other person's brain, even though they are not speaking at that point. Some scientists say that language is just a way for our brains to synchronise with each other. Our hormones even like to join the party. I'm sure you already know or have experienced your menstrual cycle synchronising with another female you spend a lot of time or live with. Magnetic resonance imaging (MRI) scans reveal that our brainwaves cohere with those of other people. Electrocardiograms (ECGs) show that our heartbeats synchronise when we emotionally connect with someone. Blood tests reveal that the hormones of others can influence our hormonal balance. And when listening to a friend tell a story, your pupils and those of your friends will dilate in unison.

We literally become the people around us in more ways than one. Which is why it's so important to be specific about who and what we surround ourselves with. But because we are human and there's this thing called 'life', we will experience times and moments when our energy is feeling low or momentarily operating on a lower frequency than desired. That's okay. It just highlights the need to be aware of what makes us feel good and what doesn't so we can deliberately put ourselves into high-vibe scenarios or cleanse our energetic fields when we don't. It also highlights the fact that those we surround ourselves with can quite literally change us, for better or worse. Find the better ones, and soak them up. As for the latter, don't worry; I've got a whole chapter dedicated to loving on ourselves on an energetic and spiritual level and how to nurture and cleanse our energetic fields coming up next! For now, it's just important to know how it works.

2. Accept compliments

No, I mean *really* accept them. Absorb them, take them in, allow yourself to receive them. When someone gives you a compliment, say thank you. Soak that shit in. Let it land in your body. Let go of the mind's narrative, close your eyes and drop it into your nervous system. Breathe it in with all you have and feel it on a cellular level.

It's so common and natural for us to hit it away. Like if someone compliments your clothes, 'Oh, these shabby things? They're as old as the hills'. If we can flip this autopilot reaction into acceptance and receiving mode, we can start to accept the love that's around us – because it's everywhere. There's love in the way the sun rises every morning. There's love in the way flowers bloom and follow the sun. There's love in the way your baby climbs up your legs and pulls at you. There's love in the way your toddler screams your name twenty times in two minutes. And there's love in your babies following you to the toilet because they need to be near you and know what you're doing every moment of every day.

If you still can't see it, know this: I love you. Yep, I do. Because you are here on this Earth. You are no accident. We are sisters. You are meant to be here, and you have a unique purpose; otherwise, you wouldn't be.

Let that sink in. Challenge yourself to take a breath every time someone says something nice about you, and before the temptation to shy away from it or brush it off blurts out, say 'Thank you'. It helps when you surround yourself with people that make you feel good because these people are not shy of sending a compliment in your direction. Bonus points for writing these compliments down at the end of the day and feeling gratitude for them. Turn the volume up on them and use them as inspo for starting to write some of your own down. For example: What do you like about yourself? What do others admire in you? What are you proud of yourself for doing today? What went well and why? I might write down that I'm proud of myself for making something to eat for lunch instead of eating the baby's leftovers, or that I'm proud for not being so hard on myself for giving the boys chicken nuggets for tea, or that I did ten minutes of the washing today. Whatever self-compliments you write down, really feel them. Lean into them and get into the practice of meeting yourself here for a moment – and then maybe one percent more each day.

3. Serve others

It can feel easier to love others than it does to love ourselves – especially for mothers with our natural instinct to give and give. I don't want to encourage burnout here or giving so much of ourselves that we end up depleted and empty. I'm just talking about flipping our focus on this and finding that the receiving is in the giving.

To turn the heat up on this high-vibe energy party, we can be the person who dishes out the good stuff. We can be the person who gives genuine feedback and compliments to our fellow mamas – and anyone else, for that matter. There's always something good to see in other people, and it's another thing to express it out loud. The more you give, the more you will receive because there's no other frequency quite like that of the giver and the lover.

When I get really in tune with this energy, it can be hard to walk past a stranger and not tell them something I like about them – complimenting a fantastic red lippy that makes someone's outfit sing or admiring some-one's sick manicure or letting someone know how helpful it was that they held the door open while I wrangled a toddler and a double pram through the narrow entry. The more you do it, the easier it is, and the more it snowballs – and the littlest things count, too: giving someone your parking spot with leftover time or thinking good thoughts and sending positive vibes in someone's direction. When it's genuine and real, you are the one creating these high vibrations and sharing them, so you can't help but radiate the good stuff. It pours out of you when you give it away. So, *you* be that person who holds the door open. *You* invite that mama you don't know that well from your mothers' group over for a play date on your new trampoline. Be the shining light that you are, without any expectations attached that you need or deserve something in return – even though it *will* come back to you in some form. The act of giving is the return because you let yourself feel the love yourself and then let it out to the world.

For some reason, giving that love to someone always feels easier. When you give love away like you're made of it, you can't help but start to feel it radiate from your bones as well. It just feels good to make others feel good.

CHAPTER ELEVEN

We Are Energetic Beings

The total number of minds in the universe is one.

Erwin Schrodinger, *Nobel Prize-winning Austrian physicist*

We had thought that we were human beings making a spiritual journey; it may be truer to say we are spiritual beings making a human journey.

Pieree Teilhard de Chardin

There is no shortage of theories and opinions when it comes to how we all came to be here and how all of existence was created. Some call it the power of the Universe; some call it God or Spirit; others might call it a load of shiz. If you are one of those people who is quite sceptical about things you can't see or touch, I'm going to give you something you can sink your teeth into. If you're reading this, I'm guessing you're open to this way of seeing the world; it might already be your vibe. But whether you're aware of it or not, you *do* believe in something, somewhere. And you have already experienced the power of an energy that is greater than yourself.

You've been thinking about a friend or person, and they've called you the next day. You've gone to the supermarket in your Ugg boots, praying that you won't run into anyone you know, and you see every woman and her dog (because it works when we focus on what we don't want as well as when we focus on what we do want). You've opened a book to the exact page that you were either looking for or needed to read. You've had a gut feeling to buy that house even though it's over your budget because it just feels right. You've knocked on wood. You've said a prayer. And you've thanked someone called God before. You've gotten a magical knowing hint from somewhere that makes you think, 'I don't know what made me think to stop by Grandma's house, but if I hadn't, she would have had her stroke on her own with no one to call the ambulance'.

If I cut your brain open, I wouldn't see these thoughts, I can't see your feelings, and I can't physically touch or see this energy. But there is a force out there that is greater than ourselves, and we all belong to it. Most people define their reality from the confines of what their five senses tell them, but there is so much more going on. We can't see gravity, but we don't throw ourselves off buildings, and we show our faith in electricity by not shoving forks and knives into the toaster. We might not know the complexities of these things and how they work, but we play by the rules.

Everything on this planet has its own energy and is vibrating at specific frequencies. Fear, guilt, shame, loneliness, comparisonitis – these are all examples of things, thought patterns, and feelings that vibrate at a lower frequency. Love, gratitude, joy, and trust are all examples of high-frequency energies. So when we are operating on a lower frequency – because, as we know, we are human and life comes in ebbs and flows – one way to let go and really up the ante is to surround ourselves with people and things that are operating at the frequency we want to be at. If we engage with lower frequencies, surround ourselves with things and people and have these thought patterns on repeat, we can't expect to operate easily on a different level. Like attracts like. If we want to achieve higher frequencies, then we need to align with those frequencies.

The idea that you're an energetic being might be a tough one to accept, but it's truly essential that you do, and I'm sure you'll find it very beneficial when you do if you haven't already. As I mentioned before, everything living and non-living in this universe is energy. When talking about human beings, we all have a personal energy field that surrounds us. Some people call this an aura – and each individual has a unique aura that is constantly moving and vibrating at a frequency that is unique to us. It's like when you know someone is standing close behind you or has a hand in your face even though your eyes are closed. That's because these people are within your energy field, and you just *know*. If you need a bit of science to back this up, hospitals measure this energy field from approximately six feet away from the human body. *Wowzas.*

Own your energy

In the last chapter, we touched on using the energy of people around us to lift ourselves up. Still, we also have to be aware that it's common for our energy to be drained by certain people, events, experiences, or self-sabotaging thoughts. Given this, it's important and critically essential for each of us to be in charge of our own energy. When we aren't, we give that control to someone or something else. There's a difference between waiting, hoping, and expecting the people around us to lift us out of our funk and taking responsibility, noticing it's not happening for ourselves, and physically putting ourselves in a different situation so we can receive the high vibes available to us. We have to get ourselves into the position of receiving and being open to absorbing all the good things around us, the same as we need to set boundaries and prevent our precious energy from being drained or stolen if we give up our power to protect ourselves.

I don't mean we go around making a big cross with our arms over our chest and not letting anyone near us. I mean, we observe and become watchful of which people, things, and situations either drain us or enlighten us. When we're deficient in energy or we undermine our personal boundaries, we're taken over by the energies of the people and things around us or by the energy of our problems and end up feeling a bit lost. Our aura must be fed with the right type of energy, so identifying this is a good place to start. Figure out what your 'fuel' is and then work out how to obtain it in a healthy way, how to refuel, not if, but when life gets in the way and our 'vehicle' needs service.

If you're not aligned with the natural flow of your own energy, you'll simply become a magnet for all kinds of other energies, some of them not so good, and your aura will become overwhelmed by the sea of energetic vibrations that surround you.

This relates to the kind of self-care we choose for ourselves. If your mother's group doesn't feel good, don't go. If you feel like staying in your pyjamas all day, do it. No judgements, just complete reverence.

When it comes to people, though, we need to be careful with what we label as 'draining' or vibrating at a lower frequency. We don't want to slip into the seductive trap of blame and shame and handballing the responsibility onto other things, like 'Cindy is vibrating way low, I'm not going to go near her'. Phrases like this suggest that some people are better than others. Like, if your friends don't even have the meditation app Insight Timer on their phone and you do, you're the more conscious one. This type of thinking is just the ego at its best. There are no levels to life. Everyone evolves differently, but we aren't above or below each other. Everyone is in their own process and exactly where they need to be, using the best of their knowledge to do what they think is right, even if we think it's wrong. Remember, everyone is always doing their best. Spending time with high-vibe people with the intention to lift your own energy is how you can successfully pull yourself out of low vibrational pools. Of course, you would have probably experienced that when you're tired and grouchy, your children and partner feed off this and can get grouchy, too. Intending to lift your vibe from someone else's hits differently. It's one thing to be drowning and pull someone down with you and another to reach your hand out, ask for help, and with the other person's guidance, lift yourself up and out of the water. My husband is just as tired and overworked as I can be, so it's not much good if I'm trying to mooch good energy from him. Instead, I can stroke his head, I can ask him what has gone well about his day, ask him to talk about things that prompt some high-vibe conversation; then, we can get the ball rolling. Otherwise, if this is too much, I schedule a date with my girlfriends. Who are always just as happy as I am to have a night out, and we subconsciously vibe off each other, lifting each other up. It's beautiful.

It's easy to give a label to people or things that irritate or annoy us, but it's not about labelling or judging. No one is bad and no one is good – when we see things through the eyes of no judgements, we resist the urge to label things. It's tricky, though, because our brain's job is to make sense of the stimuli coming in so that we can function in the world, and labelling things is just one way it does that. Picking up on and being aware of it is the key. Everyone is on their own journey and vibrating at their unique frequency. No one made us queen of frequencies, and it's not our job to go around and stick people in a box. Our job is to love and to *be* love, which requires us to resist the urge to be right and swap it for kindness and acceptance.

Once upon a time, my husband and I were going to IKEA. I thought I knew where to go and park, and I insisted to him that he follow my directions (anyone who knows me can attest that I have the worst sense of direction – no – I'm a person who needs additional resources to help me know where to go). Anyway, when he knew better to go the other way than what I was suggesting, I was mortified. I was so hurt that he 'never' listens to me and that sometimes I actually do know things. Unfortunately, this was not one of those times. He proved me wrong. Zac, bless him, saw how worked up I got about it and chose to be kind instead of gloating about being right. Of course, there are way more stories of the other way around, where I'm the right and kind one (wink wink), but just to show you that sometimes, very rarely, we gals can be wrong, too. Zac's decision to be kind instead of right is something I've never forgotten and was a building block of love and compassion. We're always going to make mistakes, more so than we'd like to admit, but our job in marriage isn't to go around pointing fingers. It's to have a laugh, choose to be kind, and know that sooner rather than later, the pendulum will swing, and it will be our turn to be wrong and want the other person to show compassion.

We know that the people who trigger something in us are the people who express what we in ourselves *suppress*. For example, say someone (okay, my sister Jane) spends generous amounts of money on beautiful clothes. Because I didn't allow myself to do that, every time I witnessed Jane doing it, I created an inner conflict with myself that drained my energy. It has nothing to do with Jane and her actions; it was *my* reaction that was having a destabilising effect on me. My irritation was the cause of my energy loss.

Another example is when Zac does things to care for himself. I go to war with myself because I know he deserves time to recharge, but because I can suppress that desire in myself, it's insanely triggering. I push myself down the list of priorities and put washing, work, and washing first (yes, I said washing twice). How can I have time for myself when there's so much to do and little people to care for? So when Zac does make time for himself, I can get resentful because it's what I desire but don't allow myself the space to do it. Again, this is not Zac's fault. It's nobody's fault. It's just a good reminder that creates more space for me when those feelings creep in. We should always spend time in quiet contemplation when we feel pee oh'd because it's often because a person or situation is mirroring our own suppressed authenticity. There's a reason we are pissed off at certain things. It's a unique lesson assigned just for us. How special!

Getting real about your energy field: conscious action steps

I'm going to call this the action section because I'm about to get down and dirty with what we need to do to be buzzing on the vibrations we wanna be and how to get outta the pits. My advice is to start small. And if that feels too big, go smaller. (Remember the one percenters.) Doing something miniscule is better than doing nothing at all because something too big is scary or overwhelming. I know we get stuck in those dark holes where you don't know which way is up, and you just go through your days with your head stuck in a dark cloud. Just simply waiting this out and knowing that things will shift soon is a kind of action. Knowing that your moon cycle is due and being a little bit more patient as you wait for your dark thoughts to dissipate – that, too, is action. Placing your hand on your heart to take a few deep breaths is action. Knowing this is just a phase and the light will soon return so you can take bigger steps is action. When it comes to self-care and self-lovin', prevention is better than a cure. Doing little bits here and there to keep you afloat is better than not doing anything – because eventually, it *will* catch up to you.

These feelings are far too real for me. When I have my darkest times, it's because I haven't been reading, journalling, doing my breathwork or doing anything for myself. That lack of self-care catches up to me and hits me in the face as a big reminder to get my shit together. Ironically, it's when I'm needing more self-love, not less. It's when I need to ask myself, *What is it that I'm needing? How can I meet my own needs?* It's a crazy tough way to learn, and I don't recommend it. Especially when it can be minimised by consistently taking steps forward – whether big or small. We can walk slowly, just never backwards.

As Voltaire once wrote, 'The best is the enemy of the good'. And good is better than not at all when we don't know what our next move is. When it comes to replenishing your energy as a new mum and feeling completely lost as to what feels good for you now, the best way is to keep softening into yourself. Keep experimenting and keep things in motion. You might be thinking, 'How *long* is that going to take?' There is no finish line because if there was something to *achieve*, it would mean that you achieve it and then stop. It's a constant cycle that keeps going around and around and will change just like the seasons. It's about being in the flow. Different activities and practices will feel different year to year, month to month, and day to day. The key is just to keep swimming.

Your aura is all the space immediately around you. If you stretch your arms out and swing them around your body, that's about the distance of your energy field or aura. When we become mothers, we experience massive shifts in our energy fields, not only because of what our bodies can do but because our perspectives change. And, I don't know, we go through probably *the* biggest transition there ever is and ever will be on this planet. So with this shift comes new ways of balancing and finding a different way to become in flow – where we pick up only what we need to from our environment with a positive and healthy filter and then radiate our glorious and loving light from within us, giving back and serving the universe and influencing our surroundings, including our children and partners.

When everything is in a state of balance and flow, we interact with the world in harmony, with joy and ease. But when we get blockages within our aura or it becomes out of balance, we can feel discomfort and out of sorts, and illnesses can even manifest. It's no secret that becoming a mother can have us feeling a little bit different than we did pre-babies, so even just knowing about our aura and energy centres and being aware of them can move us towards a better balance in life because they serve as great allies for self-reflection. I know that when I've checked in with mine when feeling a little bit lost, on more than one occasion, I've had 'a-ha' moments where everything just makes sense, and it's clear what I need to do moving forward to find my flow and balance. For example, when I'm feeling a bit scattered in my business, unclear about what I want to create and out of touch with my vision, these feelings are associated with the energy centre at my third eye. Knowing this, I can focus on this energy centre and elevate it to get back in touch with my vision and feel a deeper clarity moving forward.

Just to be clear, when I refer to balance here – I don't mean a delicate juggling act that could crumble with just a toe out of line. To me, balance is fluid and doesn't always mean a fifty-fifty split between two things like work and motherhood. Work isn't even on our radar when we're doing our best to keep an infant alive. Different scenarios call for different amounts of our time and energy; it's about finding what works for you and then pivoting when you become aware that it isn't. We know when something isn't in balance because (a) we're mothers and we know everything, and (b) it doesn't feel good.

From time to time, our aura will need a little cleansing, a little freshen up after being drained or zapped from our surroundings or internal happenings. Sometimes our energy does not flow easily because we have blockages that we need to clear, or we need to step up and reclaim our magic. This is what it means to live in alignment with your highest self. Attending to our aura is one more example – and a key one, at that – of how we can allow our feelings and show ourselves some love instead of pushing through when we notice (or don't even take the time to notice) that we're depleted.

The best way to engage with your aura to either cleanse, reclaim, or get your energy field flowing is through its key energy centres within our bodies, known in the traditional Eastern teachings as chakras. There are seven main chakras that run along our spine that start from the root, or base, of our spine and extend to the crown of our head. Each chakra vibrates at a particular frequency that correlates with a colour. Because they are not visible (except in a metaphysical sense), many of us don't know how to recognise and utilise them, but I'd like to run through them because I think it's a key concept when talking about how to feel more ourselves and empowered when we experience such change becoming mothers.

The word *chakra* means 'wheel' in the ancient language of Sanskrit, so I like to picture them as whirling balls of colourful energy within our bodies. In the Emily East Crash Course in Chakras, they are responsible for bringing energy from our external world and our environment (hint, the people around us) into our energy field and body, as well as moving energy from our body and aura into the world around us. The individual chakras in our bodies are focal points that blend the physical and spiritual bodies. And as long as energy flows freely through our chakras, we can experience life fully and without discomfort, physically and mentally.

But as we know, blockages do happen, so there are certain activities, foods, movements, and thought processes we can engage in to restore this energy flow. To function at their best, our chakras need to stay open (it's the only way the good stuff can flow in and we can let go of the bad stuff and, at the same time, radiate good vibes and interact with the world positively and authentically). When they become blocked, we can experience physical, emotional, and spiritual symptoms related to a specific chakra. And sometimes, when you don't know or can't pinpoint what's happening within you, these chakras are a brilliant, practical tool we can utilise to get ourselves moving again – literally and figuratively.

My sister Jane lived in Melbourne for five years, had her first two children there, and then moved to live in the same town as me. When she moved, filling in her days obviously looked a little bit different. She was in a comfortable flow in Melbourne: she lived a thirty-second walk away from her coffee shop that was more like family than anything else, and she had a walking track and parks in her neighbourhood. She knew where to go and what to do to entertain her boys and fill her own cup up in the process. So when she moved, she found herself twiddling her thumbs. She lived out of town, so if she wanted her coffee fix, she had to get in the car and drive for fifteen minutes, and it took some time to find new parks to go to. She wasn't complaining about any of this; it was just a transition phase she had to go through to find her new normal. A little bit like finding our new normal and daily routine as mothers, Jane went from having a squeaky clean routine one day to being out of sorts the next.

To get things moving along and to make the transition smoother, Jane used the framework of the seven chakras to self-reflect and find practices to help her feel more grounded. She resonated with the root chakra being blocked, which is responsible for us feeling grounded and connected – which makes sense, given that she had uprooted her life to some extent. To combat this blockage and to get it moving freely, one thing you can do is connect with Mother Nature and do some 'rooting' activities. Jane started walking barefoot outside; she made a cubby house outside with her children, and she even ate root vegetables like carrots, beetroot, and parsnips.

Whether I've got you on board with this whole energy thing or not, having some specific support and guidance on how you can care for yourself in big times of transition or unease can't do any harm. One of the biggest challenges I've faced as a mum is being able to identify my needs in any given moment. How do I give myself what I need when I don't know what that is? Enter: *the chakra system*. It provides a framework for me to really reflect and zero in on what my mind, body, and heart are needing as well as give me some ideas for how to fulfil those needs and feel grounded in a new and unfamiliar routine.

THE CHAKRA SYSTEM

The free flow of energy when the chakras are clear and aligned is a divine feeling. It's part of what helps us to navigate difficult circumstances without getting overly stressed and to enjoy the ride even when it seems life is spinning out of control. The guide below is designed to get straight to the point for the busy new mum. I wish I'd had something like this when I first had children, so I created it for you.

If this information is new to you and seems overwhelming, just skim and see what catches your eye. You'll know intuitively which one you need or want to focus on first. Simply reading this material can be an exercise in trusting your intuition. If one chakra, in particular, sings to you or jumps out of the page and shakes you by the shoulders, that one is for you. Or you could choose to take one chakra per week or per month and move through them in order (or out of order). This is your self-care practice, so whatever you decide and resonate with is the right decision.

Chakra balancing for me has not only been about receiving energy and coming home to myself over and over again; it has also allowed me to create a deeper connection with my spirit and my higher self. It's helped me to trust myself and my intuition, giving me the courage to choose the path of fulfilment and unlock the power that I held within me all along. I want to support you on your journey as well and empower you to take charge of your life and potential. To show you that you can discover what it is that you subconsciously might need to let go of, what is no longer serving you energetically, and claim back your power each and every time you need to. I want you to feel inspired, grounded, and ready to make decisions that feel in alignment with your soul's path and desires. And I want you to parent from that place. That is my intention for you and the intention of this little resource I have created.

ROOT OR BASE CHAKRA

Where: The base of your spine

Colour: Red

About: Provides us with a base or foundation for life; helps us to feel grounded and confident handling challenges. Our root chakra is responsible for our sense of security and stability. We express this chakra by feeling a connection to nature and our ability to survive, ground, feel stable, and trust the universe.

You'll notice it's blocked when: You're experiencing times of change, you're holding onto something that you need to let go of, you're disconnected from nature and your roots/where you're from, your household chores are too overwhelming, you're disconnected with family, you're out of routine, your bills are overdue or late, you have been neglecting your body or not taking time to honour and appreciate it.

Ways to reclaim or utilise its power: Connect with nature, walk barefoot outside, sleep naked, build a cubby house outside with your children and make mud pies, spend time in the garden. Get your hands into the dirt. Swap the playground and play gyms for bush walks and playing in nature. Pay bills on time (if you can) and take pride in your home. Make a budget. Make that skin check appointment or get your Pap smear if you're due. Dance in the nude to bongo drums (lol), dance naked after you get out of the shower, imagine the smell of freshly cut grass or go and cut your grass just so you can smell it! Sprinkle cinnamon on your breaky. Eat cherries, tomatoes, and red peppers. Cook wholesome food at home. Call your mum and dad or grandparents if you can. Ask to hear stories about when you were younger or about their childhood. Wear more red.

Affirmation: I am safe.

SACRAL OR NAVEL CHAKRA

Where: Below your belly button

Colour: Orange

About: Responsible for our sexual and creative energy and how we relate to our emotions and the emotions of others.

You'll notice it's blocked when: Your sexual libido is AWOL, your immune system is a bit down, you're not sure what brings you joy anymore, you have mum-guilt big time for caring for yourself, you feel like you're constantly on the bottom of the food chain when it comes to your family (kids and partner).

Ways to reclaim or utilise its power: Play ocean sounds or waves as you go to sleep or meditate. Go swimming solo or engage in lots of water play with your children. Buy or make new bath toys (channel your creativity and play in the water); be extra playful with mundane activities – like getting kids into the car. Why not try 'I'm going to be Buzz Lightyear to the car! Who are you going to be?' Watch comedy movies or sitcoms, watch romantic movies or read a romantic novel, engage in self-pleasure or connect with your partner, hold your partner so your chests are touching for a minimum of twenty seconds, burn incense and wear essential oils on your skin, buy yourself some flowers, practise being in receiving mode, and up the ante on healthy eating. Dance, dance, and more dance. Go out to dinner at your favourite restaurant and savour the tastes and textures you love the most.

Affirmation: I deserve.

SOLAR PLEXUS CHAKRA

Where: Your stomach

Colour: Yellow

About: Responsible for our confidence and self-esteem as well as feeling like we are in control of our lives.

You'll notice it's blocked when: You're feeling quite flat in general about life, proactivity and willpower are lower than usual, you find making decisions difficult (even easy ones), and you feel a little disconnected from family and friends.

Ways to reclaim or utilise its power: Write a mission statement for your life; do the 'Feminine Archetype Quiz' for free on my website (emilyeast.com.au) to remind yourself about what is authentic and special to you. Reflect on your boundaries (if you have any) or create some – does that mean you ask for help with the dishes? Does it mean you hop into bed an hour earlier and turn your phone off? A boundary is whatever you can put in place that honours who you are and protects your energy field. Send a text to a friend and let them know what you admire about them, or start this conversation with your partner. Or better yet, create a list of ten things you admire about yourself and pop them in your journal (extra points for re-reading them and adding to the list each day). Is there anyone you are jealous or envious of? Spend some time meditating on this, and just like a hot coal, let it go. Get a diary or calendar and plan out your goals. Read books by people who inspire you, or visit biographyonline.com to read heaps of cool, uplifting true stories. Reflect on your work-life balance – is your current situation feeling good? If not, what changes can you make? Can you seek some career advice at work to feel more fulfilled? Can you pick up or drop some hours or work from home sometimes? Can your children drop back or pick up a day at daycare? Roast marshmallows with your children over the stove at home or a little fire pit in the backyard. Bake your own bread, or if you usually buy bread from the supermarket, go to a bakery and buy some fresh, high-quality stuff. Drink lemon water. Eat bananas.

Affirmation: I am powerful.

HEART CHAKRA

Where: The centre of your chest
Colour: Green

About: No surprises here; it's all about our ability to love and show compassion.

You'll notice it's blocked when: You're not feeling loved, you feel unnoticed or not appreciated, you have unkind thoughts about yourself – judging yourself harshly, being your own biggest critic.

Ways to reclaim or utilise its power: Meditate outside, play with your children outside, and spend time taking deep breaths and being aware of the fresh air. Open windows in your house to let fresh air in. Eat broccoli and spinach. Cook apple crumble or apple pie with your children using green apples. Get a shoulder massage. Volunteer. Be more expressive romantically with your partner (super hard when this energy centre is depleted, so take things slow – perhaps start with a little kiss as your partner leaves for work or returns home or vice versa, or maybe just a cheeky bum tap as they walk past). Draw pictures and make love letters with your children about all the things you love about each other and your family. Buy and read picture books with your children about diversity and acceptance of everyone – for example, stories about Aboriginal culture or different ways families can look. (Sophie Beer, Jessica Sanders, and Tami Charles are all brilliant authors of stories about practising compassion and acceptance.) Organise a catch-up with friends or family or have a playdate and go a little deeper than surface conversations and let them know what you love about them. Do meditations based on receiving love and getting your body into a state of reception. Energetically open your heart through meditation, awareness, and willful efforts; keep this centre open. Notice throughout your day when you feel it energetically close; do the best you can to keep it open. The way you do this is simple: never close it. Closing is a habit, but exercise that control. Relax, open, and feel tremendous energy rush up inside of you. Notice comments that make you close, and practise reopening. Notice how this shifts your relationships with the masculine – there is nothing more toxic or poisonous to a masculine than a feminine withholding her heart within the boundaries of safety and respect. Let it out, sister, don't ever close. Your inner heart is magnetic, and it heals people, not just yourself.

Affirmation: I am love.

THROAT CHAKRA

Where: The throat
Colour: Blue
About: Self-expression and finding your voice
You'll notice it's blocked when: You have a sore throat, there's a conversation or something that you want to express but are having trouble with doing so (conscious or subconsciously), you feel unfairly treated, you feel guilty about something.

Ways to reclaim or utilise its power: Sing! Play your favourite belt-out tracks in the car, in the shower, or when you're cooking dinner, bathing your babies, or tidying up. Sing out loud – and don't. hold. back. Engage in conversations with others who hold different opinions from yours and listen without judgement. Go to the museum or some gardens and spend time appreciating the beautiful nature and art around you. If there's an argument or conflict in your mind that you'd like to resolve, write a letter to yourself or to another person. Do this with the intention that no one will ever read it so you can be as unrealistic or illogical as you like and totally, completely, and unapologetically yourself. Perform your daily affirmations. If there's a public issue you feel strongly about, do something to support it, like donating to a charity, following activists on Instagram and sharing some content on your page, or signing a petition. Drink herbal teas, put mint in your water, and wipe your benches with some water and a few drops of eucalyptus oil. Use eucalyptus in your diffuser. Wear essential oils (put them on a hanky and under your children's pillows). Practice meditation that includes chanting or omming.

Affirmation: I am truth. (Extra points for saying it out loud and in the mirror!)

THIRD EYE CHAKRA

Where: Centre of your forehead

Colour: Purple

About: Your inner vision, insight, imagination, and clarity of thoughts; your intuition

You'll notice it's blocked when: You find it hard to make decisions, you're finding it difficult to concentrate or focus, you're triggered when people do things differently to how you would do them, you're finding it difficult to resolve problems, your imagination is lacking, you're second guessing yourself regularly.

Ways to reclaim or utilise its power: Have technology-free time every day (set timers on your smartphone that limit the amount you use certain apps, and don't take your phone to bed with you). Engage in some mirror work by looking yourself in the eyes and saying 'I love you' and completing the sentence 'I am amazing because ...' Let these affirmations land in your body; feel them rather than just saying them. Engage with the feelings, not the thoughts. Get out of your head and into your body by dancing, dry brushing your body, or giving yourself a massage. Create or refresh a vision board. Spend time visualising your highest self; engage with her and her feelings and her energy. Who is she? What is she doing, and what is she like? How does she *feel?* Meditate. Download my free 'Activating Your Inner Wisdom' meditation by following the prompts at emilyeast.com.au.

Affirmation: I trust my intuition.

CROWN CHAKRA

Where: Just above the top of your head

Colour: White or violet

About: Consciousness. It's often seen as the last one to work on because the other chakras supply its energy. It represents the spiritual connection to yourself, others, and the universe. You appreciate being a part of something bigger. The crown chakra plays a role in your life's purpose. When it's activated, you feel enlightened and connected – and that everything is love.

You'll notice it's blocked when: You feel disconnected from your inner voice and unable to trust life and the universe. You lack the belief in a higher power, you have trouble learning or obtaining new information, you feel confused, and you have rigid thoughts and beliefs about religion and spirituality.

Ways to reclaim or utilise its power: Burn candles around your home. Practice daily gratitude – whether you ask your partner or children three things they are grateful for that day or write a list of ten things you are grateful for each night before going to sleep. Make it the last thing you do before shutting your eyes, and breathe in that gratitude as you drift off to sleep. Up the ante with your meditations to engage with this chakra; give a new app or a different style a go. Be super aware of your ego. The lesson of this chakra is to live life mindfully and be present in the moment. Practice trusting in your inner guidance by connecting with your body through dancing; with this connection, feel into the connection with the divine, source, or whatever words resonate with you.

Affirmation: I am that I am.

HOW YOU CAN BE WITH THESE CONCEPTS

When you're living an authentic life, there will be plenty of people who will doubt you or even poke a little fun. But let me ask you, What have you ever gained from playing small? That's right, not much. The greatest regret people often have is that they lack courage. They played small so they could be accepted. We worry about what people will think about us or say about us. We close our hearts to the world so we don't pose a serious threat to our ego's identity. But the way people treat us is nothing personal; it's a reflection of how they feel about themselves internally. Accepting this reality frees us up to be more ourselves, and when things go pear-shaped, it doesn't mean anything is wrong with us. We have the ability to create our reality by choosing the meaning we assign to it when 'life happens' and how we respond to it.

My motherhood journey started out with me trying to understand what I was going through by backing everything with science. But I became more and more open to the mystical. Motherhood woke me up to that on a whole new level. I started to see people and life differently. I think so many of us are now more aware of our energy and less dependent on expert opinions. We've been conditioned to look for authority figures or even people on Instagram that we wish to be like to give us permission or show us what is right for us. Slowly, we are collectively learning that our intuition is the greatest authority. It's no longer 'woo woo'. We are energetic beings, and we can care for ourselves as such. Understanding that caring for ourselves back then is not what it looks like now because now we are aware that it's more than just our bodies we need to nurture; it's our hearts and our energy as well. With this newfound authority, we are reclaiming our needs and discovering new ways to have them met. They're pretty exciting times to be a part of. Here are some practices that have helped me along the way with embracing challenges, letting go of self-judgement, asking for what I need, getting my needs met, and learning how to care for my energy. My hope is that you'll find it helpful.

For more on protecting your aura, see the information on boundaries in Chapter 14.

Embodying the Chakra System: Which chakra spoke to you? Choose one of the activities and schedule time to do that this week.

Quick fixes to cleanse your aura: When you notice that your energy field feels drained or your aura needs a tune-up, you can quite literally dust yourself off. For example, you've just stepped back into the car after visiting a friend who emotionally dumped all over you. It didn't feel good, and you're feeling zapped. Physically dust down your arms, from your shoulders to your fingers, and flick that energy off you. Do it for both arms, like you're rubbing the energy off. Continue to do your legs and face. See how that feels. When you get home, you can also light a quick sage burner or palo santo and cleanse your immediate energy field. Close your eyes, and with the intention to clear and cleanse your field, wave the smoking cleaning tool around your space while taking deep breaths.

Embracing challenge: Saying that 'easy sucks' is one thing; embodying it is another. Life gets rough, and accepting it can be easier said than done, especially running on two hours sleep. To hold space for your emotions, giving them safe passage through your body without judgement, is a powerful thing. An emotional release exercise can help you do this. Lie flat on your back with your knees bent and your feet flat on the floor. Firmly plant your feet a little further than hip-width apart, and then let your legs fold inwards and rest on each other. Gently start to rock your legs from side to side. There is no rush. Let your breath guide your body. This is a nervous system regulation technique, where the rocking signals safety to your body. The hips store emotions within them, so moving them in this way will help surface any emotional energy you are either feeling or have been suppressing. Breathe as you do this, and allow and notice whatever comes up for you. Journal on your experience afterwards.

Identifying your needs: If you feel like you can identify your needs, create a list of them and explore which ones you can meet yourself. For example, if you love being thought of and surprised with flowers, perhaps you can pencil in time this week to take yourself to a market, wander down the aisles, and pick a nice bunch. Or, if you like to be told how gorgeous and beautiful you are, create some space in your week to do some mirror work where you look yourself in the eye and tell yourself those things, or leave yourself little love notes around the house.

Which needs can you get support with: Can you identify which needs you'd like support with? For example, if you'd like to feel taken care of by someone else, add that to your list – try to make it as specific as you can, like 'I'd like to be taken out for dinner'. Come up with a couple of people you'd like to have do this for you, and go about making it happen for yourself. If that person is busy, work on asking the next person or come back to that need and get another one met first. Be creative and patient. And when it does come to fruition, let it land in your body. Breathe it in and remind yourself how loved you are and how the people around you love you and want to meet your needs.

Tip: If you're struggling to create a list of what your needs are and how you'd like to feel, sometimes it's easier to identify what you *don't* want to feel. Ask yourself how you are feeling, and then match the opposite feeling to an activity to meet that need. For example, if you're feeling lonely, that usually means you value connection (the opposite of lonely). Add to your list ways that you feel connected, like making a phone call to a friend you haven't spoken with in a while, organising a walk with a friend, or shopping with your sister.

How to ask your partner to meet your needs: Here are some examples of common feelings and how you can ask for your needs to be met in a way that doesn't project your emotions onto the person you are asking or blame them and cause them to feel defensive.

Instead of: 'You never show me any affection'. Try: 'When you touch me, it shows me that you care about me. I would love for you to hug me a bit more on a regular basis. I understand that it might not come naturally to you, but it makes me feel so close to you'.

Instead of: 'We never do anything together anymore! You're always working'. Try: 'I really want to feel closer to you, and lately, I haven't been feeling that way. Can we pick a time to do something, just us?'

Remember, the first step in getting your needs met is identifying what they are. The second step is communicating this to the other person, including how they can actually do that for you.

Practice asking for what you want: For most people, asking for what you want can be uncomfortable. But to have emotionally connected relationships, sometimes we must be willing to feel a little uncomfortable. We know that no partner or one person can meet all of our needs, and we shouldn't expect them to. Just like you can't completely meet your partner's needs all on your own. To start practising this in a small way, take turns giving each other a massage. Let me explain:

1. With your partner, choose whether you would like a head massage, a foot massage, or a hand massage.

2. When your partner is giving you a massage, practise giving them feedback about what you like and don't like. For example, 'I like when you gently bend my fingers back like that' or 'I don't like that technique; can you do it this way instead?'

3. Say thank you – when either one of you gives feedback during the massage, have the other respond by saying thank you. It's important to instil feelings of safety and curiosity when both giving and receiving feedback.

Journal question: How are my needs not being met showing up in the rest of my life (e.g., procrastination, drinking, social media, expectations of others)? What would it mean for the other areas of my life if I started to meet my own needs?

Food for thought: How do you tell the difference between you jumping onto someone's lifeboat to lift your own vibe compared with wrenching someone off theirs to join you in your low vibrational pools of emotions? Zac and I dance between these two often. When we get stuck in a feedback loop where we're nitpicking at each other, taking little digs, and noticing everything that the other is doing wrong ('you were on the toilet for too long', 'you're meant to hang the wet sock on the small clothes line, not the big one', the list goes on), this is not the time to get Zac's help to lift my vibe. We're both feeding off each other's irritations and not helping each other at this point. So, a call to my sister or a girlfriend, a quick walk around the block with them, pushing the kids in the pram, chatting away about what's annoying us, I then return to the house all lifted. Then, you can actually be the person in the relationship to lift the vibes and break the feedback loop. If you're noticing that you're feeding off someone else's vibes or you're influencing someone else's, that's not the time for this strategy. Opt in for freshening up by scheduling some time either right now or as soon as you can with someone else. No judgements.

SENSUAL SOMATICS™ EMBODIMENT OF YES, NO, & MAYBE

When we practise what it feels like in our bodies to say yes, no, and maybe, we teach our nervous system how it feels to reclaim our boundaries. In some cases, our 'no' has been dishonoured and even disregarded, and we are left feeling like we don't have choices (we people-please, self-sabotage). When we reinstil our power of choice through boundaries, deep healing can happen. Reclaiming our boundaries and relearning how not just to say yes, no, or maybe, but feeling it within our bodies is deeply important when it comes to expressing our true authentic selves. This embodiment practice might not seem like much, but I can tell you, so many emotions are evoked for me each time I do it. I move through something different, and it's been incredibly healing and helpful to re-establish the connection to the power I have over my own boundaries. Here's how:

Your NO: Stand tall with your arms extended out in front of you, with your palms facing outwards, like you're pushing something away or signalling 'stop!' Your legs are wide, one in front of the other so that if someone tried to push you over, you would stand strong. Your core is strong, and your weight is intentionally shifted forward as the energy of your 'no' is directed in front of you.

Your Maybe: Stand tall with your arms extended in front of you, resting in a diagonal position, fingers pointing down, shoulders softening away from the ears, legs in warrior stance, just like your 'no', with your knees slightly bent. Your weight is even on both feet as the energy of your 'maybe' is directed down through your feet instead of in front of you or behind you.

Your YES: Stand tall with your palms facing open, fingers extended, arms externally rotated, shoulders dropping down your back and away from your ears, and your heart space is open. Your feet are hip width apart, and your spine is long and extended through the crown of your head. Your centre of gravity is soft so, if someone came into your space, it would be easy for you to fall over backwards.

Tips: *Stand in position and feel into your body with each practice. Fully embody the posture, and say your yes, no, or maybe out loud. Shake it off, reset your body, and reposition yourself to repeat each embodiment three times. You might notice something different arise each time. Embrace whatever surfaces for you and, afterwards, journal on your experience. I promise you that even though it seems simple, sometimes the simplest things yield the biggest results (one percenters). You can even imagine yourself saying yes, maybe, or no to a specific someone or situation so you can build that strong connection and self-trust when it comes to expressing yourself and setting your boundary.*

PART FOUR

Separation vs Connection

Life doesn't make any sense without interdependence.
We need each other, and the sooner we learn that, the
better for us all.

Joan Erikson

CHAPTER TWELVE

Desire (Love Changes – How to Keep It Sexy)

If you want to impact your partner, remember to use your body before your words. Touch them. Belly up to them. Communicate your love and care through your body first and foremost. They will hear you more clearly.

John Wineland

The old paradigm of motherhood meant caring for others' needs at the expense of our own, never tending to our own emotions and feeling we had to mask them and put on a happy face all the time. Under the old paradigm, our connection to self was broken – and without a healthy connection to self, it's impossible to have a healthy connection to others. The new paradigm prioritises self-care and honouring our own needs because the relationship with the self is the foundation for strong relationships with our children and our partners as well as all the other important people in our lives. You don't have to go it alone or pretend to be perfect; the new paradigm of motherhood gives us the freedom to show up, even with our flaws – to trust that we'll still be loved and, in fact, that the people around us will also be freed from the expectation that *they* need to try to be perfect.

So far, in this book, we've covered some tools for connecting with yourself and nourishing your energy. As you practise using these, you'll automatically start to see them having a ripple effect on your relationships. In this last part of the book, we'll elaborate more on how the new paradigm of motherhood applies to relationships and explore how to use these concepts intentionally to create honest, connected, fulfilling relationships.

So, as we shift our focus outward to our relationships, let's start with something that will be familiar after all you've read so far: connecting to yourself and embracing all parts of yourself, even the parts that are difficult to accept. Repeat after me: 'I love that I'm a mess. I love that I hate myself sometimes. I love how impatient I am'. Now you try. Finish this sentence: 'I love that …' Now say 'I'm so beautiful' and feel the words coming from your body and up from your spine.

When we fully own and love the parts of ourselves that we hate, there's a sense of mastery and freedom that comes with that. But even more so when we share it. The thing is, the lie we've been sold is that love is all rainbows and unicorns. When the truth is, love can also be messy and hard and ugly. To withhold this love, whether it's sharing the good parts of us or the hard parts like the 'I'm angry at you because…', is a denial of who you really are. And I know that's not how you want to roll.

Women, in particular, have a collective feeling of, 'I'm too much', so we tend to withhold our hearts. And it's completely normal not to want to share the raw, vulnerable, and 'less desirable' parts of ourselves, especially with our lovers. Particularly if we have in the past, only to be burned. When we open our hearts with no expectations of reciprocity, and when we open our hearts when we feel like closing, there's a part within others that will respond. Have you ever noticed that?

You see, loving all parts of ourselves returns us to what we truly are. We are love. We are the highest expression of love. And because love is unified, it wants to feel oneness, just like we desire to feel oneness with our lovers, our children, or our pets. We want to feel deeply connected. Love will always find love. When we love ourselves, we become magnetic – and I don't just mean on the days when you have make-up on and your hair is clean. When you love yourself fully and hold space for yourself fully, you become truly magnetic.

This was a big part of how Zac and I began to recover from our non-existent sex life. What really began to bring my libido out of retirement was learning to hold space for myself. And I mean all of myself. With that, I began to feel more confident in my skin. To me, confidence comes from feeling the deepest parts of myself. And I became the invitation. I started to believe that my open heart, warts and all, was healing those around me and was a magnet. I would walk into a room flooded with that inner belief and affirm to myself, 'People just want to take a bite of me'. It sounds silly, but that was sort of the point: to have fun, bring a light-hearted energy to it, and feel confident in who I am, no matter where I'm at in my journey. I began to learn about my feminine gifts of nourishing energy to myself, and as it rippled out of me, other people felt it too.

TIPS FOR FEELING TURNED ON BY LIFE AND CONNECTED TO YOUR CHANGING BODY

The first time my libido went AWOL was when I was pregnant with Zephyr. Every day when I'd look in the mirror, I'd think, *'Whose body is this?'* It didn't feel like mine. I felt unable to desire sex because I didn't feel at home or comfortable within my own body. It was so foreign to me. It wasn't so much that I felt unattractive, even though I could not fit into my clothes and find things to wear that made me feel good or like myself; I just didn't feel like me. As my motherhood journey continued, my bulging belly concerns turned into saggy boob concerns. Not to mention that my nipples look like they've breastfed a whole tribe in Africa or like you could attach your leads to them to recharge your car battery. It seemed like no matter where I was in my motherhood journey, my body seemed to come up with new ways to remind me that my life, and my being, would never be the same. As life went on, I continued to embrace the importance of connecting with myself as a route to being able to experience connection with others. One of the biggest influences in doing this work was completing my Sensual Somatic™ Facilitator Training with a goddess called Desi (@sensualsomatic on Instagram). I spent three months exploring my own sexuality and sensuality and how to support other women to do the same so we can be sexually liberated and feel powerful and connected in our own skin. Here are two of my favourite practices for myself and for teaching others about trusting ourselves and exploring our senses and intuitive wisdom. Since doing this work and practices like these, I've learned to embrace my worn-out nipples, built self-trust, and been curious and actually interested in exploring my sensuality and holding space for myself in all my forms. I'm more turned on by life, and when my body speaks to me, it's talking less about what it looks like and more about how it feels. And that feels good.

If you want to rediscover that sensual connection, here are some practices to get you started.

Seated intention pose/posterior activation: Take a comfortable seat, either on a cushion or chair. Allow your spine to be tall without it being too rigid. If you need to rest against a wall, that's okay. Allow your spine to take its natural shape without forcing it to be straight. Begin by breathing into the diaphragm, allowing your body to be soft. Ask yourself, where can the body be softened just a little bit more? Allow the heart space to open and the lower belly to release. Ever so slightly, tilt your head back. This will shift the weight a little so you feel your back muscles engage. Immediately allow this sensation of your back muscles activating to remind you that you are held and supported. As you feel your back body activate, imagine yourself being held by a safe, strong energy. This can be represented by a person, a place, your ancestors, or even yourself. In this moment, if you feel called to, speak 'I am held' and continue to breathe. Do this as long as you'd like to. Having your feet up against the wall can also create this sensation – with your hips about thirty centimetres away from the wall, lie on your back and elevate your legs against the wall. Have one hand on your heart and the other on your stomach. Feel held by your body and repeat the mantra that you are held. Notice what emerges for you and hold space for whatever comes up.

Cat-cow breaths/spinal undulations: If moving your body freely sounds too scary, start with some 'cat-cow' breaths (you'll be familiar with this if you're a yogi). It's where you start on all fours, your hands and knees, and as you inhale, take a deep breath in, drop your belly to the floor, drop your lower back and look to the sky. On the exhale, reverse the pose by tucking the tailbone under, arching your back like a cat, and looking up at your belly button. Move through a few repetitions while you listen to music. Music can help guide your intuition, and the structured movements give you something to come back to if you notice yourself getting into your head. When you start to feel connected to your body, you can then explore the posture and your movements. Maybe you start to make circles with your hips or start to roll your spine back or forth like a wave. Allow space to explore the movements of your body and what feels good; at the same time, have the structured breathing and movements to come back to or build upon if and when you need them. As your hands are pushing into the Earth beneath you, you can even imagine yourself pushing the energy out of you and into the Earth. Let it take your worries and insecurities, whatever it is you're feeling around your body.

Connecting to your sensuality and unleashing your body's inner wisdom is something that I help women with. If you'd like to explore these practices and others like them, you can do that directly with me within my online community – Soul Nation (visit emilyeast.com.au and follow the prompts).

Pleasure and desire are not the same (and we want it all!)

When I mentioned that I had no libido in the early stages of my mothering journey, please trust that the issue was not that I don't like sex. I love it, actually. I enjoy it. It feels good. But even though it was a fun activity and I felt safe and loved and enjoyed the release of hormones after, I still didn't feel motivated to initiate it. Why not? To explain this, I'm going to nerd out a little bit about dopamine, a neurotransmitter whose release allows scientists to track the exact moment desire occurs.

In 1954, the importance of dopamine became apparent when an experiment by neuroscientists James Old and Peter Milner uncovered the neurological processes behind desire. The experiment involved blocking the release of dopamine in the brains of rats by implanting electrodes in their brains. To the researchers' surprise, the rats lost all will to live. They wouldn't eat, drink, or have sex. They didn't seem to desire anything, and within a few days, they died of dehydration.

From this discovery, follow-up studies started taking things a little further. Other scientists also depleted rats of dopamine, but this time, they sprinkled tiny droplets of sugar into the mouths of the rats. And the rats *loved* it. Even though dopamine was blocked, they liked the sugar just as much as they did before they had the electrodes placed in their little brains; they just didn't *want* it anymore. The little rats could still experience pleasure, but with the removal of dopamine, desire disappeared along with it – and without desire, action stopped.

What do you think would happen if we reversed this process and flooded the little rodent brains with dopamine? Other researchers had the same question and realised that flooding the brain's reward system with dopamine had the opposite effect, and the animals performed at super-high speeds. One study showed that when mice received a big hit of dopamine after poking their nose into a box, they developed a desire so strong that they poked their little heads in the box *eight hundred* times per hour!

Human beings aren't any different. We get a dopamine hit when we eat junk food, scroll through social media, or play video games. In

Atomic Habits, James Clear explains that for years, scientists assumed dopamine was all about pleasure, but now we know it plays a central role in neurological processes such as motivation, learning and memory, punishment and aversion, and voluntary movement. When framed that way, it seems there's almost no aspect of our behaviour that dopamine doesn't influence!

It's important to understand that dopamine is not only released when you experience something pleasurable but also when you *antici-pate* it happening. That's why gratitude journals are so powerful. Your reward system in the brain gets just as much of a kick out of *thinking* about something good happening as it does when it is *actually* happening. Gambling addicts have a dopamine spike right *before* they place a bet, not after they win. Cocaine addicts get a surge of dopamine when they *see* the powder, not after they take it. Pavlov's dogs salivated in anticipation of the food, even if they didn't receive it. The lead-up to Christmas can be just as enjoyable as waking up on Christmas morning, and daydreaming about a holiday can make us feel just as good as doing the real thing.

I can't help but think of online shopping here. I definitely feel the dopamine hit when I click on that beautiful button 'add to cart'. But have you ever spent, like, a good hour online shopping and adding things to your cart to then just close your browser and not end up purchasing anything, despite the time you invested? It's because the anticipation of the reward, not the actual fulfilment of it, is the part that feels good. And that's the part that gets us to take action. Whenever you think about something pleasurable, your dopamine levels spike in anticipation. The same reward system in our brain that is activated when you receive a reward is the same system that is activated when you anticipate a reward.

The key message is this: desire is the engine that drives behaviour. It is a powerful way to motivate and initiate action. Without it, we still enjoy certain activities but don't necessarily go out of our way to get them. This was the secret sauce in resuscitating my sex drive and actually *desiring* it in the first place. Ultimately, activating my sensual body through dance and the two practices outlined in the box earlier in this chapter influence the cascade of hormone communication between my physical and emotional body. For example, when my body is activated through movement, dopamine and oxytocin are released, which has a powerful effect on putting my nervous system into a rest and digest mode and activates my social engagement system. This is the mode we need to be in to engage in things like sex because it turns off our hypervigilance and allows us to surrender and trust another. By leveraging what we know about how hormones and neurotransmitters motivate our behaviour, we can intentionally give ourselves that hit of dopamine and oxytocin through dance and sensual exploration to motivate ourselves to engage in intimacy with our partners. It's no lie that when we feel comfortable and sexy, we feel good. That's also dopamine encouraging us to do more of what makes us feel good and sexy.

As the tech entrepreneur Naval Ravikant says, 'The trick to doing anything is first cultivating a desire for it'. Orgasm feels great because it releases endorphins and oxytocin – but we need dopamine to get us to the place of releasing those feel-good hormones. Being turned on is as important as the orgasm itself. It's the turn-on that influences us to act to get the orgasm – and this is the piece that was missing for me.

Attachment

Another key step in getting my libido back was creating a bit of distance. Let me share with you what I mean. My sister, a business coach for other women, invited Zac to be a guest speaker on one of her team training sessions because he runs a couple of successful businesses himself. I went and watched him, and I saw him in his element. He was talking about all things that he loved and was good at and passionate about. I saw him in a completely different light and in a way I hadn't seen him before. It was totally sexy.

We didn't spend nights apart, but there was this space between us that created that desire to be near him. Space between my comfortable self and his comfortable self. I was totally fangirling over him. If your partner is a tradie (tradesman for my non-Aussie speaking gals, like a builder or a plumber or someone who earns a living by literally getting their hands dirty) or usually wears casual clothes to work or most of the time, creating space between you could be seeing him in a suit. For us, it could be going out for dinner and wearing a clean shirt that hasn't got baby poop or vom on it. Zac loves me wearing lipstick, and I think part of the reason is that I very rarely wear make-up, so when he sees me with a polished lip, it's that novelty and something different that creates some interest. It's not about meeting any particular cultural standard of beauty – it's about the surprise. The brain loves novelty. It's exciting and gives us that dopamine hit. The men's equivalent might be if your husband always has a beard and then shaves. I know when Zac shaves, I'm all over him.

Creating desire is making the most of opportunities where we could see each other not in the everyday, familiar territory that feels warm and safe but also in new and different. Novelty is king. And it's that desire that will motivate action for us to be together and connect. It's like two magnets attracted to each other. If we pull them apart ever so slightly, we feel resistance, and they fiercely want to reconnect. That's what this space can do: it can pull the magnets apart and create that heat and magnetism.

Yes, we want safety, but we also want mystery and surprise. I want to know my husband will always have my back and love me even when my dark feminine is let off her unruly chain, but I also want him to surprise me with flowers and a touch of spontaneous romance. So how do we find this mystery and desire when we are just so familiar with each other? After your husband has helped change your blood-soaked maternity pads after you've given birth, cleaned up your red wine vom after a night out with the girls, kept a straight face after you pissed your pants jumping on the trampoline, or high fives you after successfully squeezing enough colostrum out of your nip before your milk comes in and your newborn sleeps, how do you find the space for both this unconditional 'do anything for you even though it's not very glamorous' love and the 'who the hell is this sexy lady beast in my bedroom that I have to jump on right now' love? Just like we want to open up space between emotion and reaction, we also need to create space for desire. We know a little time away from each other makes the heart grow fonder, but we don't have to go on holidays apart from each other or have a night away to create this space. We can choose to see our partners in a different light. That is also a form of space.

This is actually quite similar to a parenting concept you might be familiar with: attachment. Here's a brief refresher on attachment. As children, we naturally develop an attachment to our caregivers, and the quality of this attachment creates the foundation for every personal and professional relationship to come.

There are a few types of attachment (whose names can vary a bit depending on which psychology textbook you're consulting). I first learned and taught them as secure and insecure attachment, and these might be the terms that persist the most in popular culture, but I'm going to share with you here the terms I like better:

1. Anxious: manifests as clingy, works better with others than on their own, originates from caregivers who were unpredictable with giving their attention ('I can't do this without you');

2. Avoidant: manifests as distant, can usually sit in problems longer than most people, originates from caregivers who were distant and neglectful ('I'll do this by myself');

3. Disorganised: manifests as clingy sometimes and distant at other times, typically excels in high-risk environments, originates from caregivers who were a source of both safety and danger ('I want you'/'I don't want you'); and

4. Secure: manifests as attuned, regulated, caring, and loving; can easily repair after stress or disagreement; resilient all around; originates from attentive and attuned parents ('I love myself'/'I love others').

Picture a room full of bright colours and fun toys for children. Upon arriving in the room, a child with an anxious attachment style will be distressed when their mother leaves. A child with an avoidant attachment style won't be fazed when their mother leaves (but this isn't necessarily because they're happy; they've just learned that when they show distress, they're rarely comforted). A child with a disorganised attachment style might go back and forth between distress and showing zero emotion. And a child with secure attachment will most likely cry to begin with but then settle down because they have faith that their mother will come back. A child with secure attachment can sometimes look very similar (from the outside) to the child with avoidant attachment, but these two children's internal experiences are quite different.

I love the way this framework highlights how our feelings about ourselves also extend to others. An awareness of this framework also shows how old paradigm habits (such as trying to control all aspects of our children's lives *or* keeping our emotions under such tight control that we become completely disconnected from our children) can negatively impact our relationships with our children. Our childhood experiences set us up with one of these attachment styles, but that's not fixed (phew). Many of us grew up with parents who had their own attachment wounds, which can be easily passed down the line – which is why it's so bloody brilliant that you are here, reading this now. Becoming aware of our own attachment style can help us make more empowered decisions and be more intentional about the relationship we cultivate with our children.

Similar to our relationship with our partner, where we want safety and security but also a bit of mystery and surprise, our relationships with our children also need a balance of closeness and distance. Otherwise, we'll end up with forty-year-old teenagers living at home (think the movie *Step Brothers* with Will Ferrell and John C. Reilly). You're still doing their washing, and they're still ordering take-out off your credit card without a real sense of identity or independence. Picture a toddler arriving at a new playground. The securely attached response is when the child runs off to try this exciting new equipment but keeps sneaking glances over their shoulder to ensure that mum's still there. This strikes a healthy balance between staying at mum's side, afraid to try the new playground (a response that leads the child to miss out on fun new adventures), and running off to the jungle gym without giving mum a second thought (not so great for the child's safety from an evolutionary perspective).

When the dreaded day comes when our babies start to grow up and need us less and less, they'll turn to us for guidance, and it's our job to tell them it's okay. 'The world is wonderful and big and exciting, and you should go and explore it for yourself because it's so much fun out there'. They know that we will always be there for them, and we'll always be connected. I cried when I stopped breastfeeding my second son, Knox. As I sobbed to my mum that he didn't need me anymore, she said to me, 'They will always need you'. How did I not realise this when it was my own mother who I was leaning on during a stressful time? We always need someone, no matter how old we get. Now I can be that someone my children can always come back to. But if we say to our children, 'Don't go, why would you want to leave the love and connection and safety I have created for you here? The world is scary and dangerous; isn't it good enough for you here?' They'll end up owning a piece of our anxiety and won't risk losing our love and connection over their desire to see the world. They will sacrifice their own adventures to stay close to home. They will think it is one way or another instead of realising they can have both adventure *and* safety. We have to let them go free, follow their desires, and reconcile their needs to feel desire, love, and safety. Then they'll never really be gone. We'll keep that love and connection – and they'll always know they can come home for Christmas.

Responsive desire

In full parent mode with two under two, there was a time early in our journey that sex just wasn't happening for Zac and me. I was going to bed early and Zac was going to bed later when I was already asleep. So, we decided to give scheduling a go and prioritise intimacy. It was a temporary fix to get us more connected, and after a few months, we didn't feel the need to keep it going – but for a time, it was just what we needed.

Even if we've worked on self-love and adding some healthy mystery to our relationship, simply finding the time for sex can be a challenge in and of itself. Nevertheless, it's absolutely worth doing because of the way it bonds you to your partner. The post-orgasm rush of oxytocin and vasopressin is why we feel such a cosmic union with somebody after making love to them. Whereas the old paradigm was all about the needs of the kids, in the new paradigm, the parents' relationship matters too.

I'll admit that it used to feel like an insult turning it on in the bedroom after a big day of motherhood. After everything that we do, we're expected to look pretty while we do it and then give more of ourselves at the end of the day. Like we haven't already given enough. I feel that. But I've come to learn that by creating space for ourselves, getting our needs met, and keeping set boundaries – I *want* to prioritise my own pleasure and joy. I *want* more of these things. I *need* more of these things. I'm open to receiving more joy in my life instead of being stuck in doing mode and leaving no room for them. It became less about more giving and more about surrendering to my own pleasure. There was a time when I was saying no to my own pleasure, no to my own joy, no to more connection. But as time goes by and I continue to heal, I'm welcoming these things more and more into my life.

Not long ago, I was walking past a Bras and Things shop and was suddenly taken aback by the big pin-up pictures in the windows of these beautiful women pushing up their breasts and looking amazing. I thought to myself, 'God, women really do everything. We make human life, and literally, every part of our bodies and our lives change, and while that's all going on, we look sexy doing it. These big boobs are what nourish our babies, but then they're also sexual playthings'.

When this starts to feel burdensome, I keep in mind that I have a choice – and I consider *why* I'm doing what I'm doing. If I want to wear mascara today, then I will. If I want to put on some self-tanner or some sexy knickers, then I will. But I won't feel good doing it if the reason behind my actions is reaching expectations. I'll do what I want when I want it – but one thing I want to do is be close with my partner. I want to love him, and I want to be connected.

Although some people have what researchers call 'spontaneous desire', where lust hits them like a lightning bolt and they have to devour their lover there and then, this is not the only way to have a healthy sexual desire. As parents of young kids, if we wait for spontaneous desire to arise, we might be waiting a *looooong* time. There is another type of desire, 'responsive desire', which New Jersey-based sex therapist Christine Hyde explains using this great metaphor: responsive desire is like being invited to a birthday party. Your friend asks you to a party, and of course, you say yes because it's a party and it's your friend. Then the date gets closer, and you start to think about how you're going to get there, who you will even know there, what you will wear, and who will look after the kids. But the date arrives, and you put your party pants on, and you get yourself to the party, and what happens? You have a good time.

Sexual connection is the same thing. Put your party pants on (or, in this case, take them off), and you're going to have a good time. Zac was hesitant when I first suggested that we schedule a sex date. His thoughts were that if we took the spontaneity out, it wouldn't be as hot or spicy. On some levels, there is something attractive about having someone want you desperately and taking you by surprise. But in real life, that wasn't happening for us, and relying on my desire to drop out of the sky while doing laundry would just mean more dry spells. My sexual desire was as rare as the lunar eclipse. But the good news is, scheduling sex taps into my responsive desire to connect and be with Zac. I hop into bed, let his skin touch my skin, and then I remember, 'Oh yeah, I like this. I like Zac'.

Research has pretty solid evidence to say that couples who sustain strong sexual connections over multiple decades have two things in common: (1) they trust each other, and (2) they prioritise sex. Trusting each other means this: you've got my back. Relationship researcher and therapist Sue Johnson boils trust down to one question: 'Are you there for me?' In our times of emotional turmoil and the ebbs and flows of life, we can trust that this person will love us and be there no matter what, in the good times and the bad. Identifying your needs and having them met by your partner is a clear way for this to become obvious to you. The second factor, prioritising sex, has certainly been a connection saver for this busy mum. If you rock the spontaneous desire, then you go, girlfriend. Power to you! But if you're like me and need a little nudge and reminder that sexual connection is important for my relationship, then my tip is to make sex intentional. It might not sound as juicy, but when you think about it, is there anything sexier and more romantic than being prioritised and deliberately chosen as something that matters? Carve out time to be together because foreplay doesn't start five minutes before the real thing. It starts about thirty seconds after the last orgasm. It's happening all day, every day. Prioritising sex doesn't only look like having actual sex with your partner. It can also be in the form of feeling sexy within your own skin. It can look like cuddling with your partner or kissing, sensual dance, exploring your own senses and sexuality, self-pleasure, turning yourself on, feeling good about yourself, and then building on this energy to bring to your relationship. It's getting those dopamine hits happening, sometimes on your own, before bringing that motivation and desire to your relationship. That, too, is prioritising sex. And I know that when I started to prioritise my own sexuality and do things like dancing and exploring my sensuality, I desired more sex with my husband and was ready to go and get it. Further to this, understanding my inner cycle also gave me valuable insight in the times of the month when I would be more randy than most. This was another way for me to best leverage my energy, and realistically when to schedule sexy time.

I was having a conversation about sex with a close girlfriend of mine who has a daughter the same age as Zephyr. She was telling me that with the stressors of parenthood, sex just didn't sound appealing, especially when she and her partner niggle at each other during the day. Then one morning, her partner got up and emptied the dishwasher, cooked their daughter breakfast, and got her ready for the day – something that she usually does by herself. My friend told me this was like porn for her, and thinking about how wonderful and thoughtful he had been turned her on.

I guess sometimes it's not about what turns you on so much but about what turns you off. Little digs at each other here and there, a few tense conversations, or a comment under someone's breath can gradually pull us apart. These little moments are inevitable when couples spend as much time together as they do and are so sleep-deprived and emotionally and physically challenged when we become parents. The key is to know how to find our way back to each other over and over again.

Sex educator Emily Nagoski, author of the book *Come As You Are*, has shared that she is often asked: 'How do couples sustain a strong sexual connection over the long term?' To explain what a strong sexual connection is and how couples maintain it, she first explains what it is not. You might be interested to learn that this strong and sustained sexual connection doesn't come from having a lot of sex or from having wild and adventurous sex. One study found that the best predictor of whether couples were satisfied sexually and with their relationships was not based on how often or where or how kinky it was but whether or not they cuddled afterwards. *Cute*.

These things don't have to come from sex, and the only way that they do is when we completely surrender to the moment. Our brains have to go along for the ride – vasopressin, dopamine, and oxytocin are only released when our mind follows along. If we are stressed or worried or our mind is elsewhere, then loving feelings and attachment while making love will be missing along with our wandering minds. Losing yourself in the moment with another person can be liberating and is more of a practical thing to do to be closer to your partner. Yet practise a little bit of mindfulness. Our logical brain shuts down (if we let it), and we can immerse ourselves in good feelings and intimacy. Cuddle afterwards, and hold your lover tight. Literally envision those happy hormones leaving your body and circling you both. A big lavender light of love and glitter fills the room, and you can feel it radiate your cells from the top of your head to the tips of your toes. Particularly your chest and your heart space. Your heart beats stronger as you feel the love and attachment you have for the other person, and for a moment, you forget about the dishes in the sink and the sticky orange juice spilt on your floor. Give yourself permission to shut off and be present with your own body's love potion and the swirling magical energy of your partner. Get that good hormone release and see what it does to your mood, how well you get along and show each other affection afterwards. Resist the urge to get up straight away after sex because you have a million things to do; relish the moment just a little longer together.

Every human being is doing the best they can

At a base level, our desires are driven by foundational needs. Dopamine drives us to eat and reproduce; without it, we would die, just like the rats. Psychologist Abraham Maslow developed a 'hierarchy of needs' that can be very useful in helping us understand what's motivating us and others. The needs for safety, love, and belonging are just above physiological needs in Maslow's pyramid. If we're hungry or thirsty, we won't have much attention to devote to social connection – but once our physical needs are met, the need for connection with other human beings is the next most urgent category. It resides in the bottom half of the pyramid and needs to be met before we can give thought to higher-order needs such as intellectual stimulation and professional fulfilment.

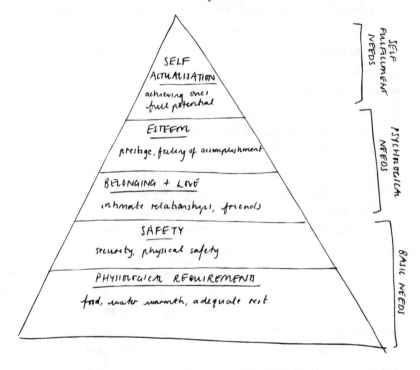

Maslow's Hierarchy of Needs

Here are some underlying motivators that affect us all:

- To conserve energy;
- The need for air, food, and water;
- The need for love and to reproduce;
- To connect and feel a sense of belonging and inclusion;
- To feel socially accepted and approved of;
- To reduce uncertainty;
- To achieve status.

The thing is, much more of our behaviour is driven by these basic needs than most of us realise. Every behaviour has a surface-level motive and a deeper, underlying driving force. If you ask me why I see a shirt in the store and say: 'I want this cute top for my boys; I'll get them one each', my answer would probably be something like, 'Because my kids have complexions to be jealous of and can pull off anything'. I wouldn't say, 'Because I have an innate need to win other people's approval, having my kids looking dope is one way I can do it'. Having other people think my children look fashionable is a way of seeking acceptance and belonging. Understanding our deeper motivations can help us show more compassion for our own behaviour and for others' – a factor that often gets in the way of the connection we desire.

When reflecting on our actions or when we're in the moment, we can be a bit kinder to ourselves and our children when we know it's a normal instinct to feel or act in certain ways. You didn't lash out and yell at your partner because you're a horrible person; you just needed to feel loved and recognised. Your sister didn't steal your favourite top because she's evil (although this may be questionable); she just wanted to achieve status and feel socially accepted. You didn't serve your children chicken nuggets for dinner from the freezer because you're a lazy mum (you cooked them first of course, you're not a monster); you just needed to conserve your energy because you need to give all you've got left to the upcoming bathtime ritual.

We might go about chasing these feelings in different ways, but the point is we all chase them. Sometimes we don't understand why people do what they do or say what they say, but by understanding our driving behaviours, we can use this insight to our advantage rather than to our detriment. You can have more empathy, compassion, and particularly patience with yourself and others (for example, a tired and somewhat mean three-year-old) when you know why people act the way they do (helpful when navigating your relationships with in-laws or dynamic shifts within the relationship with your partner).

You can adopt this strategy and use it whenever you have a disagreement, are triggered by your children's actions, or even when you're unpacking your own behaviour. The key is to pin their (or your own) action with an underlying motive to connect on a deeper level. It's not easy, but if you can look past the surface and find the root cause of the behaviour, just like when we know our babies aren't the devil when they're teething or tired, we start to get to know each other on a deep and intimate level. We can have more empathy and patience from moment to moment.

Think of someone who really bothers you and ruffles your feathers, maybe another mother in your mothers' group or on Instagram, maybe your sister or partner, or maybe a particular habit or behaviour your child does (like when my children tell me to stop singing – ouch). Someone who can take you from a good mood to a crappy one almost instantly. When it comes to the people who bother you and challenge you the most, whether it's over something big or small, just remember this: everyone is doing their best.

Look at the motivations above that are alive within us all. We are all striving for the same thing – we just go about it in different ways. Our job is not to judge and point fingers but to be compassionate and raise the vibration of ourselves and the universe. Even those people who bother us and do things we don't understand (Will Smith publicly hitting Chris Rock at the Oscars comes to mind), we get extra points for reminding ourselves that even people like them are doing their best. Sending hate and feeling hate for this situation only lowers the collective vibration of the 'verse. Instead, even though I find it shocking, sending hate and shame doesn't help the situation.

Try compassion on instead. How does that feel? Compassion can be hard, but it opens us up to ask questions instead of silently judging and to realise that everyone wants the same things. Everyone wants peace; we just have different thoughts about how to get there. We don't have to be conscience police. Don't freak out when people choose a different path than what we would choose. Drop the wrongness of anyone doing it differently than you would do. Drop the judgement. Everyone is doing their best. Let's spend our time and energy lifting our vibration rather than judging and fighting those who don't believe the same as we do. No one made us queen of appointing right and wrong. The universe has that job covered. Accept others for who they are; accept them for being on a different journey. There is no hierarchy. We are all the same. We are all human. And we are all doing our best. We evolve differently from others but not above them. There is no 'better' or 'less than' in a relationship with other people. Everyone is exactly where they are meant to be.

At the beginning of this chapter, we spoke about how it's important to love yourself as a foundation for loving others, but actually, the street goes both ways. When you can show others compassion in the moments when they may not be their best selves – when you can find that common ground and understand that they're motivated by the same basic needs and desires you are – then that opens up space for you to show yourself the same compassion in moments when you're not your best self. You already know comparisonitis is poison when it means you don't measure up – but it turns out it's poisonous even when you compare yourself and come out ahead.

CHAPTER THIRTEEN

The Divine Balance of Masculine and Feminine

Remember, the goal is not to 'be more masculine or feminine'. It is simply to relax more fully into who you truly are while developing your 360-degree capacities to feel, relate, understand, and direct – as a gift to yourself and the world. Nothing to change. Only expand.

John Wineland

So you're ready to raise your consciousness. You know you need to make a shift for you and your family to be seen, heard, and each authentically expressed. But if I took a peek at your diary, what would I see booked in? Would I see any self-care or downtime? Any empty space for creativity and inspiration? Or does this sound more realistic: you're doing every single task in your family unit and household; you have no room in your diary because it's filled with play dates and appointments; you're feeling burnt out and drained; you know you should get some help, but you're resistant to spend the money or to ask for it; you're saying yes to things that are actually a 'soul no'.

Oh, I get it. I've been there, too, and still visit there from time to time. But I've learned that if we continue to do motherhood that way, trying to prove to ourselves and everyone else that through constant productivity, doing the washing until our fingers bleed, piling on the pressure and stress, and allowing what we do for our children determine our sense of value in the world – we are going to burn out. Our bodies will start to break down. And we definitely won't have the energy for spiritual growth and letting go of the ingrained habits that represent the old paradigm.

The 'doing it all' approach to motherhood is driven by masculine energy – specifically, the wounded masculine (we'll dive deeper into what that means as this chapter continues). When I was living in this energy, I was constantly hustling and on the go, drinking all the (cold) coffee, eating all the sugar, listening to all the parenting podcasts, making sure the dog was walked and the kids had fresh air, doing all the things. I would serve my kids lunch and not take the time to nourish myself. I forgot how to care for myself in the midst of caring for others. I stopped moving my own body, giving *myself* fresh air, or taking *myself* for a walk. In focusing on *all the things*, I was blind to the fact that my relationship with Zac was suffering because I was so stressed out. And at the end of the day, I'd peel myself off the floor with a spatula and, without any time to recover, be ready to get out of bed and do it all again tomorrow.

Reaching my breaking point prompted me to dive deeper into learning about the concepts of masculine and feminine energy. And oh, em, gee, it was game-changing. Suddenly, a lot started to make sense. Until then, I had assumed that doing something 'the feminine way' meant I would have to let go of control or go with the flow like a dead fish. Without direction, without agency. And my family would miss out on things, and everything would fall apart. But since I couldn't continue the way I was going, I decided to surrender anyway and try something different.

I completely let go of the old way. I cleared out the podcasts and parenting experts I was following online and aligned with my intuition and soul. I prioritised feminine practices and ways of being. I filled my feed with soulful coaches and healers instead. And let me tell you, things are different now. I feel super chilled writing this book. It's been a beautiful reminder that I want to create it with my feminine energy, not the burn-out, push energy that felt so familiar to me and from where I thought things get done. Every morning I breathe in the cuteness of my children and play cars with them. We eat breakfast together on the couch, and if I can't get the toddler dressed, we stay in our pyjamas. When Knox is sleeping and I can get Zephyr to rest, I'll read a book instead of trying to squeeze in more housework or emails. Most mornings, I meditate for around twenty minutes. And the days I'm at home writing or creating, my schedule has spaces and gaps that allow for spontaneity, play, and inspiration.

I now mother and create with greater ease and flow, which is reflected in the way I birth my work into the world because I'm working in an integrated way. Opportunities that I never would have imagined come knocking because there is physical and energetic room for them. Have my family strategies gone out the window? Does this mean I'm living in a house filled with piles of dirty washing and an overflowing mailbox? Hell no. With the feminine way, all these things have been simpler and more effective. I take care of my body; I make sure I'm eating well – all the time. Not just when my kids are in care. I don't feel exhausted by all the washing or managing the billionth meltdown for the day. In fact, I could go as far as feeling energised by them (believe it or not).

I can hear your question: is mothering and keeping a house straight (not to mention a career) even effective in this way? Can you actually get things done from being 'in your feminine?' Damn straight, sister, and it feels good. For one, I'm not *trying* to do it all myself. I know my needs, and I get help when I need it. I know I'm not meant to do it all myself, and I create space for myself to do what I can and know that whatever that is, is enough. But you'll probably find that softening into this energy, you'll be more 'productive' than you ever were. You might even find that your definition of 'productive' will change. I know mine did. If my ultimate goal is to live a meaningful and joyful life, then I had to stop using 'productivity' and 'being efficient' as the primary metrics when evaluating the use of my time. Instead of thinking about what I get done during my day, I'm asking myself, *How did I feel? Did I laugh today? Did I feel joy?* To me, these are the things that add up to a meaningful life. Sometimes tidying my home brings me joy; other days, swapping the washing for a spontaneous trip to pick the boys up early to get ice cream brings me joy.

My patience and compassion for myself, my children, and my husband feel like they have doubled since I started shifting my energy around this piece and doing things differently. I'm more connected to my intuition and inner wisdom, so I make decisions more easily. I spend less time in my head overthinking and doubting myself when I both mother and work. And I want this for you, too. You deserve a life that you adore, makes a huge impact on your children, and helps you feel free to be yourself without feeling like you've been hit by a bus at the end of each week. You're a queen, and what you have within you matters and should be seen, heard, and loved. In a way, feminine energy allows us to be *stronger* in who we are as we relax into it, reclaiming our inherent gifts and honouring the very fabric that makes up our being.

We are meant to be different

Masculine and feminine go together like peas and carrots – they need each other to get ahead because we were all designed to be different. When you're building a house, for example, you don't just need a team of builders. You need electricians and plumbers, painters and other qualified people. You need different people with different skill sets, not just one type of person. You need a wide range of skills and abilities to support each other's work, to help each other out and get the best feeling and functioning house possible. Masculine and feminine are like plumbers and builders; we need both to get a good foundation.

There are many gender differences in the brain, but the most obvious is probably the corpus callosum. In Part Two of this book, we discussed the two hemispheres of the brain. The two halves are connected by nerve fibres known as the corpus callosum, and (as Dr Jenny Brockis writes in the fascinating book *Future Brain*), on average, this structure is eleven percent bigger in a female brain than a male brain.

What does this mean? Think about how much women usually love to talk. Our verbal capabilities, our articulation and ability to find the right word quickly, are no accident. Because our corpus callosum is thicker, we can link the thinking part of our brain to the verbal part of our brain super efficiently. This superpower of being able to articulate and verbally express ourselves goes up particularly in the middle of the menstrual cycle when estrogen levels peak. Still, even when we're not peaking, we're better than the average man.

Why did we evolve to have this biological difference? Because language was and still is our tool. We hold little babies up to our faces, and we talk to them, and we sing to them, and it's our job to develop their language and their little malleable brains. When we talk to our babies, the same part in our prefrontal cortex that lights up when we speak lights up in our babies as they listen (another example of how mirror neurons work). It also highlights the need for us feminine beings to be social, to communicate with each other and come together as a collective, to support each other, to hold space for each other, and cheer each other on. It gives us a huge sense of well-being when we are chatting away, which you probably would have already experienced directly. We can have three or four conversations going at once when we're catching up with a girlfriend, and we can easily shift and interchange between topics.

Let's continue to rewind the clock a bit and think of the cave days. Gender differentiation was important back then to ensure our survival – we were made to reproduce and survive. It can be really helpful to understand our biological and physiological make-up because often, not always, it can be insightful when understanding our own and other people's behaviour. If we know particular attributes or behaviours have an inbuilt purpose, just like women are meant to talk more because language was our tool in surviving and moulding little babies' brains, then it's easier to be compassionate and understanding in stressful times – particularly in the trenches of parenthood.

My poor Zac has been a bit like an experimental guinea pig over the last few years, particularly when it comes to the workings of his brain. Men have tunnel vision and tend to focus on just one thing at a time. This is because they were designed to be the hunters and protectors, so they needed to remain laser-focused on the task at hand to ensure our survival. They had to remain focused on the animal they were trying to protect their family from or the one their family was going to eat, and ignore other distractions – because if they missed out on the kill, we would all either miss lunch or *be* lunch. It was very important work, and they could not stop for anything until the job was done. Both tasks of hunting and protecting needed undivided attention and focus. When killing a predator like a mammoth or a bear, there's no time to be thinking about whether or not you left the iron on or if a bear has stolen your kettle of fish. Single-minded tunnel vision is what made men good at keeping their family and tribe alive and fed.

Which brings me back to Zac. I was folding the washing in our bedroom one day, and a suit shirt was in the basket. Instead of putting it away in the spare room cupboard, where we keep the fancy things, I left it on his side of the bed so he would put it away himself, and I carried on putting the rest of the washing away. The suit shirt didn't get put away at first. We played a game of me putting it on his pillow and him putting it on the floor and out of the way every night before hopping into bed. This went on for a few days until I asked him, 'Can you put away your suit shirt, please?' His response, with my best David Attenborough impersonation, was *'fascinating'*. He said, 'What suit shirt?' I found this remarkable. To him, he had one thing on his mind – getting into bed.

It's an amazing thing, really. You know when you start putting washing away and you put the clean towels in the bathroom, then you realise your bathroom mirror needs a wash, so you go to get the Windex, which you left in your bedroom after washing your mirror, so then you start to put your makeup away that was left out, so now you're sitting on your bathroom floor trying all your old beauty products and chucking out what you don't use. Mind you, the washing still has yet to be put away, and the bathroom mirror is yet to be cleaned because we can't block out or walk past things we can see that need to be done. Women think holistically and see the big picture. We are highly imaginative, and because the parts of the female brain are more connected, we tend to collect more pieces of data when we think, put them into more complex patterns, and see more options and outcomes. Call it genius, call it organised and holistic – call it overthinking or controlling in a less favourable (but sometimes still accurate) light.

The male brain, on the other hand, is great at blocking out unnecessary information that isn't needed for doing the task that's right in front of it and moving in a more step-by-step thinking pattern – hence Zac's ability to continue to move his own shirt off his bed to get into it every night without any awareness. He's not thinking about where it goes or what he could do with it; he's getting into bed.

Have you ever noticed that most men can't talk on the phone while doing anything else? It's hilarious; my husband, my father-in-law, and my dad all do it. They go outside or away from everyone when the phone rings. Or if they're driving to a new destination, they turn the radio down so they can *see* better. Women, on the other hand, can talk on the phone, have one hand washing the dishes and the other one cooking dinner with a baby on one hip while emptying the dishwasher with our toes.

When the men hunted, women stayed behind and cared for the children. We connected through communication and language, and we were the organisers. We were in charge of deciding where the berries and veggies came from, when to move on to another campsite when the seasons changed, or who would be a good match for whom that would keep bloodlines clear.

It's easier to be compassionate and empathetic when we know crazy behaviour has an inbuilt purpose. Even though it looks very different today, it was inbuilt to keep our species alive and evolving. Getting your son's attention while he's watching TV to let him know dinner is ready isn't as easy as saying to him, 'Dinner is ready'. Say it as many times as you like; he won't hear you. He's got tunnel vision for the TV. Try putting your hand on his shoulder to get his attention, and then tell him. It's the same with older boys, aka men and husbands. If you want a conversation, ask him to put his phone out of sight and perhaps turn the TV off in the process or wait for him to finish his email. It will save you energy and possibly avoid an argument.

Now, of course, there are exceptions. Some men love long conversations to catch up with their guy friends; some women have laser-sharp focus to tune out distractions but aren't so great at multitasking. Human beings vary along as broad a spectrum as the colours of the rainbow, and we also adapt to our environment (e.g., a man who grew up with sisters or a single mum who's had to learn to play the roles of both mum and dad). But there are patterns to the way we evolved as a species for gender differentiation and specialisation. Beyond that, in any romantic relationship (whether between a man and a woman or not), it is helpful when the two partners have energies that balance one another out. When we recognise that, we can choose to play up our own strengths and rely on our partner's respective strengths instead of (a) expecting them to be just like us or (b) trying to do it all ourselves.

The best example I was given to explain masculine and feminine energies was to think of it like a glass of water. The masculine is the glass. Its role is to hold the water, to contain it, to love it, to allow it to be. It provides protection and structure and presence. The water, the feminine energy, is fluid; it's moving, it's being, and when it's held, it has purpose. Without the glass, the water would flow recklessly in any direction. Or, it could be like a fire hydrant with so much force and destructive impact. The glass, without the feminine, is empty. It's got no love in its heart. It has nothing to protect or nurture. When it comes to motherhood, a truly vulnerable time, the mother needs to be protected. It's the masculine role to protect the mother so she can mother – whatever that looks like.

Just like it takes a good mix of left and right brain attributes to raise well-rounded, grounded, and open-minded children, it also takes a good mix of feminine and masculine energy to raise insightful and intelligent, resilient and confident babies. Not only does it support our children, but having an understanding and awareness of both energies expands our capacity to learn and love ourselves as well as how best to support and evoke the gifts in the people we love.

The masculine feels valued, motivated, and empowered when they feel like they are needed. The feminine feels the same way when we are cherished, appreciated, and – may I say – adored. If you're standing in your feminine, perhaps for the next week you could experiment and practise biting your tongue and restrain yourself from giving any unasked-for advice or suggestions. Just to see what happens. It may make the masculine in your life more attentive.

The energies can sometimes get scrambled, and it can take some work to find a balance, but this concept can help us understand why our partners react the way they do. For example: when we stand in our feminine, we are givers. Operating from this energy, I offered to call someone to help Zac assemble the trampoline in our backyard. It surprised me that he was offended – until I realised that to him, my suggestion meant he was incapable and I didn't think he was enough. Obviously not my intention; I just thought I was being helpful.

Another example: I find it really hard not to offer advice or solutions to Zac when I am the one home all day and have learned a thing or two about our children. Little tips and tricks that make our life easier – like what TV show gets a toddler to sit still for two seconds so you can get them dressed, or what is the only spoon that they will eat with at the moment, or how they'll only eat frozen peas, not cooked. When Zac does things for the children that I usually do, it can be hard not to intervene sometimes when he's doing it differently than how I would do it. Particularly if he starts to struggle with something that I have already struggled with and found a solution. But I've learned it's so important to surrender and stand in my feminine for many reasons:

1. It empowers Zac when he can solve the problem himself and makes him feel good. (Backing off and letting him take care of things is you softening into your feminine. And also, who says your solution is the only way or even the best way?)

2. If I offer advice, it can make him feel inadequate and like he's not capable – it's emasculating, I may as well chop his balls off.

3. Children (and mothers) need to know there is more than one way to do things. It develops adaptability and resilience and is an opportunity for us to soften and let go of control, to be taken care of.

I quite often find that without offering advice every two seconds, thinking that I am helping, Zac's more likely to come and ask me for it when he needs it. Not just with parenting. He was writing an important email to a client one day, and I'd like to say that I have experience in writing and would love to help. I was biting my tongue when opinions and advice came to mind. But instead of offering my advice or help, which would have been disempowering for him (and who is to say that my advice would have been better anyway?), he eventually came to me for another opinion. He was way more receptive and open to hearing my suggestions and working together than if I had offered them unsolicited.

The Divine Masculine	*The Divine Feminine*
Testosterone	**Estrogen + Progesterone**
Fixing things	Vulnerability
Independence	Dependency (influenced by
Problem-solving	menstrual cycle)
Task-oriented	Caring
Self-sufficient	Loving
'I can do it myself'	Open
Doing	'I need help'
Present	Being
Structure	Expressive
Aware	Movement
Decisive	Intuitive
Protect + Provide	Free-flowing
	Care, Nurture + Organise

All of us tend to switch between standing in our masculine and feminine energies throughout the day, like using the strategy and mindset of the masculine to build businesses and then showing compassion and vulnerability to lead a team within it. While letting someone else put your washing away so you can lie on the bed and rest with your newborn requires you to soften into your feminine, while coaxing a toddler into the car seat more often than not needs your masculine energy. But over time, our society has prioritised and rewarded masculine energy more. In addition, both the masculine and the feminine energies have a 'divine' version (when they're at their best) as well as a 'wounded' version (when they're not). Running myself into the ground with the 'doing' energy was pure wounded masculine.

The Wounded Masculine	The Wounded Feminine
Forceful (my way or the highway)	Repressed truth
Dominating	Feels unworthy
Overdoing	Shame and guilt
Controlling	Feels like I'm 'too much'
Demanding	Always apologising
Overthinking	Overexplaining

The gold is found in marrying the masculine strategy and mindset with the feminine magnetism, energetics, and embodiment. Put it this way: masculine energy goes for what they want, the feminine draws it towards her with her seductive magnetism. The shadow side of these two energies is that 'going for what we want' can easily turn into going for it at all costs, burning ourselves out to the detriment of our health. The feminine feels shame and guilt for slowing down, expressing our truth, or showing any connection to our sexuality. In truth, the feminine has been suppressed in culture for generations. Our expressions have been shamed; we've been burned at the stake for being too loud, too different, too 'ourselves'.

The new paradigm of motherhood embodies the gifts of the feminine. Meaning, we operate in the divine feminine, not from the shadows of it or the 'wounded feminine'. The thing is, femininity has been suppressed for so long that we've learned to lean more into our masculinity to the point we've overdone it. We protect until we over-protect, we work until we're overworked, we do until we overdo it. We think gifts of the feminine, like vulnerability and an open heart, are a weakness and not how we build empires, businesses, or run households.

The old paradigm of mothering mostly operates from the wounded masculine. To build a business, to become CEO, to be a stay-at-home mum who juggles organising the house and everyone in it, or anything that we become 'successful' at has required us to work hard and push ourselves to acquire it. It's that 'doing' mode treadmill. We go around and around and around, do, do, do, and go, go go, so fast and so much that our health and joy get pushed further and further away from us. And what's more devastating is that while we're spinning all the plates in the air, we burn out, and it's incredibly hard, if not impossible, to receive joy and pleasure. There isn't any room for it physically or energetically. We push through and get things done at all costs. We apologise too often, shame and guilt take up more of our time than they need to, we overthink, and we feel overwhelmed.

It's time for the feminine way to rise. And this isn't about shaming or dominating men; it's about balance, sister. The rise of the feminine isn't about women embodying more masculinity; it's about dismantling the old way so the new way (divine feminine in union with divine masculine) can be born.

Empowering each other

I think somewhere along the way, we've come to think that because we can *have* it all, we must *do* it all as well. We can make the cake, we can bake it, we can eat it, and even do the dishes afterwards. But that doesn't mean we can't ask someone else to put the dishes away once in a while. Being dependent on someone or something is not wrong. It's not weak, and it doesn't make us incapable. It means we're smart enough to know when to use our masculine energies or evoke them in others and when to tap into our feminine essence. We can have it all; it's not a matter of having one or the other but deciding how and when we want to take care of ourselves and when we ask for someone else to take care of us.

Before having children, we've most likely spent our time in masculine-fueled workplaces, and we tend to carry this energy into motherhood, as it's so familiar to us because we've been conditioned to think that's how we succeed. Before babies, the masculine mindset of protecting and providing for myself was highlighted in the monetary sense. I earnt my own money, and I spent it how I wanted. It was a big shift for me leaving work and my income behind to stay at home with my children. With money comes freedom and choices, and with money not coming in like it used to, it felt that my choices were fading, my freedom was fading, and so was my self-esteem and the feeling of contributing. This poked around my emotional holes of not feeling important or of value. I didn't feel like I was adding value to my house; I felt like a burden and like I had to stay small. Even though I was doing my part for the family, staying at home with the kids so Zac could go earn a living for all of us, sometimes it didn't feel like a team effort. It felt like the money he was earning had nothing to do with me and it wasn't mine to choose how to spend it.

But here's the thing, healing my relationship with money was actually what led me to do this work. Overcoming playing small, wanting to feel important, and opening up to Zac about how I needed help was the catalyst for investing in my first coach, and now friend Rick William. And from there, I started my intense healing, which led me here. Here's the other thing that I've learned: I can play on the floor for an hour, clean baby vom off the carpet four billion times, clean the never-ending filthy high-chair, read the same tractor book until the end of time, perform the entire song list of *Encanto* (with no intermission), and cook dinner to boot, and all of these things are valuable. All of these things are important and vital, which can be easily forgotten when we don't actually get *paid* for these things.

It's easy to get caught up in thinking that these things aren't valuable because they don't pay the bills. I've struggled with this way of thinking for so long, and it doesn't feel good at all. What helped me move through it was being open with Zac about my relationship with money and realising that it was a very masculine way of thinking. Protecting and providing for my family has many different looks and doesn't only look like having an income. It's reminding myself that we are a team and Zac earns the money *because* I stay home raising the children, which I know is the most important job of all time. Zac wouldn't be earning money if it wasn't for me, and I wouldn't live in a house with running water if it wasn't for him. We're now more open about how we complement each other and play on our strengths. I don't think I could manage our finances like he does, and he doesn't think he could stay at home and manage our house and family the way I do. We complement each other, and we appreciate what each other brings to our family. To help activate this reciprocity, have the conversation at least once a week that goes like this: 'Your biggest contribution/gift to this relationship is …', What I love about you is …', and you could even add, 'What I would want even more of is …' to help balance anything out that you are feeling.

There are certain times of the month when women produce differing levels of estrogen and progesterone. Depending on the amounts in our bodies, it can feel good for us to depend on someone. That time of the month might be a good time to go and get a massage or facial or whatever it is that you like to do. Ask your partner or your parents or a babysitter to watch the kids for a bit. Depend on someone *else* to make you feel good when you need to. Dependency actually increases those delicious hormones like estrogen and progesterone, which are associated with behaviours like nurturing, caregiving, and empathy. So if you get the mum-guilts for depending on someone else or doing something for yourself, remember that doing so is rewarding your mind and body with more of the good stuff that makes you the perfect mum: an inbuilt cocktail of wondrous motherly hormones. Slowly teach yourself and remind yourself that dependency can be a beautiful and intimate thing. Relying on and trusting others makes us vulnerable and open to receiving the love we deserve.

How to have those difficult conversations

My desire to talk and connect through conversation is the total opposite of what Zac feels he needs at the end of the day. He needs space and time to unwind, which can leave me feeling a bit lonely and invisible. It can be a bit of an internal conflict for me when I feel like I need conversation, but I know Zac needs space. So how have we learned to meet in the middle? How can I have my conversation while he also has his space? Just having this understanding of one another's needs is profound in itself. Recognising that we are different allows so much space for empathy, compassion, understanding, and connection. It's not a 'one or the other' situation. You both can have your needs met together.

Pre-framing to acknowledge one another's needs can go a long way. For example, I might say at the beginning of the conversation, 'I'm expressing my feelings not because I want you to fix anything or offer advice; you are doing nothing wrong, and I'm not blaming you. I just need you to listen'. As women, we are intuitive and might expect our partner to pick up on our needs implicitly. Still, we can balance this feminine perspective with a masculine one that is literal and direct by explicitly stating what we want and need from our partner.

This kind of pre-framing also has the benefit of giving our partner a choice. I don't want to unload without asking first, to find out Zac has had a horrible day and just needs to tie some loose ends up from work before I can have his attention. By asking first, I give him a chance to finish his emails, make those last phone calls, or do whatever he needs to do to be able to give me his full attention and the same laser focus he applies to getting into bed at night (suit shirt be damned).

When I feel like I need to express my feelings, I usually need a hug to go with it, so I ask, 'I need you to give me a hug, and I need you to listen. If you feel like you need to say anything, can you just repeat back to me what I'm saying and how I'm feeling in your own words? Is that okay? Then after I'm finished, maybe you can express to me what you need. Maybe you'll want a hug, or whatever it is you need. We can do that, too'.

The masculine wants to perform. They want to be that person you can rely on to give you what you need – so don't be afraid to help them out by identifying exactly what you need. Expecting them to know it on their own is tempting and very seductive because it makes it easy for you to slip into patterns of blame and not take ownership of your feelings. When they don't read your mind (shocking) and don't live up to your expectations, they piss you off without even knowing it, and you can put all the blame and responsibility onto them, and none of it be your responsibility.

Taking responsibility and living your truth is much harder work. The masculine doesn't take hints; they don't overthink like the feminine can. So saying exactly what you need in the moment is a way to honour yourself and get what you need as well as give the masculine clear ways to support you. It's a win-win. It might take more patience from both ends, but it's worth it, trust me. And the more you do it, sometimes the masculine starts to do it all on their own. But remember that fixing things and offering support is what the masculine loves to do and how they feel important. As infuriating as it can be, just remind yourself that they are doing the best they can, too.

Providing a safe space to get both our needs met is a powerful thing. In my experience, this conversation goes swimmingly when emotions have had some space to breathe. However, when emotions are still firing and feel very real and big in the moment, it's so much easier said than done. I know when I'm feeling upset or angry that I need to lay the foundations of the conversation before I lay it all out, but as we know, emotions can feel irrational. I can let my feelings out with no context at all, and Zac jumps in with his fix-its and advice because I haven't laid the foundation and identified to him what I needed in the moment – which is just for him to listen. So before you know it, I'm coming across as attacking, and Zac immediately goes into defensive mode. Leaving us both dishevelled and worse off than when we began. At first glance, the idea of pre-framing might seem like a way to keep our emotions under wraps instead of letting them out, but actually, setting the foundation this way is *more* conducive to me expressing my emotions because I do so at a time and in a way that Zac can take them in and really hear me.

If you don't get what you need from the convo, reflect and have another go later. I personally can beat myself up after attempting to share my feelings with Zac and have it blow up. I feel like a failure when I leave the conversation half finished and unresolved to go have a cry in my room because it just feels like it all gets too much. I beat myself up thinking that I could have approached the conversation differently or that maybe I shouldn't have tried to have the conversation at all. All I want is to feel closer, and I manage to make us feel further apart. And then I get mad that Zac just couldn't help himself and offered advice or defended himself during the conversation. I think that I must have come across as attacking for him to get so defensive. Can you feel my mind going crazy? Around and around with thoughts and feelings that contradict each other.

In these moments, what brings me peace is being kind to myself and knowing that I can have another go tomorrow night or whenever it be and that my nervous system is responding exactly the way it has learned to do. Once I understood this, it was easier not to 'make myself wrong' for withdrawing and retreating. Even though my mind is telling me to stay and finish the conversation (train wreck that it may be), my body (and specifically my nervous system) is telling me otherwise. When Zac and I are not in ventral vagal connection, when fight-or-flight kicks in, we've lost our connection, and we're no longer moving toward a positive solution together. Leaving to be by myself in the bedroom, where I can self-soothe and move into a dorsal vagal state, is a perfectly natural response and probably more helpful, in the long run, for our relationship than staying in the conversation but dissociating. That would mean I'm not truly in my body and in touch with my emotions – and that's when conversations tend to go off the rails. The dissociated state means our nervous system has picked up on something it perceives as a threat to our survival; in those moments, we aren't thinking clearly and are likely to lash out in unkind ways. This is not the state where connection is possible, and it's not the state we want to bring to our problems to try and solve them. Regulating our nervous systems, bringing the best parts of ourselves forward, and then using those parts of us to solve problems is so liberating. But you know what makes you a spiritual jedi?

Regulating your partner's nervous system when *you're* dysregulated. *Ouf.* To get the best out of Zac, trying to talk to him when he is dysregulated is as useless as his nipples. I've found cuddling him, touching his lower body in particular – his legs, his feet – really grounds him and regulates his nervous system. Once I've done that, even in the midst of my own painful dysregulation, I'm a fucking queen. And it brings out the best in both of us.

Suppose I, instead, choose to stay in the conversation during a moment like the above. In that case, I might honour what's happening to me by saying something like 'I want to leave this conversation now because I feel uncomfortable, but I'm going to stay here with you' or 'I might leave for a moment to get some space, then I'll come back, and we can talk some more'. With loving persistence, I will get to a space where I can stay in that conversation with Zac without the pull to leave, and we will resolve whatever it is that we need to. The gentle stretch of our nervous system over time reminds us that we are safe in this moment rather than asking too much of ourselves too quickly. But if it does get the better of me and I end up in the bedroom alone, I can acknowledge that I resisted the urge to leave several times, and the more I do it, the stronger my emotional muscles will get. Instead, I can alchemise my own emotions by practising some self-care (my favourite is dancing) so I can bring my best self to the conversation when I try again.

We can practise this as often as we need to to get it right. I remind myself that I'm normal and I'm doing the best I can. I give myself space, I put my hand on my heart, and I whisper the things that I need to hear, 'You are loved, you are seen, and you are heard'. I give myself what I need, and then I feel less pressure to get that from someone else. (Sometimes, I also talk to a girlfriend or sister about it, which always helps me release the energy from my body before I give the conversation another go with Zac.)

When I'm triggered by my children, leaving the situation to regulate my nervous system often isn't even an option. (This is why motherhood offers us such intense opportunities for psychological growth; one could say we have no choice.) A few deep breaths here and there, modelling what I'd like my children to do when they become dysregulated, and letting them watch me come back into regulation (or, if necessary, apologise if I don't) allows me to keep going – not in a 'push through and endure your pain' way but in a 'here's an opportunity to regulate myself and show my kids that even though life is pushing me and I want to scream or curl up under my bed covers right now, I'm choosing to do something different' way. A phrase that helps me: 'I am safe at this moment'.

If you've had good intentions to have a heart-filled conversation with your loved one but it doesn't go so well – and, really, who hasn't had this experience? – then my suggestion would be to give yourself some space, be kind to yourself and know you're doing the best you can, and try again later when your feelings are a bit more neutralised and you have your wise mind in action, with left mind and right mind integrated and a calm nervous system that can attend to the balance of masculine and feminine energies and the needs of your partner. Create some space to put your ducks in a row. Remember that your emotional brain doesn't seem logical, and our emotions will often outrun our logic because that's what our brain and body were designed to do to keep us safe. But with time and practice, we can show our nervous systems that we are safe in these moments when we crave more connection. If you feel the pull to either yell or withdraw or whatever your nervous system wants to do, acknowledge it and gently try something different. Remind yourself that you are safe at this moment and let your whole body feel it, and use this power to keep the conversation going until both of your needs are met.

The best conversations I've had with Zac happen when I truly surrender into my full expression with an open heart and say what I'm feeling. I let him *feel* me; I speak from my body, not my mind. When I speak from my mind, he responds with his mind. But when I speak from my heart, I evoke his divine masculinity to hold me. I've literally been crying, punching the pillow, and letting him fully see and feel me. I've let go of any feelings of being 'too much', and in this space, Zac has no words. He just holds me. And I can tell you, it's pretty healing. The tears turn into healing tears. Too many times, I've brought my masculinity to the conversation, and I've expected him to bring his. But it doesn't work like that. I've wanted him to take charge of the situation; I've wanted him to hold me. But I've literally opened my heart like a fire hydrant and sprayed it with such force and been, like, 'Hold me!' I can picture him trying to fight through the immense pressure of the water, searching for my heart and my needs. Softening into my feminine by turning the force of the water down a little and letting him see me, for me, is how I let him in.

You know how I said 'like attracts like' when we were talking about frequencies? Well, that works for absolutely everything, except when it comes to the masculine and feminine energies. If you bring your feminine to a relationship, a situation, or a conversation, you will evoke the masculine energy in another. The divine feminine that softens and shows vulnerability will instinctively evoke the masculine to hold space for her.

If you want the masculine in your life to rise, you need to bring your feminine. You're not going to evoke his masculinity if you overpower it with yours. And if you want him to stand in his feminine, evoke it by standing in your masculine. When it comes to masculine and feminine energies, it's the opposites that work. If I want Zac to bring his divine masculine of protection, holding space for me, to be the glass that holds my water, then the best way is for me to soften into my feminine and let him. If he's standing in his feminine and I want his masculine, then I have to 'out feminine' him so that I evoke it within him. And vice versa. The water needs the glass, and the glass needs the water. It's like two ends of a magnet. Two positive ends will push each other away, just like two masculine energies. One positive end and one negative end will attract each other and be intimately connected.

It's time for the feminine to rise

The children coming in and the children here now are demanding this new paradigm, demanding that we lead our households and lives with divine feminine energy. They must be nurtured in different ways and be allowed to be in their full expression without the shame adults and the world project onto them. Their true selves must never be suppressed because they have codes that need to be anchored into the collective so they can do their job of bringing more light into the planet. You may have already experienced that your children, and the children that have yet to be born but are on their way to us, won't be able to thrive in environments that live off processed food, lack of nature, and suppressed emotions and playful expression. I believe that the generation we are birthing will lead us in this new world in this new way. They'll be different from the leaders of today. They will align more with their mind, body, and soul. You will feel a lightness with them because they're ready to create new waves for humanity. But they can only do this if we do this work, if we start to soften and just *be*. The old paradigm is something we need to shatter to fully support these children. They're going to teach us, and already are teaching us, in ways that we can't even imagine, but we have to be willing to get rid of the old belief systems we've held onto for most of our lives. And it's not only the way forward; it's the way now. Our job is to create environments outside the matrix most of us have been brought up in. The world we have known until now is not the one we're raising our children in. And I know you feel this; otherwise, you wouldn't have been called to read these pages.

When you honour your own intuition and feminine gifts, you raise your vibration. When you embody the wisdom of your feminine intelligence and honour your emotional boundaries, you rise. And when powerful women gather with the sole purpose of lifting each other up, *she* rises. The feminine. Mother Earth. All the ancient wisdom from our ancestors. This book is an invitation to listen to the whisper of *her* within and embody your inner knowing. The old paradigm crumbles when more and more women rise to embody their feminine power.

I've never felt more connected to this than when I've been a part of group coaching containers. Because my feed is filled with healers, I've come across some incredible women doing incredible work. I've put myself in short courses and group coaching and have literally been held by women rising all over the world. As we get on group zooms, everyone is there to cheer each other on and authentically express themselves. Without a word being said, I feel like I have allies all over the world. I feel more deeply connected than I ever have. I feel a true sisterhood. I embody my feminine. I see others doing the same, and I know I'm not alone, which is a nice turn to take after spending too much of my motherhood journey feeling lonely and misunderstood.

I had a moment not long ago that brought this home to me. I took my three-year-old nephew to visit my mum (his nan) for a day out and left my two boys at home. I've looked after him and my other nephews before, but it felt really different this time. I had an epiphany (another poo story because everyone can relate, and I have a lot of them). I took him to the toilet, and he was chat, chat, chatting away while on the toilet, so I had a bit of time to think while I waited. My initial thought was, *'Man, I was having a day away from wiping bums'*, but it turned into a feeling of responsibility. I recalled when I taught primary and secondary school children, if a student had come to ask me for help but they weren't in my class, I wouldn't send them back to their teacher or tell them I was not the one to help them – of course, I helped them. I believed that all teachers were responsible for all children. Why did it take me so long to bring this into motherhood? This felt like a full-circle moment in that I felt connected to the collective. I felt a sense of collective responsibility – not that I had to do it all alone but that we all could depend on each other. I was at the library one time with both of my boys, and Knox ran off. Another mum was there and without thinking, she said to me that she'll watch Zephyr for me, so I can go help Knox. I didn't know her, but it was a shared responsibility for all children. And it felt so good to trust and honour each other, and to have each other's backs. We get it. Even if we were strangers, we shared the collective sisterhood. And even if you're a single mum raising your child without a partner, there is a greater collective raising your child along with you. *This* is how the new paradigm is unfolding. It's not just my sister's job to help her son go to the toilet (a super glamorous task). It's not only her role to raise him either. He doesn't belong just to her; he's a child of the world. And it's not just the mother's job to raise our children. She needs to feel safe, she needs to be held, and she needs to be protected so that she can be a mother. And we can't do that alone.

CHAPTER FOURTEEN

What Makes a Good Life?

Although living alone can offer conveniences… physical health is not among them.

Julianne Holt-Lundstad

To be human means to be wounded. The story of one's life grows around wounds that open to what is truly, deeply human.

Michael Meade, *The Water of Life*

Robert Waldinger is the director of an 84-year-long study on adult development, which in itself is incredible. Most studies don't last longer than a decade – the participants start to opt out, the funding dries up, the research changes course, or the researchers pass away and no one picks up the pieces. Despite these obstacles, still to this day, about sixty of the original 724 men who participated in the study are still alive and participating – all well into their nineties (it's insane). In fact, the study is now in its second generation, including children of the original participants. The study is remarkable for the insights it provides into what makes a good life. Because of the study's longevity, we don't have to rely on participants' observations and memories to draw conclusions – we have information about what they actually *did* throughout the course of their lives.

The study began in 1938, tracking young men who were sophomores at Harvard University. A second cohort was added in the 1960s, tracking men of similar age but had been born into some of Boston's poorest neighbourhoods, where running water was a luxury. Some participants become lawyers, bricklayers, teachers, and doctors. There was even one president of the United States (John F. Kennedy – part of the Harvard cohort, not the cohort added later). Some climbed the social ladder all the way to the top, and some made that journey in the other direction. Some developed alcoholism; some developed schizophrenia. The researchers didn't just get these men to complete a questionnaire. They interviewed them, filmed them talking to their wives, spoke with their children, collected medical information from their doctors, took their blood, and scanned their brains – all to get the clearest possible picture of their lives.

So, what has this study taught us? What have we gained from the tens of thousands of data points gathered from these lives? Well, the lessons aren't about wealth or fame or how hard the participants worked. When the study began, the researchers assumed that the biggest predictors of healthy ageing would be things like personality traits, intellectual ability, and physical characteristics (like skull size). But these weren't the most important factors. Neither were money or fame. The biggest factor that separated men who aged well and lived the longest from those who did not was the quality of their relationships. The men who were the healthiest in their eighties were the ones who reported being the most satisfied in their relationships at the age of fifty. The clearest message we've learned from this study is this: good relationships keep us happier and healthier – period.

Social connections are really good for us, and loneliness kills. This study shows that those closely connected to family, friends, and their community live longer. The study has also taught us that for those who are more isolated than they want to be, their health declines earlier, their brain functioning declines earlier, and they live shorter lives compared with those who aren't lonely. Relationships are good for us, and loneliness is toxic.

It's not enough to be in a committed relationship or surrounded by lots of people (although that is generally better than being completely isolated). You can be lonely in a crowd, and you can be lonely in a marriage. It's the quality of these relationships that counts. Marriages without love and affection could be worse than separation. Living amongst good, warm, and loving relationships is protective.

From this study, we also know that physical pain is more tolerable when we have those we love around us, and it can be magnified if we are feeling lonely. Good relationships can buffer us from physical pain. Not only this, but our brains function better when we have love and support. Our memory declines at a slower rate when we are happy with the relationships in our lives.

We don't have to be happy with each other all the time. We don't have to agree on everything or get along one hundred percent of the time. We just have to know we can count on the ones we love in times of need. We need to know they have our backs when things get tough for us. We need to know we can lean on them and they will love us at our best and our worst. I haven't just described a healthy relationship with your partner here, but also a healthy relationship with your children. You need this from your partner, and your children need it from you.

If you consider the ways you spend your time and attention as investments in your future self, where will you invest? The Harvard Study of Adult Development tells us that, more so than investing in career and financial success, we should invest in our relationships.

I have this fear of getting old. I fear that when I get old and look back on my life, I will be a harsh critic and think I didn't reach my full potential. But I'm learning that it's not about what I achieve, what I do, or how much money I make doing it – it's the ones I love and spend my life with that matter. I'm guilty of focusing on the wrong things. I fear that if I give my children my everything, I'll be left with nothing when they leave to live their own lives. Shouldn't I be building myself and my career now so I'll still have something when I'm not a stay-at-home mum anymore? *Nah.* Giving them everything of me is exactly what I need to do. Because when I am old and grey and look back on my life, that's what will be important to me. I don't have to wait until

I'm wrinkly to see that. I can feel it now. Raising my children and the relationships I have built doing it are the best gifts life has given me. And giving that my full attention will, and does, make me feel full and satisfied. I am living the dream.

But relationships aren't easy, and they can be messy. Why? Because we are human. We like quick fixes. And relationships can be anything but simple. Relationships are messy, complicated, and super hard work. I've learned to lean into my relationships, the good, bad, and ridiculous – because I know that at the end of the day, they are life-long. Lifelong in that we will always be in relationships – loving ones, romantic ones, casual ones, fleeting ones. Even if we go and live solo on a mountain top, the impressions relationships can leave on us are real and ongoing. So I am committed to doing the work it takes. I'm committed to saying sorry and admitting I'm wrong. I am committed to choosing kindness over rightness. I commit to coming back after an argument and a dramatic exit and slamming doors with my tail between my legs to sit next to Zac and ask him how *he's* feeling. I'm committed to staying open and loving when my toddler is having his fifteen billionth tantrum for the day – or when I lose my shit, I'll work hard at tapping into my calm again. I am committed to doing the work. I know that I will be happier and healthier as a result and the people around me, including my children, will be too.

Much of what's led up to this chapter in the book factors into healthy relationships. Being present in the moment instead of constantly trying to check items off the list in 'doing' mode will certainly improve your relationships. Observing and accepting our feelings helps us have honest conversations instead of being driven by emotions we keep pushing beneath the surface. Learning to practise self-care and treat ourselves with love is a prerequisite for extending similar treatment to others. All in all, the new paradigm of motherhood is conducive to relationships based on true, deep connection – the most meaningful kind. The rest of this chapter will explore two additional tools I've found helpful for creating the type of relationships that add years to our lives.

Set boundaries

I used to roll my eyes when I heard the word boundaries. Maybe it's because Kourtney Kardashian used the word so much that it lost its meaning for me – but a more likely explanation for it being such a trigger for me is that I personally lacked them. I thought I had them in place, but I really didn't. I've come to realise that my lack of boundaries was popping its head up in all areas of my life.

I felt the need to please and rescue people and to be overly generous with offering my resources. I was also super indecisive – I'd ring my sister every time I needed to make even a minor decision, like which night of the week to wash my hair or which takeaway I should send my husband to get. This indecisiveness came from a lack of connection to my inner wisdom and intuition, resulting from not having clear boundaries in place. Let me say it again differently: Without solid boundaries in place, we can't honour our intuition because we'll be too busy asking everyone else to weigh in on decisions we could be making for ourselves.

The internal pull to put other people's needs and preferences before my own left me feeling like an empty shell of my being. I denied my own needs for so long that I didn't know what they were, let alone how to communicate them clearly to the people I loved. So, I constantly felt unseen and like my needs were at the bottom of the pile – a situation I'd created for myself and which led to the buildup of resentment in my relationships.

Then I learned about boundaries, the lack of which was causing all kinds of unwelcome things to show up in my life. It was the common denominator that tied everything together – which was kind of wonderful, really, because I could address them all by taking small steps to put boundaries in place.

For all the discussion of boundaries in popular culture, I think a point that's often missed is that the goal of setting a boundary is to give you space to connect with your true, authentic self and give power to your intuitive voice. It means you look internally for the answers you seek and rely less on other people's opinions and thoughts.

Boundaries aren't just about learning to say no. They're so much more than that. A boundary is a personal limit that is expressed so our needs will be met directly. With boundaries in place, we can more easily access our intuitive voice, better regulate our emotional states, and protect our all-important energy field. In this place, we feel more comfortable sharing our thoughts, opinions, and beliefs with others. We don't feel compelled to please or agree with others all the time or even look outside of ourselves for the answers we seek (like when I'd ring my sister to help me make every little decision). We need boundaries so that we can develop and maintain authentic relationships.

The signs of having loose or no boundaries are:

- Compulsive people-pleasing;
- Indecisiveness or constantly asking others for their opinions before trusting yourself;
- Generally feeling uncomfortable or guilty when you say no (so you say yes most of the time!);
- Being a chronic fixer/helper/rescuer of other people; and
- Having difficulty asking for help.

If that's your current reality, imagine a way of being that looks more like:

- Being aware of your own values, thoughts, opinions, and beliefs;
- Knowing how to communicate your needs to others;
- Knowing what you want or need and being able to express it;
- Being able to say no and accept when others do the same; and
- Being able to regulate your emotions and, at the same time, allow others to express themselves, too.

All of these and more can be achieved when you become clear about your personal boundaries – physical, mental, and emotional.

If you're new to boundary-setting, I suggest starting small. The first step is to define and identify your boundaries and notice where they're lacking. Spend time witnessing this in your relationships and activities. Notice how you feel throughout your day. When does your chest tighten? When do you feel drained or energised? When do you feel expansive versus limited?

Just doing this alone – connecting to the sensations in my body and getting out of my overthinking mind – strengthened my ability to connect to my inner intuitive voice. It allowed my inner wisdom to take over that overthinking and indecisive part of me. I was then able to communicate my needs to the people in my life. I've come to realise that always meeting the needs of others is an unattainable goal and ultimately results in me neglecting my own needs, putting me back into that space of not being able to say no or set boundaries. Once I get my needs met, I'm more full, energised, and ready to show up and be present for my children and relationships.

So, I invite you to be the witness in your own life. Do you have clear boundaries? Are you left feeling full and energised by the daily actions of your life and within your relationships? Or are there moments of tightness in your chest or tension in your jaw? Those are the moments to pay attention to, and they're invitations to set a boundary.

It might be as little as saying no to a coffee or play date. It might be as little as letting your partner know you are locking the door when you have a shower and me time so you don't get little visitors. It might be as simple and small as asking a friend not to make certain comments about other people's looks or weight in your presence. But it's important to note that boundaries are not just about shutting people out. Sure, in some cases, they can be about limiting or completely stopping contact with a person if they repeatedly dishonour your boundaries. But when boundaries are met, both parties are honoured, which truly expands your capacity to love others and be loved yourself.

LET'S TALK ABOUT FRIENDSHIP BREAKUPS

Usually, we think that once we are friends with someone, we should be their BFF. The ending of a friendship means we've failed, or someone has done something wrong or bad.

But that is certainly not always the case. As we evolve, so do our friendships. You might notice that as motherhood has you redefining your values and spirituality, they may not align as much with the other person. You might find yourself feeling depleted after spending time with them or like you're disconnected from them or drifting apart. Ultimately, throughout our lives, friendships will end and change as we do, and as we become more in tune with our needs and more protective of our energy, what we are looking for in friendships will evolve. I certainly found myself spending more time with other women with kids or other women in the healing space. But as some friendships changed or even ended, it brought a lot of shame, confusion, and guilt around it. Like I should be putting in more effort, or like I was being a bad person. In my experience, I worried about what other people would think of me or that they might be saying horrible things about me behind my back about why we don't spend as much time together as we used to. But the truth is, it's natural for friendships to end throughout our lives. There may not be a concrete reason for it, like a fight, falling out, or something that has gone wrong. It's important to grieve and to let ourselves feel the sadness of the change in friendships. It's completely normal, especially if we always thought this person would be in our lives. But we can thank them for the chapter they were involved in and how they supported us, and still hold loving space for them even though things are different now. We don't talk about friendship breakups and how painful they can be, but with time and healing, we can have more clarity around why the friendship looks different now. We can also create space for new relationships that leave us feeling energised, inspired, connected and authentic to ourselves. There's a real difference between keeping a person in your life because your ego is resisting change, worrying about what the other person will think of you, and bringing self-awareness and compassion to yourself when making changes to how you spend your time and energy. Here are some reflection questions to help navigate your changing friendships and deciding how to spend your time and energy:

1. Do I feel authentically connected to this person? Am I able to completely be myself and feel seen and heard when I'm with them?

2. Do I feel judged or accepted within this relationship?

3. What was our main source of connection? Was it gossiping, drinking, or venting to each other? Is this connection not serving you anymore?

4. Do they respect your boundaries? Do you feel like you can respect your own boundaries when with them?

5. How do you feel after spending time with them?

6. Does this connection facilitate your own evolution/ growth?

Get to know your inner child

One of my earliest memories is from Christmas Day when I was about five years old. My twin sister and I are the youngest of five siblings, so it was a noisy and busy household. On this particular Christmas morning, everyone was getting ready to go to my grandma's house for lunch. We were packing our favourite toys to take, and my mum was fussing in the kitchen, cleaning up after breakfast. I wanted to show and tell her my favourite toy that Santa had left me, but she was lost in the chaos of organising five children into the car on an overexcitable morning and didn't hear me.

As an adult, I get it. And as a mum, I now get it even more. She was busy, and it was impossible for her to give one of five children her undivided attention at that moment. Heck, there are times when

I've chosen not to give my full attention to my toddlers when they ask, 'Look at me, Mum!' because I'm loading the dishwasher or I'm lunging to catch a toddler gone rogue in the high chair. But little Emily, my inner child, felt unseen in that moment. The false belief that no one understood me or saw me or noticed me followed me into adulthood, and it was through inner child work that I finally traced it back to memories like this and understood where it had come from.

All of us have an inner child. The child part of ourselves, the 'little Emily' that we carry within us, who has experienced our past and upbringing. This little child has wounds from unmet needs growing up. It could be from a comment here and remark there or even bigger wounds like abandonment or feeling unloved. I never doubted the love my parents felt for me. I grew up in a safe and secure household. But no one gets out of childhood unscathed.

From Maslow's Hierarchy of Needs, we know that when a child has their basic survival needs met, they can start to seek love. Their primary goals are to be seen, heard, and loved, and they will mould into anything they need to to feel that. For example, if it wasn't okay to be angry in a child's early years, they learn to keep their emotions hidden to be loved. If they receive love and attention for being quiet and staying small, then that's what they learn to do. You can see how this type of programming can start to show up in our adult lives.

When I started inner child work myself, I felt like I was healing myself from the inside out. This work revealed all of my coping mechanisms for what they were. I could finally see all the ways I'd been covering up underlying issues, compensating instead of addressing the root cause. Picture a situation where there's a horrible smell coming from somewhere near your patio. You're not able to enjoy sitting out there anymore because it seriously reeks of something gross. I'd come up with all these brilliant ways of covering up the smell – lighting incense, burning candles, setting up fans, blaming it on the kids. But only once I admitted something had crawled under my house and died could I address the problems that were keeping the air thick, stinking up my life. Inner child work was a way for me to crawl under the house and finally get my hands and knees dirty to drag out what was buried so far underneath.

You are not your triggers

What I mean by a trigger is a situation or circumstance that activates or touches an unhealed wound. And what do I mean by an unhealed wound? I mean, a part of your being that has been hurt before and hasn't quite recovered is still showing up for you in your life.

My mum and dad don't live close to my sister and I, so we have to share them whenever they come to town. We're getting better, but have often had conversations about where they're going to stay, when we will all be together, and when we'll both get some quality personal time with them. On one visit, in particular, Jane was about to have her third baby, so Mum and Dad were coming down to see her and help her. At the same time, there was not much sleep happening in the East household, and Zac was going away for work. I desperately wanted their help, and I desperately wanted them to stay with me. But, having a baby certainly trumped my situation, and they stayed and supported Jane. Even though I knew this was what they needed to do, I was still triggered by this situation. My reaction was to withdraw. I wanted to make myself small, and I didn't want to talk to anyone or answer any of my phone calls. I wanted to shut the world out. It may sound dramatic, but I was sleep deprived and had unhealed wounds, so I just wanted to tell the whole world to f off. *I don't need anybody; I'll do it myself.* Dramatic, yes. But did it feel real for me? Also, yes. I sat with feeling like I wasn't important for almost the whole day. Feeling like nobody cared about me, that no one wanted to help me. On this day, I realised and spoke the words to myself, 'I am not my triggers'. I knew in my heart that what my mind was telling me wasn't true. I knew the tightness in my chest and my clenched jaw wasn't the real me in this situation. I knew my mum and dad thought I was important. On this particular day, I wasn't acting like the real me. I was a wounded version of myself. Realising that separation was liberating for me. I literally jumped up from the couch, left the old skin still lying there, and was energised to bring this new insight into my life.

You see, growing up in a large family, there were times when my voice was drowned out. Like the situation I described from my childhood Christmas, I felt unseen and unheard in that moment, which translated to feeling unimportant. This example shows how this inner child experience is still showing up for me now. The best part of this understanding about what triggers me and how I can separate myself from that is how I've been able to communicate this to my husband. The same week as this happened, Zac expressed that he was worried about me and my mental health. And with complete clarity and conviction, I could explain to him my triggers and where they come from. I could explain that it had nothing to do with him, and without blaming him, I took responsibility for my triggers. Honestly, it was so liberating. For years, my experience has been trying to have these conversations but not really knowing what to say. I couldn't explain what was happening with me. I didn't understand it, let alone have the words to express it to someone else. And if I did manage to have a go, I would come across as blaming, and Zac would get defensive, and we'd have an argument. I would re-traumatise myself and end up worse than when I started, and it cemented the fact for me that I needed to keep to myself and stay small. With this new understanding, insight, and self-compassion, I could tell Zac how he sometimes triggers this wound of feeling like I'm not important and need to stay small, so then I could set a clear boundary around it. For example, although it might sound small and insignificant, when I tell Zac that I'm cold and he responds, 'It's not cold', I immediately feel like I'm not heard and that I need to keep my truth to myself. So, Zac and I talked about setting a boundary around how he responds to me in that kind of situation. You can see how this plays out for me in small scenarios and how it has the potential to blow up. This conversation brought us so close together. He was so thankful that I'd told him and he then had clear ways to support me. I felt so proud of myself for how far I'd come and for having the courage to have conversations like this, which at first seemed scary, only to end in deep love and connection.

When you are triggered, you'll know it. It's like an avalanche of emotions. I've discovered a few of my wounds doing this work, and by expanding my capacity to know myself and understand myself, I have gifted myself with the highest degree of self-compassion and pride. This has brought me closer to my loved ones, which is all I've ever wanted. Being able to identify a trigger, we then have two choices. We can set a clear boundary around protecting that part of ourselves or that wound, or we can take triggering moments as opportunities to heal.

Can you think of the last time you were triggered?

Perhaps your partner forgot to call you on their way home to let you know when they'd be back because they were distracted. While the logical side of you knows that's human – the wounded part of you feels rejected, so you send an angry text or make an aggressive phone call. Or perhaps someone leaves a rude comment on your post, and even though the logical part of you knows it has nothing to do with you and they're probably in a bad place, the wounded part of you remembers being mocked, shamed, or insulted and is ready to self-protect. Maybe you just felt unheard, so you reacted in ways that would make sure you were because, in your past, you often felt unheard or ignored. These are examples of the fight nervous system response.

The flight response is the same branch of the nervous system as the fight response and might look like turning your back on a difficult conversation. For example, your partner comes home excited to share that they've been promoted. While the logical part of you is happy and wants to celebrate, the wounded part of you is angry because you feel you are never noticed for the work you do within the household and all the effort you put in.

The freeze trauma response can look like people-pleasing, going along with other people's perspectives and not your own. It might manifest as zoning out, letting other people make all the decisions, avoiding situations that could cause conflict, being unwilling to say no, or being overly polite and agreeable or hyper-aware of other people's emotions and needs while denying your own.

A trigger is when your body goes into self-protection mode – whether that be to fight, flight, or freeze. Events in our daily lives often remind us of times when we went into self-protection mode, and it can result in us repeating the same responses that we had back then. And while these responses may have kept us safe before, sometimes safe can also mean stuck. Understanding the emotion underneath the trigger can help us build self-awareness and let our bodies feel safe when we aren't actually in any real danger.

Being triggered is a normal, natural, and healthy part of the human experience. It doesn't mean something is wrong with you. When you feel a trigger, pause and take a breath – even if you've already reacted and had a trauma response. Take a moment to notice the sensations in your body. Notice when your ego attaches a narrative to your experience and creates a whole story about it. Immediately, you can practise kindness and compassion towards yourself – put your hand on your heart and say, 'I'm feeling intense emotions right now'. Then, practise some self-lovin' and some self-soothing that doesn't include your phone. You could do some breathing in the moment or wrap your arms around yourself and give yourself a big hug. Learning how to manage your triggers is the key to self-confidence, emotional maturity, and overall compassion and empathy for yourself and others.

INNER CHILD WORK

Tell me about your childhood. What's your story?

This is how we begin to let the inner child in. Your highest self is investigating. Fully step into your inner child, resisting the logical/adult perspective that wants to creep in.

What happened? What did your parents do right? What did they do wrong? Why? How did you feel?

Just like a three-year-old, keep asking why after why after why. Bring her out of your heart and put her in front of you. What would you tell her? What does she need? Can you give it to her?

> I like to hold her little face in my hands and tell her she's important and seen. Then I see her hugging me, and then she runs off to play again and returns to my heart.
>
> It's not easy work, but like with the Conscious Anger Release technique in Part Two, you can provide a safe container to express and hold yourself.
>
> Set a timer, maybe play a song, and when it's over, intentionally move out of that space and return to your higher self. Without this limit, we risk getting stuck in the emotion. We want to open our hearts and bodies to let it release. The shower is brilliant for this, or maybe the bathroom because it's usually a small space with privacy.

I resisted this work for so long because I felt guilty about the idea of blaming my parents. I love them, and we have a close and loving relationship. But I learned that that's not what it's about. And as a mother, now I can see that. We aren't going to escape childhood completely unscathed. We can be a very loved person and still feel unloved. We can be surrounded by people who love us and still feel lonely. We can feel depressed despite all our privileges. Life is messy. It's contradictory.

When you open yourself to feeling and releasing heavy emotions or old ways of programming, untrue beliefs that you formed as a child, you create an open, flowing channel that allows energy to flow through you. You feel a sense of unity and wholeness and merge into the universe. You know in your being that you are made up of exactly the same thing as everything else in this universe. You are no different from the trees, the birds, the soil. We are all the same, made up of the same energy. We are all one.

And as soon as you feel like there is only 'us' and no 'other', nothing is out of your reach. There's nothing you can't have because you are everything. You become a magnet for everything you dream of.

As with so many other lessons in this book, parenting points us towards the inner child work we need to do. Our children are brilliant catalysts for discovering what we have hidden deep within ourselves that can surface in less desirable ways, like the suppression of our emotions or the outbursts of anger or resentment towards our partners. Our children evoke such strong emotional states within us that they're little invitations to heal our own inner child, or to set boundaries to protect certain parts of ourselves. And when we pay attention, we too can leave the familiarity of our deck chairs, go soul searching under the house, and drag anything untrue or unwanted out of there. To be the best parent we want to be, we must also learn to reparent ourselves. We must forgive ourselves daily and hold space for our own emotional waves.

My toddler threw a plastic octopus at my head the other day when I was getting him out of the bath. It hurt, and I yelled. I snapped, yelling, 'Ouch! That hurt! Don't throw things at me!' I was familiar with this anger outburst, so I was immediately able to come back down and hug him. I apologised for yelling and told him that throwing things can hurt. Emotions were still dissipating, so I apologised for yelling again later that night. It was genuine, and it inspired a beautiful moment between the two of us. He hugged me and said, 'I'm sorry for throwing the octopus at your head, Mummy'. And it was in that moment that I felt proud of myself. It took away any guilt I felt for reacting in such an angry and explosive way, and it brought us closer together.

While blowing up is never ideal, choosing not to repair and apologise is even less so, not just for our own sake but obviously for our children. Apologising to our children when we make mistakes sets them up to take responsibility for their own mistakes, and they learn how to apologise sincerely. It shows that connection and trust can come from 'mistakes', not from being perfect all the time, and there is always room to repair and reconnect. Parenting mistakes are inevitable. Of course, we can strive to be as brilliant as we can be, but when we slip up, we need to teach our kids by example how to make things right and learn from them. Apologies might not happen in the heated moment, and when nervous systems are activated, we know it's not the time to chat.

Once the moment has passed and you or your child has come back to regulation, that's the time to reconnect.

Don't be disheartened if your child can't apologise in the moment. Forcing them to apologise doesn't teach integrity either. It lacks authenticity and compassion and teaches them that it's okay to be dishonest about big feelings. They start to learn that they can't trust their own big feelings and it's okay to pretend to be remorseful. We don't want to normalise our children betraying themselves or being uncomfortable. Instead, giving space and time to calm down, modelling apologising, avoiding labels like 'mean' and 'nice', and coaching them through the situation are all helpful strategies. An apology might come later, once they feel better. Through the awareness built by inner child work, we can see what we might have needed as children at a certain moment. When we connect to the feelings we had as children, we can finally forgive our parents for not being perfect – and this is what enables us to forgive *ourselves* for not being perfect and to build a more authentic connection with our children.

I can't tell you how many times I modelled 'hitting hurts – sorry, Mum/sorry, Brother/sorry, Dad …' to not get an apology back. It can feel like I'm not doing the right thing. But when your two-year-old comes to you out of the blue and stops playing with his cars for thirty seconds to apologise to you for something he did yesterday, you'll know that what you're doing matters. And it feels way better than a forced apology.

DEFENSE

The same goes for forcing children to use their manners and say 'thank you'. It lacks authenticity, and implicitly teaches them that it's okay to be dishonest to get something you want. The general rule with children saying thank you is that it shows us that they are thankful and appreciate what we do for them. However, gratitude is not something that can be forced. When you withhold something from your child with the aim of getting a 'thank you', what is happening internally is you are triggering the child's defence mechanisms. Their little nervous systems are triggered, and we're pushing them further and deeper into a state that doesn't support the emotional connection it takes to be grateful. Think about it, if you were forced to do something you didn't want to do, does your social engagement system turn on? Are you in an open and vulnerable place when you're pushed into a corner? Definitely not. You're more likely to be defensive. The answer here is to be the example and model the behaviour you want to see. Say thank you when you want them to say it; say please when you want them to say it. For example, when you hand them lunch, 'Thank you, Mummy!' When they ask for another snack, 'I'd like another snack, please, Mummy!' Monkey see, monkey do. And we know that children, anyone actually, are more influenced by what they see than what they are told. The question is, is your behaviour worth imitating? When we dig our heels in, refusing to meet our child's demands because they won't say thank you, we can't be that surprised when they dig their heels in, too.

The level of cooperation your children have is equivalent to the amount of connection they feel. If they feel connected to you, cooperation levels are higher. But if you've fostered sides, if you've fostered confrontation where it's a 'my way or the highway' kind of vibe, this encourages disconnection more than anything else. This leads to your children growing up learning that they can't trust themselves, that they can be inauthentic to get what they want or pretend to be grateful to get their needs met. In the process, they also learn they can't trust you. *Ouf.* That hurts. This doesn't mean you give them whatever they want, whenever they want. You can still have clear boundaries and stick to them. It's helpful to know that you are not in control of their behaviour, but you are the adult in charge. And there is a difference. The language 'When … then you can …' is more powerful than 'If you … then …' For example,

'*When* you sit down at the table, *then* you can have your snack'. Using 'if' removes a child's power to choose and creates a power struggle/bribery situation. You can't *force* anyone to be grateful, a child or an adult, just as you can lead a horse to water, but you can't make them drink. The more you engage their social engagement system through connection, the more likely you will foster and develop real gratitude and appreciation. So, the question we can ask ourselves is, do we want a long-lasting, genuine connection and relationships with our kids? Or do we want a forced sign of gratitude (which is not gratitude or appreciation at all) and to keep up appearances?

Do you find it difficult to apologise to your children? Some of us feel this way because perhaps our parents didn't make a habit of apologising to us growing up. Or maybe our self-worth is attached to how well our children use their manners. If we weren't given a safe container to make mistakes or openly express and work through our emotional states, we don't learn how to process difficult emotions. The key is to become aware of our own needs first, the needs that perhaps weren't always met when we were children, so we can learn to set clear boundaries and clearly communicate how we're feeling. With an understanding of how our childhood environment shaped the relationships we have with ourselves and our children, we can begin to model what healthy relationships look and feel like to our children. When we learn to regulate our emotions despite what our little ones are doing (or throwing), we provide a place where our children feel safe and secure to fully develop a strong sense of self. Children without safe and secure relationships in their homes become adults with low self-worth, negative self-talk, and higher levels of addiction or other dysfunctional coping mechanisms. It's important stuff. I love when Zac hugs me and tells me he loves me in front of our children. It makes me feel good, and our children implicitly learn so much from it. But they learn just as much when I yell and then make things right again.

Current parenting research stresses that secure attachment is determined not so much by optimal attunement and responsiveness as it is by repairing the connection when it's broken. When we repair, we have the experience of connecting with and finding ourselves again after feeling like we were lost. It's not just about repairing our relationship with our child, but it knits back together our battered sense of self after feeling taken over by our emotions.

Our emotions can be our best teachers. By sitting on the front deck, trying to enjoy the view and ignoring what emotional stench was arising, my personal development was restricted. I kept feeling the same emotions and being given the same experiences over and over until I finally came to learn their lessons. I was stuck in emotional recycling. Pushing emotions down or trying to cover them up only meant they would resurface over and over again until I was ready to take on their assignment and develop into a person who could transform any negative emotion into opportunities to learn, grow, and love more.

Inner child work and learning to set boundaries are both practices that lead inward – but make no mistake, this time spent 'working on yourself' is anything but selfish. If anything, it's selfish *not* to do this work because it has such great potential to impact the most valuable thing in our lives – our relationships.

HOW YOU CAN BE WITH THESE CONCEPTS

When it comes to relationships, there can be a temptation to aim for perfection and keep our 'real self' under wraps. Know that these superficial relationships are not the kinds that lead to lasting happiness. That's the old paradigm speaking, sister – you want relationships that are not about appearances but real and genuine connections.

My relationship with Zac got its spark back when I learned to embody my feminine gifts of magnetism. When you feel completely in love with who you are and fully enjoy being yourself and living in your body, others feel it too. Even fear or insecurity, or self-doubt expressed vulnerably, can be magnetic. It's not the heavy or ugly emotions that are the problem; it's the delivery. When we hold space for ourselves, let the emotions alchemise, and fully open our hearts, we are a magnet, baby.

And, of course, the resentment that comes from a lack of boundaries is anything but sexy – as is that foul smell coming from under the porch when we haven't handled our underlying issues. Always remember that the work you do on yourself will come back to you tenfold with the richness it creates in your relationships.

The story I'm telling myself is ... 'I've noticed you spend a lot of time on your phone when you get home. The story I'm telling myself is that you'd rather be on your phone than with me, and you find me boring. Is that true?' This little sentence starter has gotten me out of trouble more times than I can count. It's the perfect way to take ownership of your feelings and perceptions without projecting them onto your partner (or whoever you're having a difficult conversation with) and throwing blame. It allows the other person to feel safe and not defensive so they are more likely to be in a regulated state to connect with you. It also gives them an opportunity to clarify, and it stops the patterns of accusing and shaming that are perhaps going on in your mind.

That's not true. I made that up ... When facing inner conflict, perhaps you're doubting if you should try to have a conversation with someone or deciding whether or not you should speak your truth in case you hurt someone's feelings. Instead, try this on for size: 'That's not true. I made that up'. Using the phone conflict above as an example, instead of the inner turmoil of feeling not wanted or like I'm boring, when those thoughts are amplified in my head in the lead-up to the conversation, I can tell myself that it's not true. There is a difference between calming your mind and body when it starts to mislead you and disregarding your intuition and going against how you feel. Your intuition comes from deep within you and when you are still. Obsessive and untrue thoughts fill your mind when you are feeling uneasy. We can't stop the mind from thinking, but this little line has helped me shift my focus from my mind to my body, where my intuition and inner wisdom reside.

YOUR CONNECTION TOOLKIT

Here are some quick little tips and tricks to boost your connection and love with your loved ones and yourself.

Sex: One of the many wonderful things about sex is that it forces us to be fully present in the moment. If our minds are on the dishes or the laundry or the carpool schedule, desire is nowhere to be found. Although it won't fix problems in a broken relationship, it is a shortcut to the connection that can help build or maintain a bridge during challenging times. Staying true to ourselves in the process, we can love harder when we make it a priority.

Hugging: Hugging for twenty seconds is enough to release the happy hormone oxytocin. Twenty seconds might not seem very long, but it's longer than most hugs. Next time you hug, don't pull away so quickly. Push past that lingering awkward hug phase and hold on. Bring the other person in and envision your love hormones seeping out of your pores and a light shining from your heart so bright that it touches everyone around you. Physically connect your heart space with their heart space, and imagine both your lights merging together to shine brighter together. Make it a morning ritual or a habit to get into every time your loved one either leaves or arrives home to give them a big squeeze. Or maybe it can be the first thing you do when you wake up.

Dating apps: No, this suggestion isn't for those in a committed long-term partnership – but for you single, amazing, wonderful, and hero mothers out there, dating apps are pretty cool. I'm not speaking from experience, but from what I know about human behaviour, we are more likely to have long-sustained marriages when we marry later in life. The younger we are, the higher the likelihood of getting a divorce. Why? Because who we are in our thirties and forties is a more accurate reflection of who we really are compared with when we are in our twenties. So you might marry in your early twenties, but you have a lot of evolving and growing to do. Not to say you can't grow *with* or alongside a person, but sometimes we grow apart. Dating apps let you sleep with someone and then decide later. As the saying goes, why buy a book when you can get a library card? There's no normal now when it comes to what a family looks like. I have a girlfriend who did IVF on her own to have a baby, and her plan is to find her perfect match *after* she's done the new mum thing. I love it. It's very Kourtney Kardashian and Travis Barker to have kids, then marry and blend families later. And instead of hoping someone likes you when you meet up, reverse that question and remind yourself of your worthiness and think, 'I hope I like *them*'.

It's the little things that are the big things/embrace the one percenters: I don't need to remind you of how important the one percenters are. When it comes to relationships, those little one percenters make a world of difference, and, let's face it, they're easier to do. For example, when I'm feeling a little unnoticed or disconnected from Zac, a nice way to reconnect is to organise a date night and spend some time together. But do you know what else? Sure, I can organise date nights and get a babysitter over so we can go out for ice cream. These are big gestures that are important but aren't super necessary. I can tell you that giving Zac a kiss every time he walks in the door, home from work, day in and day out, has a much more profound impact on how connected we are compared with one date night every two months. Instead of throwing a kid in his arms as soon as he crosses the threshold, acknowledging that he's home and *then* giving him a flatulent baby has a huge impact. Saying 'I love you', kisses and hugs before bedtime, a kiss first thing in the morning, a cheeky butt grab as they walk past, a quick 'thanks for doing the dishes' or 'your hair looks nice like that', taking the rubbish out when it's their turn, or taking something small off their plate are all tiny little things that add up to have an extraordinary impact. And also, it's cheaper than hiring a babysitter. Those nights out are fabulous, but relied on alone, they can hold a lot of weight – it's a lot of pressure to put on yourselves and on that one night. Don't wait for date night, and don't wait around for nights where you can get out of the house. Start connecting one percent better each day, and you'll be golden. And when we lose ourselves in parenthood, just get back on the rocket ship to the moon tomorrow. Express your feelings on a daily basis so that when you have big ones, talking about them is the norm.

Take ownership: Start practising giving yourself what you need. Place your hands on your heart when you notice yourself either withdrawing, feeling stressed, yelling, or whatever it is that doesn't align with your highest self and say to yourself what you so desperately want to hear. For me, it's most often 'I see you, I feel you'. Then just get topped up by your loved ones. If you're anything like me, it's just a big relief and weight lifted off your shoulders. It seriously is revolutionary.

Know your worth: You were born worthy, sister. Ever since you took your first breath – otherwise, you wouldn't be here. Know you are enough, all on your own. You are a mother, and is there anything more sacred or spiritual than that? Don't think so.

Get sexy: Remember back to the time when you were falling in love with your partner? What made you feel sexy? What types of things were you doing? For me, I used to sleep naked or in less clothing. Then I wore a straitjacket of pyjamas, but this limited the amount of my skin on Zac's skin. When I started to do this work, I realised that my skin on his skin is how I feel sexy. So I went back to sleeping in a singlet some nights. I started to feel closer to myself and made room for intimacy.

Self-touch: Touch is one of the first somatic languages we learn well before birth and early into our most impressionable developmental years. Through self-touch, particularly soothing touch that focuses on re-creating sensations of safety, being held and nurtured, we have the power to self-regulate our nervous system and evoke our sensuality and curiosity when exploring our bodies. Right now, cup your hands onto the back of your neck and hold yourself there. Squeeze your neck and perhaps massage it a little, moving your hands down your shoulders. Caressing, holding, and exploring parts of your body that have an exceptionally high concentration of nerve endings (erogenous zones) like the neck, inner thighs, back of the arms, hips, back of the knees, and belly, not only soothes your nervous system but opens the door for you to explore your senses and soften into your being.

Rid your resentment: If I were to identify a list of universal 'turn on' killers, resentment would be near the top of the list. Resentment destroys your ability to connect with the person you're feeling resentful towards and, if left unresolved, can poison other situations as well. As we broke down earlier, you can identify and notice when resentment builds or your partner triggers you, creating space for your needs to be met. Speaking of which, we can also make space for other people's needs to be met, too. Just like we can create space for ourselves, it's very important that we also do this for the ones that we love. Give them a permission slip to go and do something that will give them more energy when they come home. Everybody wins.

One simple question: 'What does support look like for you right now?' One of the most generous things we can do for our partners is to be their allies in comforting, soothing, and grounding their nervous systems. Often, parenting is so demanding and high pressure that, instead, we find ourselves in the midst of fights, disagreements, and just daily stress, and it's difficult to make time and energy to do this. That is why asking this question is such a beautiful practice. It's about moving beyond being right or getting something that you want at that moment. The good news, and why this practice is so powerful, is that when you support your partner to relax their nervous system, they will likely be willing to hear what you have to say or reflect on what you need from them. But when both of you are in fight or flight or freeze, a place many of us constantly parent from, it's easy to get stuck in a space where it's everybody for themselves. So asking your partner, 'What can I do for you?' or 'What does support look like for you right now?' and taking one small thing off their plate can make a huge difference.

A shared breath: You can sync your partner's nervous system and yours by doing some shared breathing and literally move stress to calm together. Making it a priority to ground your nervous system when both you and your partner are agitated is some black belt spiritual shit, but, in my experience, it has been an intimate and healing practice. You can do this when you're agitated or schedule it for some time later. There are two ways to do this:

1. Breathing together: Sync your breaths. Breathe in together and breathe out together. Depending on your lung capacity, you might have to adjust a little to match it. You might need to elongate your breath to get it going.

2. Circular breathing: Unlike mirroring each other's breath, this is about giving and receiving each other's energy and love. You can do this lying down in bed together or sitting in

front of each other on the couch. First, one of you breathes out while the other breathes in, and then vice versa. As you breathe, do so with the intention of the exhalation giving energy and the inhalation receiving the other. Keep it up until you find a natural rhythm of giving and receiving, inhaling and exhaling. It creates a circle of energy and love exchange. At first, this was difficult for me. Surrendering to love is harder than it sounds, especially if you've had your heart broken before. But with time, I let myself feel fully held by my partner's healthy masculine presence instead of trying to control it. It felt more natural for me to exhale with the intention to give love than it did to surrender to it because that is the part we can control. Even when we think we're surrendering, we are often still subtly trying to control things in order to protect ourselves. *Ouf.* A simple practice that has so many levels. Give it a go.

Meeting each other's needs game: Set a timer for five to thirty minutes, depending on your time and space. During that time, ask your partner to meet your needs. For example, you might say, 'I want a back massage, and while you're doing it, I want you to say all the things you love about me'. Don't be shy to give feedback to your partner. If he's doing a crappy job massaging you, give him direction. It helps to agree before you start that his response to your feedback will always be 'thank you for your feedback'. But remember, you will swap and both have a turn at being the giver and the receiver. It's a fun game; you can do it when you're short on time or have a lot of it. Practising in this context also makes it easier to ask for your needs to be met in the bedroom, which can light the fire of desire and intimacy for those like me with missing libidos. Being comfortable asking for what I want, knowing I will be held in my naked and vulnerable state, makes me feel more and more connected each time.

Magic Mike: If all else fails, just watch any Magic Mike movies. That will get your motor running.

TOOLS FOR DIFFICULT CONVERSATIONS

Lay the 'ground rules' or foundations for the conversation: Create a safe space *before* the conversation, 'I want to tell you how I feel. Can you just listen? I don't need anything from you, but if you feel like you need to say anything, can you just repeat back to me what I'm saying?'

Express your feelings: 'I'm feeling lonely. I'm feeling sad'. Know within yourself that this is a normal feeling and a valid feeling. You are allowed to feel like this.

Acknowledge your old patterns: If things get heated and you feel the pull to yell or storm out and withdraw, acknowledge that. Admit it to yourself and even say it out loud. Then do something different. If you're pulled to leave, stay. If you're feeling the pull to scream, soften your voice. Train your nervous system to do something different. Go against the grain. Swim upstream. Recognise your old patterns and conditioning and go against them because, as the saying goes – nothing changes if nothing changes. But do it gently, one step at a time, and remind yourself that you are safe. If it's too much, honour yourself and do what you need to do before you come back and give it another go.

Meet each other's needs: Ask for anything else you need, 'I'd love a hug right now. I'd like you to help me with the dishes now, and then I'm going to go to bed'. When your needs are met, let that land in your body. Remind yourself that people are able and *want* to meet your needs because you are loved. Then you can ask, 'Is there anything you need from me right now?' Give them that, and then bask in your awesome ability to connect with each other.

Lather, rinse, repeat (as needed): If you do storm out or listen to the pull of your old patterns, be kind to yourself and give it another go once you've practised some kindness and compassion towards yourself. Flex that emotional muscle and give yourself some time to build your emotional fitness. Give yourself what you need, and then start again from Step 1. I'm rooting for you, girl!

IMPORTANT NOTE: These conversations have become exponentially different since I've done my own healing and worked on my own triggers. Childhood healing, moon rituals, dancing, all the work I've done and outlined in this book has enabled me to heal parts of myself that were getting in the way of my connection with others. I'm less reactive, less likely to leave the conversation; I'm more in charge of my nervous system; and I'm ruled less and less by my ego, my mind, and my wounds. I can handle these conversations with more awareness, grace, and ease *because* of the self-awareness I've cultivated and the work I've done to heal myself. A lot is going on in this book, a lot of ideas and suggestions. But even if you pick up just one or two things, it's my hope that these conversations and connecting with others will get easier for you, too.

PRACTISING BOUNDARIES

1. Set your intention, your why. (I'm doing this because ...)

2. Define boundary. (I want my mother-in-law to stop ...)

3. Set boundary. Dr Nicole LePera in *'How to Do the Work'* has a brilliant framework for having this conversation, and it goes quite similar to this: 'I am making some changes so that (*insert your intention for your new boundary*), and I hope you can understand that this is important to me. When you (*insert the problematic behaviour affecting your aura*), I often feel (*insert your feelings*). I understand this is something you may not be aware of. In the future, (*insert what you would or would not like to happen again*). If (*insert original problematic behaviour*) happens again, I'll (*insert how you will respond differently to meet your own need/ protect your aura*).

For example: 'I am making some changes so that my children feel free to be themselves, and I hope you can understand that this is important to me. When you say, "Don't do that or I won't play with you", I often feel like you're shaming them into behaving a certain way. I understand this is something you may not be aware of. In the future, I'd like you to validate whatever it is they're feeling and hold space for them. If you keep saying things like "You have to be nice", implying that they're not, or that you won't play with them, I will step in and validate their feelings myself or perhaps even remove them from the situation'.

Tips: Have the conversation when emotions are not heightened and you both have time and space for the conversation. Often, bringing this up when going for a walk or a drive or working on something together like cooking in the kitchen can make it less daunting and confrontational because you're not looking directly at each other and you have an activity to keep you together.

Another tip: When communicating, try focusing on how you will begin to respond differently rather than on changing the other person. If applicable, you can compromise! You also want to honour the other person's boundaries, too.

If you feel guilt or shame and start to slip back into your old patterns, remember that this is all a normal part of change. This is powerful work, and it can feel uncomfortable. You're creating space to allow yourself as well as the ones you love to be seen, heard, and loved and authentically themselves. That's pretty important work! Reclaiming your authentic self as well as honouring those that you love, *ouf,* it's a big combination.

4. Keep the boundary. Refer back to your intentions when keeping this boundary, and keep working on it! To help with this, make that one small promise we spoke about to build self-trust and know that you've got this. Take care of yourself and, if you need to, make some more time for fun and play, working that social engagement system of yours, so you can openly and lovingly communicate and stress less. You're doing the best you can, and so is the other person.

my little angels,

You were birthed into a wonderful, scary, miraculous + wild world. It's not the world I was born into, so I promise to let go of the beliefs I've had + held onto for most of my life about how raising you 'should' look. Because I know, + I know you do, too, that you won't thrive if you don't, and you will demand more of me + more of our world.

You deserve a new way to live, a new way to be raised. I promise to do my best not to project my beliefs + rhythms on to you + to let you express your own when I slip into old patterns + worn-out ways of being, somehow, I know deep within me that you won't allow me to stay there for too long. You will show me so directly that this is not the way to support you. To create an environment outside the matrix, outside of what I was birthed into, the box I was told to stay in, + allow you to be fully you.

I will never suppress what you came here to show us. You came here as a collective to bring more lightness to the planet. You came here to raise us. You came here to show us that processed foods, lack of nature, suppressed play + suppressed emotions, no matter how dense or uncomfortable, are not the way forward.

I promise to nurture your connection with yourself, + the connection to the creator. I will quickly learn that to do that for you, I must shatter the old paradigm, one moment at a time. Through love + compassion, we can do this together. You're not here to fix the old systems, or to fix me. You will implement completely new ones + rebirth a new me. A connected me. A heart led me. A me that knows when my ego is speaking + is ready to do the work + heal those old parts of myself that I've kept in the shadows for so long. And I know that you will show me how you will bring up parts of myself that I didn't know I had, the wonderful, the awe inspiring, + the down-right scary. But know you are showing me these things for a reason. You are here to wake me up to my wholeness so I can create that for you - too

I'll make mistakes along the way, I can't protect you from everything, even though it pains me. My job is to love you through anything life guides you through. Thank you for being here. Thank you for making me a mummy. Not just a mummy, but your mummy. Thank you for leading me back to myself, the parts I was so disconnected from. You've shown me the infinite well of resources I have within me, + as hard + wonderful it is being your mum, I know that it's not just about you + it's not just about me. It's showing this planet the ripple effect of the love we have for each other

Our legacy will live on long after we're gone So, in many ways, we will be together forever

And so it is my darling babies. From now until eternity, I love you

Love mummy xx

THE FINAL CHAPTER

Fly, My Little Acorn, Fly!

Please know I do not claim to speak for you. I cannot speak your truth. Only you can. And I encourage you to do so. I am one woman, with one perspective. It is my intention that in speaking my truth, I hold space for you to speak yours so that this new cultural narrative is woven from many, many voices that have previously been marginalised. In breaking my silence, my dearest wish is that I make it a little easier for you to break yours.

Lucy H. Pearce

When away on holiday with my parents, Dad was putting some leftover food away. He reached for the plastic wrap, and I chimed in, asking him to use a reusable container that we already have instead of adding more plastic wrap to the landfill. It sparked a (loving) conversation where he thought it was interesting that I was willing to throw shade about plastic wrap when I use disposable nappies on my babies. I'd like to say I'm planet-conscious, but by no means am I the poster girl for it. Sometimes our superpowers are our biggest weaknesses (just like my relationship with gratitude).

My point is that being human is messy and complicated. We tap into our humanity's divine beauty and power when we're at our most authentic. This means not pretending to be perfect (and, for that matter, not pretending that perfection is even possible). It's about being honest with ourselves and with others. It's about recognising the parts of us that are in such opposition to who we think we are that we even turn a blind eye to them or are too afraid to admit we have these thoughts, actions, or behaviours. Like being a lit naturopath who heals people with natural alternatives, then goes through the drive-through for some nuggies or a cheeky cheesy on the way home. Or a meditation teacher who can walk on fire also flips the bird to someone who cuts them off in traffic, yelling, 'Learn how to drive, dickhead!' Being human can be saying one thing and doing another. It can be being concerned about climate change, recycling like a maniac but still having plastic wrap in the cupboard.

Being human is about being honest. It's being okay with having goals and dreams and ideals but also hypocritical tendencies. Both these parts are equally loveable and equally human. And perfectionism is the furthest thing from authenticity and living a fulfilled life. Being human is the most spiritual thing we can do. Because we accept the wholeness of who we are. We can embrace the mess. That's what people relate to. Tell me a story about climbing Mount Everest and all the challenges you faced and overcame, and I'll be inspired, sure. But tell me how frustrated you are when your partner doesn't replace the toilet roll or, worse, has it facing the wrong way? Now *that's* a story everyone can relate to. *That's* what it means to be human. Loving ourselves and owning ourselves in totality. That's where the magic is.

You can meditate for forty-five minutes without losing focus and still snap when your kids throw spaghetti sauce on your walls. We can honour all of ourselves, big feelings, little feelings, messy feelings, contradictory feelings, and embarrassed feelings. *That's* the magic of being human. And that's what I want you to keep in mind as you come to the end of this book and reflect on how to integrate it into your life. Because I know all too well the perfectionist voice that comes back in so quickly to start saying things like 'You've finished the book, but you haven't implemented a single thing!' or 'You wrote in your journal for four days, but you've already failed at keeping it going!'

I want to encourage you to tell that voice to bugger off. It's not the real you. And you don't have to practise the concepts in this book perfectly for them to have an impact in your life. In fact, trying and slipping up – and then having a conversation with yourself or someone else where you admit you slipped up and ask what you can learn from it – is where the magic is at. Perfectionism is *so* old paradigm.

Being a mum is, without a lick of competition, the hardest thing I've done and the hardest job there is. But at the same time, I also know it's the best job I'll ever have and the best work I'll ever do. This is the best time of my life – raising children. As challenging as it is, I know I'll look back and miss the feeling of a newborn squirming and vomiting on my chest, or a toddler having a tantrum on the floor because, well, you have no idea and sure as hell can't figure it out. You've tried all your tricks, but you just can't seem to get him to calm down, and it feels like your ears might be bleeding. I don't want to spend my days waiting until nap time. I want to thrive, and I want to thrive *now*. Not when my kids don't need me anymore and I can finally start to live *my* life. I can have it all, not *despite* being a mother but because I *am* one. This is the existence I crave, and the gap between where I was and where I want to be, in terms of enjoying the small moments of my life, was what drove me to write this book.

Becoming a mother is the most spiritual experience there is. It is a divine feminine initiation. And with any initiatory experience comes painful lessons that can feel frightening and lonely. But such an experience can also crack us open and return us home to our inherent purpose.

In writing this book, I wanted to show you that we can do much more than merely survive. Getting to know ourselves is a magical lifetime journey that never ends. It's infinite. By doing so, we can intentionally build a foundation of love, happiness, and meaning for our children to blossom. Not only our children but our whole families. It's given me great comfort knowing that I am a rough draft of the person I am still becoming. So I hope this book moves the needle in a way that reaffirms the power of extravagant love and excessive grace in you and your life.

Because we can be both a masterpiece and a work in progress at the same time. Connecting to self-care and your divine inner feminine can give you and your relationships new life. When we blossom, so do the people around us because we show them how. Let's give away love like we're made of it (because we are).

Motherhood connects us to the past through the mothers who came before us and to the future through our children. This is an important part of connecting to something infinite. It gives us purpose and meaning beyond ourselves. Bearing children is a significant way to contribute to the world and humanity. We allow life to move forward through us and beyond us. We are a part of, and belong to, something incomprehensibly expansive. We have the ancient nurturing instinct flowing through our veins that all mothers before us have had, and what we will continue to pass on is nothing short of miraculous.

As our children grow and leave home and perhaps have children of their own, we are reminded of our place in the sweeping arc of time and our place in the cosmos. We will remember bathing a newborn on the kitchen bench and smelling their sweet hair as we watch them, fully grown, venturing into the world to meet their own destiny. We're reminded of mortality and experience the inescapable turning of the great wheel. Motherhood connects us with the cycle of life – the cycle of life *and death* – in a complete, infinite fashion.

We are nothing short of a miracle, and one of the biggest gifts motherhood can bring is the reconsideration of our relationship with the infinite. This relationship connects us to our spiritual centre and contributes to the development of mature spirituality. Whether or not we consider ourselves religious, having this divine connection to something larger than ourselves that is confirmed as our mother confirms our place in the universe. And I thank you for your contribution.

I want to leave you with this thought. Imagine a tiny little acorn that has dropped from a tree. See yourself picking up this baby acorn, holding it in the palm of your hand, and staring at it with loving curiosity. You ask yourself, how does this tiny little acorn grow into a two-hundred-foot monster tree? It's almost too hard to comprehend. You see beauty in this little acorn and what Mother Nature has created.

Now imagine that the little acorn fell from the tree but landed in a patch of soil that didn't have the right nutrients for it to grow. It was depleted in some areas and wasn't given what it needed at times. That little acorn still has the potential to grow into a mighty tree over two hundred feet tall; some things have just been missing.

You might have been thinking that the acorn is your child – but you, my love, are the acorn. We each enter the world carrying something unique that asks to be lived through us. Just as the destiny of the oak tree is contained in this little acorn, we arrive in life with something to offer and the ability to become who we are destined to be. What is waiting to be awakened in you is ancient, surprising, and meaningful. Being a mother allows this to unfold beautifully. And remember, it's a process of 'rewilding' yourself. You don't have to become someone different. Who you are meant to be is within you.

You have never been lost, and you have never been broken. You don't need to 'find yourself'; you can stop the search. And you certainly don't need fixing. You have the mightiness within you. The real work is going out into the world and claiming what's yours and what you need to live your truth. Claim what you once lacked so you can step into your highest power and raise your vibration. Then do you know what happens? You bear fruit, and you give back. Once grown into a beautiful tree, that tiny baby acorn will only bear fruit when it has what it needs. If it doesn't have the right nutrients, it can't bear fruit because it's not within its means. It has too much work to do, just staying alive. And we are the same. Give yourself what you need, be resourceful, be kind, be comfortable, be uncomfortable, be human.

Motherhood transforms us; it burns away what no longer serves us. It demands that we show up for ourselves and our children. It's a call to become the person we were meant to be. Motherhood is an invitation to claim your inner wisdom, stand in your knowing, and express your unique codes.

The world needs more people like you raising kids and their vibration all at once. Raising high-vibing, conscious children who will continue to be the fruit of our trees. So go into the wild, you beautiful little acorn. Pursue your authentic path and let your individualisation story unfold. You were born for this.

Imagine you're standing at a crossroads. You have two roads to choose from: one path says 'Victory', and the other is 'Fulfilment'. Victory is the path that mumbles to your partner 'I told you so' when they've been looking for the butter for twenty minutes, whining that it's not where you said it was, only for you to get up from where you've literally just sat down, to find it. Exactly. Where. You. Said. It. Was. Fulfilment is the other option, where you get up from your seat anyway, show your husband where the butter is, and pass it to them with a smile that says 'happy to help' (note, a smirk that *says* 'I told you so' doesn't count). As good as it feels in the moment to say those words, in the long run, you're sacrificing fostering meaning, connection, and fulfilment.

If we choose to go down the path of victory, there is an endpoint and a finish line. The goal is to win. We experience the thrill of competition, and people will gather to cheer us on. But then, when it's over, the cheering stops, and we all go home – and we need another race to experience that thrill again. But if we choose the path of fulfilment, the journey will be longer. There will be times when we trip and fall and times when we just stop because we're tired or to enjoy the view. Crowds gather to join us on this journey as well, but this time they don't go home. They are with us for the ride and can keep going without us, even when our time is done.

This example captures the idea that we can choose to view life as a competition – to define success according to the outcome and how we stack up against other people – or we can choose to define it on our own terms. When we are connected to our true essence, we're no longer motivated by the desire to be better than anyone else. When this lands in our bodies, we're not distracted by the noise around us because we're so focused on being in alignment and living in full body–mind–soul congruence, adding value that can't be measured or calculated.

And much like this metaphorical race, when we become mums, there is no endpoint. We are mothers forever. For as long as we all shall live, and beyond our physical time on Earth. There is no finish line, just ebbs and flows of surviving and thriving. It's all a part of it. We don't survive *or* thrive; we do both. You don't *win* at being a mum (although there does seem to be some competition from those on the victory path – and I must say, I enjoy the friendly banter between my sisters about whose toddler knows the most words or rolled over at the youngest age … what was I saying about being messy and imperfect?).

If we graphed our days' high points and lower points re feelings, our feelings of connection, how we felt about ourselves, and how we treat ourselves, the graph would realistically be full of ups and downs. Now map the same concepts over a week or a year, and the peaks and pits are still there. We feel differently about each part on any given day. Softening into the new paradigm of motherhood doesn't mean there aren't ups recorded every day or the weeks or months will be the same. But with a commitment to learning about ourselves, being brave enough to shine a light on our shadows, and letting go of our obsession with control, we can ensure we are on the upward journey, and our life and days just keep getting better and better. My hope is that one day you will wake up and ask yourself, 'Can it get any better?' and the universe nods with a cheeky smirk that says, 'Babe, you have no idea'.

RECOMMENDED BOOKS

If you liked my work, it's because I stood on the shoulders of these giants. Many ideas and learnings came from the wisdom these visionaries shared in their own books. In no particular order, get your eager mits on these:

Mindful Birthing by Nancy Bardacke

Metahuman by Deepak Chopra

Atomic Habits by James Clear

Mothering Our Boys by Maggie Dent

Becoming Supernatural by Joe Dispenza

Man's Search for Meaning by Viktor E. Frankl

Strive by Adam Fraser

Everybody, Always by Bob Goff

Letting Go by David R. Hawkins

Heal Your Body by Louise Hay

Doctor You by Jeremy Howick

Earth Is Hiring by Peta Kelly

How to Do the Work by Nicole LePera

Make It Happen by Jordanna Levin

Motherhood by Lisa Marchiano

Buddhism for Mothers by Sarah Napthali

The Slight Edge by Jeff Olson

The Pocket Guide to the Polyvagal Theory by Stephen W. Porges

The Power of Fun by Catherine Price

Flourish by Martin E. P. Seligman

You Are a Badass at Making Money by Jen Sincero

The Untethered Soul by Michael A. Singer

The Surrender Experiment by Michael A. Singer

Own Your Energy by Alla Svirinskaya

ACKNOWLEDGEMENTS

Thank you to everyone at Awaken Village Press who has worked on this book, including Amanda Johnson, Clint Brown, Vanessa Perrodou, Daniel Huenegardt, and Andrea Gibb. Special mention to Elizabeth Gudrais – given the fact that my manuscript was written in the throes of early motherhood, thank you for helping me shape it into what it is today. And to Andrea, who designed the cover – you brought my vision to life and gave me what I didn't even know I wanted. I'll never forget the first time I saw your design and how exhilarated I felt knowing that 'this was it'.

To the mother hen – who fiercely loved me and protected me throughout this journey and offered her gentle nurturing nature to me. Amanda, thank you.

Thank you to the very first members of my Book Launch Community – for your feedback, support, and ideas – Megan Bett, Caitlyn Gormann, Amy McKenzie, Lauren McCartin, Melanie Brennan, Kristy Brereton, Renae Rogers, Raych Findlay (also thanks for all the memes you send me that are often quite dark and hilarious), Lauren Thoolen, Kate Burton, Emma Gentle, Brogan Carter, Sharna Holland, Kirah Clark, Morgan Maude, Grace McInnes, Emily Churchill, Sophie Cameron, Chloe Reilly, and Tamieka MacErvale.

Thank you to Melissa Storey – your edits, in particular, are appreciated. Your hair smells like a meadow, and you're always bringing the high vibe energy where you make me feel important. Thank you.

Thank you to all the people in my life who provided love, friendship, sanity, and support as I wrote this book, including but not limited to Carlee King, Stevi-Dee Alexander, Bonnie Barkmeyer, Aleisha Storer, and my old school besties, French, Sair, Rach, and Lol.

My two sisters, Rachael and Jane. What can I even say? Thank you for being there for every single thing that I do and for always making me better. For being there with me to commiserate – and celebrate! – adulthood, motherhood, ambitions, and just life. Rachael, you truly are an angel sent from heaven. And Jane? My soul mate. For speaking the language that only you and I know. I really can't express how much I love you both.

To my family – my beautiful mum, Janine – always being that life-long learner that you wrote in my resume many times! For always being the first to sign up for anything I create. And Dad – the way you look at me, I feel like I can conquer the world, and I know just how much I'm loved. To my two older bros – Jeremy and Matthew – for the love and laughter.

Thank you to my coaches and healers in this process. Rick William – you've been an essential contribution to this book because of the support you have given me. I reached out for your help in the earliest days of my motherhood journey when I felt like I couldn't go on, and I wouldn't have made the transition into who I am without you in my corner. Thank you for showing me how to heal my nervous system, and for your generosity and ongoing friendship. Narelle from White Feather Guidance, and Louise Gerry, who is so much more than my naturopath. And to Desi from Sensual Somatics™. What a powerhouse you are. Thank you for your wisdom and for just being so dope. Being in your presence and space has been so healing and liberating for me.

Most of all, to my boys – Zephyr, Knox, and Zac, for inspiring this book and making it possible for me to write it. You are pure magic. I could never have written this book without the support of my husband, Zac. Who, from day one, has encouraged me to go for what I want and supported me on every level to get where I am now. I love you all so very much.

ABOUT THE AUTHOR

Emily facilitates transformational experiences for heart-led women and mothers. She's spent the last ten years exploring her own personal and spiritual growth, which was propelled forward when she became a mother. It was a truly pivotal point in her life, shifting her centre of gravity and relinquishing her values. Emily realised that her definition of a 'good' or 'successful' mother didn't match that of others or society: believing that there is beauty in being sent to the scary depths of our being in motherhood, being confronted by our shadows is not something to hide from or continue to repress but an opportunity for a sacred awakening if met with curiosity, open-heartedness, and compassion. When we remain open to our inner life as we navigate the trial of mothering, we will also gain great insights, priceless wisdom, and an abiding experience of wholeness. It will alter the very nature of our relationship with life – and ourselves. To be a 'successful' mum, Emily maintains that the only work we have to do is reveal our inner wisdom, and when we do, we will receive anything we ever wanted, including being the mother we so truly desire to be. Emily is a coach, somatic therapist, trauma-trained positive psychology educator, speaker, and yoga instructor and has learned many tools along the way. She lives in Victoria, Australia, with her husband and two boys and shares her work worldwide.

Hey, sister!

First off, thank you for taking the time from everything else going on in your life to read this book. I truly appreciate it and hope that a little self-discovery outlined in this book will have the same transformative effect on your life as it has on mine.

If you found this book valuable, please jump on to Amazon or wherever you purchased the book and leave me a review. It would mean the world to me.

And please, stay in touch! I love hearing from readers. You can always reach out on Instagram or the contact form on emilyeast.com or join our online community, Soul Nation!

With love, Emily XO

Emilyeast.com.au
Instagram: @emily_east
@soul.nationn